Unanswered Cries

Unanswered
Cries

A True Story of Friends, Neighbors, and Murder in a Small Town

Thomas French

St. Martin's Press
New York

Design by Dawn Niles

Library of Congress Cataloging-in-Publication Data

French, Thomas.
    Unanswered cries.
      p. cm.
    ISBN 0-312-05526-9
    1. Murder—Florida—Gulfport—Case studies. 2. Murder—Florida—Gulfport—Investigation—Case studies. 3. Tosi, Larry. 4. Gregory, Karen. I. Title.
HV6534.G85F74 1991
364.1'523'0975963—dc20   90-49299

First Edition: May 1991
10 9 8 7 6 5 4 3 2 1

For Tad

Author's Note

This is a work of nonfiction. All of the people, events, and details described in the book are real; there are no composite characters, fake names, invented quotes, or imagined conversations. The information was gathered over the past five years from interviews with more than seventy-five people and from more than six thousand pages of court documents, personnel files, and other records. Most of the quotes are taken from notes or transcripts of official proceedings, but by necessity some are reconstructions based on people's recollections.

I have tried, as best I could, to depict the emotional trauma that follows the murder of a loved one. However, it is a limited depiction that only begins to describe the depth of grief and suffering involved in such a case. If you are among the thousands of homicide survivors who are searching for help and understanding, I would encourage you to check with local victim organizations or with the victim advocate at the nearest police department to find out what services are available to assist you. In addition, there are several national organizations that may be able to provide support or referrals. Among these are the National Organization for Victim Assistance, 1757 Park Road NW, Washington, D.C., 20010, (202) 232-6682; the National Victim Center, 307 West Seventh Street, Suite 1001, Fort Worth, Texas, 76102, (817) 877-3355; and Parents of Murdered Children and Other Survivors of Homicide Victims, 100 East Eighth Street, B-41, Cincinnati, Ohio, 45202, (513) 721-5683.

Book One

Book
One

S he lay alone in the hall for a night and a day and another night. Finally someone saw her, and the police arrived and raised a circle of official yellow around the yard, and the neighbors stepped forward with their excuses, then retreated behind the walls of their front doors. The forensic experts came, and the forensic experts left, and at last the case was left in the hands of one who would not let go. During the day he would sit at his desk, examining and reexamining the photos of her on the floor, and ask her to help him see whatever he had missed. At night he would return to the house, wandering inside, hoping the empty rooms might reveal whatever they remembered. The weeks stretched into months. He eliminated one suspect after the other and ran down one blind alley after the other, and still he was no closer to understanding, until that day he stumbled across a single moment of stupid good luck. Then came the lie detector tests at the station, and the reenactments in the dark, and the anonymous phone calls that could not be traced, and the rounds of weary accusations and denials.

After all of that, he arrested a man and put him on trial for his life.

An investigator asked one of the neighbors:

"Does he look like a murderer to you?"

The neighbor said:

"What does a murderer look like?"

Part One

Ghosts

One

She might have stood a chance if she hadn't been living in a place where almost everyone is from someplace else. If Florida were not such a colony of impermanence, overflowing with people from other corners of the map—if more of them had been born and raised there, or at least learned to think of it as home and not just as some place to wait out the rest of their lives or hibernate for the winter or work on their tans until something better came along up north—then maybe the neighbors would have known more about the dark-haired woman moving into the house on the corner. Maybe they would have seen her emptying her car and carrying in the boxes and then politely walked across the street with a cake or a fresh-baked loaf of bread, as neighbors back home are known to do, and introduced themselves and told her that if she ever needed anything, anything at all, to just come knocking. If a few of the neighbors had done that, if they'd taken the time to find out her name and memorize her face, then maybe one person would have picked up the phone and called the police that night when her scream woke them in their beds.

The rain had been coming down hard that evening. This was May 22, 1984. The long Florida summer was just settling in for its annual siege on Pinellas County, a crowded little peninsula that dangles like a huge fishhook off the center of the state's west coast. Bounded by the Gulf of Mexico on one side and Tampa Bay on the other, the county is home to St. Petersburg, Clearwater, Largo, and twenty-one other municipalities, all of which melt together into one subtropical sprawl of sand and concrete, an overpopulated jumble of bone-white beaches and bumper-to-bumper traffic, of two-bit tourist traps and alligator-inhabited retention ponds, of serene retirement communities where the buildings are painted in cartoon colors, and waterfront condos where the air-conditioning is always set on arctic, and towering palm trees that sway in the wind beside convenience store parking lots.

Summers there are surrealistically intense. The sun hangs only a few hundred feet above the ground; cascades of blinding white light ricochet off windshields, sidewalks, and buildings; humidity builds almost visibly in the air. And when the rains come, steam literally rises from the streets. From late May through September, that's how days usually end, with a gathering of dark storm clouds—some of them forty thousand feet high, black as night, hurling jagged strikes of lightning—then the surge of release. This Tuesday evening was no different, except that the rain did not seem to want to stop. As people sat in their living rooms, staring at the TV, they could hear the showers falling in waves against their windows.

Karen Gregory was busy that night. A thirty-six-year-old graphic artist with long brown hair and piercing eyes, Karen was carting some belongings from her apartment on Pass-a-Grille Beach to a house in nearby Gulfport, a small city tucked away in the southwest corner of the county, near St. Petersburg, on the shores of Boca Ciega Bay, which opens into the green expanse of the Gulf. The house was owned by David Mackey, Karen's boyfriend, who worked as an administrator of a counseling program for Vietnam veterans. After dating David for more than a year, Karen was moving in with him. She had been living with him unofficially for awhile, spending most of her time at the house even as she kept her apartment at the beach, but now she and David had decided to formalize the arrangement. For days, she'd been loading her things into her Volkswagen Rabbit and hauling them over to Gulfport.

The house was modest but amiable in a nondescript kind of way. It was a small white frame house, one story—almost all of the houses in Pinellas County have only one story, as if everyone had agreed that two were too much to hope for—with three bedrooms, an enclosed porch, and a gray-shingled roof topped with a trio of fat, silver-colored wind turbines that spun in the breeze, sucking hot air from the attic. Out in the yard were a couple of birdbaths and a hibiscus with bright red blossoms and, just to the east of the house, a magnificent live oak tree with branches so thick and wide they cast a shadow over nearly half of the house, leaving the other half basking in the light. The house sat on the northwest corner of Upton Street and Twenty-seventh Avenue South, facing Twenty-seventh. The avenue was paved with red brick, so that whenever a car passed by, its tires made a faint rumbling, like thunder rolling somewhere off in the distance. Many times that was about the only sound along that stretch of Twenty-seventh. There weren't many kids around. Most of the surrounding houses were owned by older people, a good number of whom were snowbirds who lived up north most of the year and migrated to Florida only during the winter, which meant that their Gulfport homes stayed empty for months on end. It was a quiet street, in other words, in a quiet, middle-class neighborhood, only a few blocks from the water, well away from the rush of traffic and the rest of the world. To make sure it stayed that way, the neighborhood was filled with special signs, one of which was posted in a front yard across from David and Karen's house:

WARNING. THIS IS A CITIZENS CRIME WATCH AREA.

In the middle of all this, Karen and David stood out. For one thing, they were younger than most of their neighbors; for another, Karen was white and David was black, and they were moving in together in a conservative town where interracial couples have been known to attract stares and veiled remarks. Still, after living in the house for several years, David had never encountered a problem. A native Floridian, he felt comfortable in Gulfport. It was close to the complex where he worked, it was smaller and more personable than St. Petersburg, and it was one of the few places left in the county where the streets were still lined with trees. David liked it there.

That Tuesday evening, while Karen went on with her moving, David was out of town, spending most of the week in Providence, Rhode Island, at a conference for other veterans counselors.

So Karen made her run without him, packing up the Rabbit one more time and hauling another load from the apartment. Early that evening, when she finished, she went to visit Neverne Covington, a close friend who also lived in Gulfport. Neverne was leaving for Boston the next day for a wedding, and Karen, who had agreed to feed her cat and water the plants, needed instructions.

Karen arrived at Neverne's house sometime between 7:30 and 8:00. She was wearing a white T-shirt, a baggy pair of faded green shorts, tennis shoes, earrings, and a silver necklace and a gold chain. Although she'd already snacked on something back at the house, she agreed to have a little dinner with Neverne. They ate—Neverne had made a salad and some ratatouille with polenta—then sat around, talking and drinking wine. To this day, Neverne remembers the brand of the wine—Robert Mondavi Muscadet D'Oro—because she has not been able to bring herself to buy a bottle since.

The two women chatted for hours. They cracked silly jokes. They made plans to go wind surfing. Karen talked about her new job; after months of working mostly as a waitress, she had just been hired as a graphic artist at Datacom Associates, a St. Petersburg firm that produced technical writings and illustrations. She talked about how challenging this job was and how much she preferred it to waiting on tables. She talked about how excited she was to be moving in with David and how good it felt to be settling down and planting some roots in a nice little town like Gulfport. She felt things finally were going right in her life.

Finally, sometime after midnight, Karen announced she had to go. The new job and all of the moving had left her exhausted. She said she wanted to go home and take a shower and get to sleep.

"I'm going to miss you," she told Neverne.

Her friend laughed. "I'm only going to be gone for a week," she said.

"I know," Karen said. "But I'm really going to miss you."

Then she hugged Neverne, climbed into the Rabbit, and drove away into the darkness.

Arthur Kuiper was up late reading that night. Kuiper worked as a restaurant manager at the Don CeSar, a huge bubble-gum pink hotel out on the beach. He lived on Upton, only a couple of houses behind Karen Gregory's home. That evening he had been out to dinner at an Italian restaurant and drank several cups of espresso, and now the caffeine was keeping him up. He was sitting in bed, reading and listening to the radio, when suddenly he heard what he later would describe as a short, high-pitched, agonizing scream.

He looked beside the bed at his clock, which may have been two or three minutes fast. It said 1:15 A.M. He got up, switched off the light, turned off the radio, and looked out the window. He wasn't sure what he'd heard or where the sound had come from. He stood at his open window for fifteen minutes or so, watching and listening. But there was nothing else. The neighborhood was quiet. Even the rain seemed to have slowed down.

Martha Borkowski, a secretary who lived across from David and Karen's house, was having trouble sleeping too. She was lying in bed when she heard the scream and, immediately afterward, the slamming of a door. She thought someone was slapping a woman in a car.

"When I heard it, it just went through my mind that that girl does *not* smoke," she later would say. "Because her lungs were so incredible."

The scream also woke Glenda Harness, a bank teller who lived with her boyfriend on the southeast corner of Upton Street and Twenty-seventh Avenue, catercorner from David and Karen's. Looking out her bedroom window, Harness saw an older man—another neighbor who had heard the cry—standing across the street in his doorway, gazing out; a few moments later his wife pulled him back inside. Harness went to the kitchen and looked out toward the garage, where her boyfriend, George Lewis, often worked late into the night. But the garage light was off and she could not see him.

Lewis was a firefighter for the city of St. Petersburg and a volunteer firefighter for Gulfport. He was also the neighborhood's unofficial watchdog; it was in his yard that the citizens crime watch sign was posted, and whenever something suspicious happened in the area, he made a point of checking it out. Believing that George might have gone to investigate the scream, Glenda grew frightened. She went and found a large flashlight—she wanted something heavy in case she needed a weapon—and then sat at a table with her arms around her knees, waiting for George to come back. When he finally returned, he told Glenda he'd heard the scream too and had gone down the street trying to find out what was wrong. But he said he hadn't seen anything unusual. The two of them talked about it for a moment, then went to bed.

All around the white house on the corner, neighbors had been startled by what they'd heard. The scream had been so loud, and the neighborhood so still, that it had carried for several blocks. In all, more than a dozen people had heard it. None of them called the police.

In the days to come, trying to account for why they did not call, they would give a dozen different answers. Some simply had not wanted to get involved; others had explained it away, telling themselves that nothing was wrong. One woman would say she thought it was cats parading in her backyard. Two other women had thought it was someone crying out from a nightmare. Others, as they lay awake in their beds, had told themselves that it was animals fighting, or a neighborhood nuisance creating a racket, or kids getting rowdy.

"But it really wasn't that type of scream," one man later recalled. "It was . . . well, I'll never forget it, anyhow."

Early the next evening, more than fifteen hours after the scream, Martha Borkowski returned home from work. She noticed that across the street, the front door of David and Karen's house—a jalousie door that led to the enclosed front porch—was open. She didn't think anything of it, though. That door often swung open.

An hour or so later, as it was getting dark, Borkowski looked out her front window and saw a man she did not recognize drive up to David and Karen's house in a van. Across the way, George Lewis saw him too.

The man was tall and thin and rather gangly, with a beard and curly dark hair. He pulled into the driveway, parked under the oak tree, and walked up to the front of the house. The jalousie door was still open. He stepped onto the porch and knocked on the inside door, which led into the rest of the house and which was closed. When no one answered, he left the porch, walked over to the corner, and looked up and down the street, as though he was searching for someone. He went to his van and sat for a few minutes, then walked back to the porch and knocked on the inside door again. When there still was no answer, he returned to the van and drove away. Before he left, he scribbled a note on a piece of paper and placed it on the windshield of David's car. The note said:

Karen & David,

Hello. Stopped by about 7:15 or so but saw no signs of life. Many things to do tonight so I probably won't be back but I have something you wanted. Will be home not too late.

At the bottom was a phone number, and a name.

Peter

That same night, David Mackey was trying to reach Karen. David was still at the conference in Rhode Island, and when he finished with the day's work he called home. There was no answer. He called again later, several times. Still no answer.

By midnight David was growing worried, so he called Anita Kilpatrick, Karen's roommate from the apartment on the beach. Anita said she hadn't seen Karen and suggested that maybe she'd gone to see her sister Kim, who lived in Dunedin, about twenty miles northwest of St. Petersburg. David called Kim's house, but Karen wasn't there, either.

The next morning—Thursday—David picked up the phone in his hotel room and tried again to reach Karen at the house. He called early, around 7:30, so he wouldn't miss her before she left for work. No answer. He tried again. No answer. Next he called Datacom. But Karen's boss said no one had seen or heard from her, either that day or the day before. He did not know where she was.

David called Anita Kilpatrick again. Both he and Anita were upset now. Clearly, something was wrong. Karen was not the type to skip work, especially a new job.

Anita started checking with police departments and hospitals to find out if there'd been an accident. But no one seemed to know anything about a Karen Gregory. Anita waited for David to call back. She was sitting on her couch when suddenly these pictures entered her mind. She saw Karen struggling with a man, shoving and fighting with a man who was taller than Karen. Then she saw Karen lying on the floor. Anita pushed the pictures out of her mind and told herself she was dreaming. She tried to read the paper but couldn't concentrate. She kept reading the same sentence over and over. She got up from the couch and started pacing.

Meanwhile, David was calling Amy Bressler, a neighbor who lived just up the street from his house. He asked Bressler to look out her living room window and see if Karen's Rabbit was parked in the driveway. Bressler looked over. Yes, she told him. Karen's car was there, along with David's.

Now David was sure something was wrong. He asked Bressler to go over and check on the house, saying he would stay on the line until she came back.

Bressler put down the phone. She walked over to the house and knocked on the nearest door, a side door. No answer. She walked around to the front door. It was closed, but she noticed that several of the jalousie window panes had been broken and that glass was scattered along the walkway. She knocked on the door. No answer. She walked around toward the back and saw that a bedroom window was open, the curtains moving in the breeze. She called out.

"Karen?"

No answer. With the curtains drawn, Bressler could not see inside the bedroom. But there was a slit, four or five inches wide, in the screen of the window—it had been there as long as David had owned the house—and so she put her hand through the opening and pushed back the curtains. An unmade bed was directly in front of her. She looked to the right, toward the bedroom door leading into the hallway, and saw a woman lying on the floor. The angle allowed her to see only the lower half of the body, but it was surrounded by blood.

"Karen?"

Bressler ran back to her house, where David was still waiting on the other end of the line. She was crying now. She was hysterical. She said she had to get the police.

"Something really horrible has happened," she told him. "I don't know what it is."

At 8:39 A.M., slightly more than thirty-one hours after the neighbors had heard the scream, Bressler called the Gulfport Police Department. Unsure whether the woman she'd seen on the floor was alive or dead, she reported what officially was recorded as a "nonresponsive person."

She was waiting in the street a few minutes later when Officer Cheryl Falkenstein drove up in a cruiser. Falkenstein got out, walked past the broken glass on the sidewalk, and tried the front jalousie door. It was locked. She walked around the house to the back bedroom window, pushed aside the curtains, and saw the woman on the floor.

"Can you hear me?" the officer said. "Are you OK?"

No answer. By now a team of paramedics had arrived and joined Falkenstein at the side of the house. They needed to get inside quickly—for all they knew, the woman might still be alive—yet the doors to the house were locked. So they decided someone would have to go through the window. They removed the screen and Falkenstein crawled inside head-first. She walked toward the woman, saw that she was not breathing, then quickly walked past her toward the front porch, where she unlocked and opened the jalousie door for the others.

Falkenstein, a twenty-two-year-old rookie, was badly shaken. She had been with the police department for only five months, and in that time she'd never seen anything like what she was seeing now.

All of the lights in the house were off. Inside the back bedroom, the one into which Falkenstein had crawled, a fan was sitting on the floor, still blowing. On top of the bed, stained with blood, was a blue flowered Hawaiian shirt. Next to the bed were the faded green shorts Karen had worn to Neverne Covington's house two nights before. Karen's tennis shoes were there too, with the laces still tied. Not far from the shoes was a black umbrella and a stack of magazines. On top of the magazines was a phone, and as Falkenstein and the others looked around, the phone began to ring. It kept ringing, even as the minutes passed and no one answered. It would stop for a second and then start again. It just kept going.

A few feet away, on the carpet just past the bedroom door, lay Karen. In the darkness of the hall, the paramedics had to use their pen lights to see her. Even so, it was obvious that there was no need to check her pulse. She was on her left side, almost in a fetal position, with her face turned toward the wall. She was still wearing the jewelry she'd had on that night at Neverne's, and the same white T-shirt, too, but it had been pulled up to just below her breasts. A black teddy was bunched around her waist. She wore no other clothing.

It was difficult, there in the hall, to be sure exactly what had happened to her. Her neck and head were covered with dried blood, covered with so much of it that it was impossible to see the exact nature and number of all of her wounds. But it was clear that she had been stabbed repeatedly. On her lower back and one of her legs, marked in blood, were several handprints, placed at such an angle that they could not have been made by Karen. Scattered around her along the stretch of hallway carpet was a series of bloody bare footprints. Not far away, on the tile floor of the bathroom, was another bloody footprint—a partial one, about the size of a silver dollar.

Blood had been left all through the house. There was some on the sill and curtains of the window where Officer Falkenstein had crawled inside. There was more on the bed. Outside the bedroom, across the walls and floor of the hallway where Karen's body was still lying, there were large stains and smears. Out on the front porch, three drops had dried on the floor. On the door that led from the porch into the rest of the house—the door on which the visitor had knocked the evening before—there were smears below the doorknob. In the window panes of the front jalousie door there was a hole, and around the hole were some hairs that were the same shade of brown as Karen's. The broken glass from the door was strewn along the front walkway, all the way to the curb and out into the street. In the driveway, on the windshield of David Mackey's car, the visitor's note was waiting to be read.

Inside the house the phone was still ringing.

It was David, calling from his hotel room. He'd been pacing, staring at the walls, trying to imagine what could have happened. He'd waited several minutes, waited as long as his patience would let him, then repeatedly dialed the number at his house, letting it ring and ring until finally someone answered. It was a woman whose voice David did not recognize. An Officer Falkenstein.

"Is Karen there?"

"Yes."

"What's happened?"

The officer hesitated a moment.

"She's dead, sir."

Two

Every week, more than four hundred people are murdered in the United States. Their bodies, pale and useless, are found in ditches or on darkened streets or in the dew-covered grass of vacant fields or inside the imagined security of their houses. Karen's was curled on the carpet of her new home, an expression of vague sadness on her face.

Her death, like most of the other four hundred, was hardly considered front-page news. The morning after the discovery inside the house, the *St. Petersburg Times,* an aggressive paper that usually gave prominent play to any local homicide of even passing interest, would relegate the incident to page 5B. The accompanying headline assured readers—in that shorthand peculiar to all newspapers—that the victim's identity was not as noteworthy as the fact that something unpleasant had occurred in a place where unpleasantness is unexpected. "Woman slain in tranquil area," it said.

The message was clear enough. This was not the most important case in the world, or the most striking, or the most shocking. As brutal as it was, the violence that had been committed inside the hallway was not extreme enough to stand out against the daily blur of death and destruction. It was not as singularly disturbing as, say, a gunman cutting down twenty-one people in a McDonald's. In this instance, only one person had been killed, and that person was not particularly young or particularly old or particularly helpless in any especially heartrending way. In fact, she did not meet any of the criteria usually required—in either a newspaper or a true crime book—for someone's death to merit special attention. She was not a movie star, a pregnant mother, an heiress, a rising executive, or an attractive college student with a brilliant future. She wasn't rich or glamorous, wasn't even remotely famous, wasn't the daughter of anyone powerful.

She was simply a thirty-six-year-old woman trying to make a life for herself, and when she was killed, it was what people sometimes casually refer to as "a little murder."

Yet there was nothing little about it. The fact that Karen's death was not as newsworthy as some did not lessen the pain of those who loved her. And it did not change the number of lives about to be swept up in the case that followed. For beneath the surface of this one ordinary murder there awaited a story that would shatter the illusions of safety to which each of us clings. Karen had died alone and anonymous, screaming for her life in a neighborhood where people had pledged to look out for one another. But her cry would linger on, exposing the astounding web of everyday existence, showing all of the ways we rely on those around us and all of the ways that reliance is betrayed. More than anything else, her cry would lay bare the limits of trust.

She was one of those chameleons who can transform themselves into different people. Sometimes she could almost pass for a teenager; other times she seemed older than her years, enveloped in an air of worldliness, as if nothing could ever surprise her. She had olive-colored skin, thick brown hair, fierce brown eyebrows, and crystalline eyes that some swore were green and others swore were blue. Occasionally she'd lock those eyes on people and mesmerize them with a hint of a smile that was both warm and slightly mysterious. Her "Mona Lisa look," one of her friends called it.

She stood about five feet five and was trim and tightly muscled. She wore little or no makeup. A couple of her teeth were slightly crooked, and whenever she laughed hysterically, she instinctively would cover her mouth so that no one would see. She liked to call her friends "sweetheart" or "honey" in a half-affectionate, half-silly way. She was a vegetarian. She was crazy about reggae music. She made a mean batch of baklava. She would not miss the film *Black Orpheus* if it played anywhere nearby. She had a pronounced fondness for socks, possibly because she had once lived in the cold of New England. Her favorite color was purple. She loved to talk long-distance with her friends and would rack up phone bills big enough to rival her rent check. She enjoyed telling outlandish stories and often began them with declarations.

"Honey," she'd say, "you're not going to believe *this*."

Her name had not always been Karen Gregory. The "Gregory" came later, when she was in her twenties and was making a declaration of independence. She was born Karen Marshall on March 29, 1948. Her father, Delmar, owned an appliance company, and her mother, Sophia, was a homemaker. They lived in upstate New York, in Menands, a village outside Albany. Karen was their first child. Two years later came her brother Roy, and then there was a pause of five years before Kim arrived, and then two years after that came another brother, Mark.

Being so close in age, Roy and Karen were thrown together constantly. They took their First Communion together at the Sacred Heart of Jesus Catholic Church in Albany, and a few years later, when it was time for confirmation, they did that together too. They played together and got in trouble together and fought constantly for attention, affection, and superiority.

Karen brought a sweet but diabolical determination to this battle. She would blackmail Roy into bending to her will. She would tell him that he could sit in her room, which had a collection of music boxes and other treasures and which to Roy seemed like Oz, if only he would do the dishes for her. She would grant him a few moments to gaze at the latest issue of the Mickey Mouse Club magazine if only he would dust the stairs for her. She threatened him. She made deals with him. When necessary she used force, squeezing the back of his neck. On those rare occasions when he would scratch out some small victory, she would spend days plotting revenge. Typical big-sister tactics.

One evening, when Karen was about nine and Roy seven, the two of them were sitting in the living room, watching TV and eating dinner. They were having grilled cheese sandwiches—both would later remember that fact distinctly—and their parents were eating in another room. Karen was about halfway through her sandwich when she announced she was not going to finish it.

"You have to," said Roy.

"I'm not going to," said Karen, and with that she took the sandwich and threw it into a wastebasket. Roy was astounded. One of the cardinal rules of their household was that one finished everything on one's plate. As Roy thought about this, his astonishment quickly gave way to the realization that at last here was a moment where he had the upper hand. He ran into the other room and announced to his parents what had happened.

Their mother asked Karen whether she truly had thrown away her sandwich.

"No," Karen said. "Roy did it. He did it, and he's blaming it on me."

Again Roy was astounded. In their house there was only one thing worse than throwing away food, and that was lying. You'll never get in trouble telling the truth, their father had told them, and Roy had believed it. Yet here was Karen, lying to their parents' faces. She wasn't descending to hell. She was grinning.

Roy began crying and running around the room. Karen remained calm, pointing out to their parents that Roy's loss of control only proved his guilt.

"That's why he's so hysterical about it," she said. "He did it, and he's trying to cover it up."

Their mother would have none of it. She told them that if neither of them would confess, both would be punished. Roy couldn't stand that, either. Being punished for something he had not done was bad enough. But the injustice of their both having to suffer for the same crime was even worse. Karen may have been his rival in a struggle for power, but she was still his big sister, and he worshipped her. So he confessed. He told his parents he had thrown away the sandwich, and they sent him to his room. As he left, Karen looked at him with an odd expression on her face. Finally, he had astonished her.

For years Karen reigned over the lives of her sister and two brothers. They looked up to her with a mixture of respect, admiration, and fear. She indulged them and bullied them and made them laugh with imitations of the absolutely ancient nuns who patrolled the halls of the parochial high school they attended. Not that there weren't any signs of weakness. Karen was shy and nervous with outsiders, and for a time she had a stutter, which was made worse when a doctor advised her parents to mock the problem out of existence. Even so, Roy and Kim and Mark saw her as invincible.

Her style of babysitting, Roy remembers, was decidedly military. She would issue an order and they would follow it. She was wiry and strong, and when she wrestled with them she always won, even as they grew older. She was an excellent student, especially in art. She had legions of girlfriends who would retreat with her to the sanctuary of her room. Kim, who wanted to hang out with Karen and the other older girls, was usually kicked out during these sessions. Sometimes, though, Karen's friends would appeal for clemency and Karen would allow Kim to stay.

The room really belonged to both sisters. Karen had a big bed, Kim had a smaller one. Kim was afraid of the dark and would ask Karen if they could have a night light. Karen would say no. But if Kim awoke in the middle of the night from a bad dream and asked to climb into the big bed, Karen would say yes and hold her there in the dark.

At the same time, like children in many big families, the Marshall kids showed off a collective talent for scaring the wits out of one another. They inherited it from their father, who had inherited it from his father, who'd had a thing about hiding behind doors. The kids perfected their own techniques. Karen was no amateur—she jumped out of closets to great effect—but Roy raised the art to a new level, taking his inspiration from episodes of "The Twilight Zone" and experimenting on Kim and Mark when their parents and Karen were gone and he was appointed babysitter. One night he turned off the lights, went into the kitchen, and found a knife and a bottle of ketchup. He poured some ketchup on himself and the knife and then cried out as if he'd been attacked. When Kim and Mark found him, he was on the floor playing dead. Kim got mad. Mark cried. Later, Roy would remember the moment and be ashamed.

As the oldest of the four children, Karen did everything first. She drove first and went to college first and moved out of the house first. She was the trailblazer, as Roy put it.

She attended Nazareth College, a Catholic women's college in Rochester, New York. She had to fight to persuade her parents to allow her to leave home; finally they agreed, but they insisted that the institution be Catholic. At Nazareth she studied art and was pleased when one of her sculptures was placed on display on campus. She made lots of friends and lost her shyness. The girl who had once stuttered now stood at the front of a class, making ten-minute presentations.

This was in the 1960s, and as Karen became more independent she began carrying signs and joining marches. Her parents were embarrassed when they picked up the newspaper one day and found a photo of their daughter sitting with some other Vietnam War protesters. When Karen came home to visit, she would take a seat at the dinner table and launch into extended debates with her parents over the war.

One of the touchiest subjects between Karen and her parents was Catholicism. Karen had more than her fill of it at Nazareth. The nuns, she said, cared only about the rich girls. Roy, who was feeling the stirrings of independence himself, had similar feelings about religion. He and Karen joked about how if they ever again tried to walk into their old church, Sacred Heart, the big oak doors would slam shut in their faces. Still, despite the nuns, Karen lasted the four years at school, earning a bachelor's degree in art education. Her parents could hardly wait for graduation. But when her mother called to say they would be driving to Rochester for the ceremony, Karen told her to forget it.

"I'm not going to go up on the stage and get my diploma," she said. "Let them mail it to me."

"Are you crazy?" her mother said. "We're making that trip to Rochester. If I have to break both your arms, you're going up on that stage."

Karen still refused. So her mother called out the heavy guilt artillery: she told Karen that if she wouldn't do it for her parents, she should do it for her grandmother, who had sewn her a beautiful white dress for the occasion. Did Karen want to break her heart too?

That did it. "Okay," said Karen.

The big day arrived and the Marshall family took their seats in the audience. One by one the graduates filed out. Then came Karen, wearing her black robe and underneath it her new white dress. But there was something else.

"What's Karen got on her feet?" asked her grandmother.

While the other women wore dress shoes, Karen was clunking across the stage in boots. Years later, when the family recalled this moment, there would be some disagreement as to whether these were combat boots or hiking boots. Either way, Karen stood out. Her mother was dumbfounded. Her father sat there and burned. Roy just laughed. Once again his big sister had found the perfect revenge.

From that day on, Karen went her own way. She taught art to elementary schoolchildren, worked with patients at a mental hospital, and eventually got engaged. She'd met a young man named Steve Kruse. She told her mother they wanted the wedding to be outdoors.

"What mass are you going to be married in?" asked Sophia.

"I'm not," said Karen.

Her mother refused to attend. She had no intention, she said, of going to a wedding without a mass. So Karen and Steve were married without the family. Her parents did not even know when the ceremony took place.

Karen and Steve lived in a little place in New Hampshire called Fitzwilliam. It was an isolated place, so isolated that sometimes it seemed Karen was on a long vacation from the rest of the world. In Fitzwilliam it was as if the sixties had never ended. Steve worked at a co-op, trading work for food, and Karen tended a garden and prepared their meals from scratch. A few years later, though, the marriage ended. Karen was still friends with Steve, but they had drifted apart. When they divorced, she dropped his last name and took a new one—"Gregory," Sophia's maiden name. She told her father that she had used his name for more than twenty years and now she wanted to try her mother's.

Even after the divorce Karen stayed in Fitzwilliam; she ended up living there for more than a decade. She worked at a children's magazine and then at a computer magazine, eventually falling in love with a potter and moving in with him. She made pottery of her own, cooked vegetarian dishes, and lived in a big house crawling with cats and the smell of incense. When he went up to visit her, Roy kidded his sister, saying she had become the queen of the hippies. "Miss Whole Wheat," he'd call her, and she'd run laughing to her closet and pull out a dress to prove she owned such a thing. It was her only one. Naturally, it was purple. "See," she'd say. "I don't wear blue jeans all the time."

By January of 1983 Karen was ready to leave New Hampshire. Tired of the snow and the cold, she decided to move to Pinellas County, where Kim and her husband lived.

"I need a change," she told her sister. "I really need a change."

It wasn't easy starting over in Pinellas County. It's not easy for many people, because the county is an odd, mixed-up kind of place where it's hard to get your bearings. According to the maps and any reliable thermometer, it's located in the extreme southern portion of the United States. But in reality, it's packed with so many transplanted northerners—many of them from the Midwest—that it no longer feels even remotely connected to the South. It's more like Ohio, only with bigger cockroaches. Worse, almost all of the land's natural character has been bulldozed into oblivion. So much of the county has been paved over that it has come to resemble one gigantic parking lot.

And yet there are glimpses of the beauty and wildness that once enveloped the region. Alligators float motionless in lakes beside mobile home parks, occasionally emerging to swim in backyard pools; bald eagles nest where they can and ride the thermals above the subdivisions; sleek gray bottle-nosed dolphins gather in the bay at dusk, when the wind has died and the glassy water is tinged with purple, and then slice through the surface with their young, dallying only twenty feet from shore. And for all of the cement sameness of the place, there remains something mysterious, something unfamiliar etched into the landscape in a thousand tiny ways. Fireflies are scarcely ever seen, but the sweltering space above the highways is filled with lovebugs, which are black and flecked with red and which fly in couples, endlessly copulating even as they smash into the grills of speeding cars. There are no pools of worms on the ground after it rains, but on warm afternoons scores of small brown lizards patrol every yard and sidewalk, bobbing their heads up and down, puffing out their dewlaps, engaging in precisely patterned rituals of display. During the day, billowing clouds of the most heavenly white drift in the distance; at night, stars hang over the Gulf, shining through the vapor trails of the fighter jets that constantly roar over the water. And always there are the beaches, with their squadrons of sea gulls and armadas of stingrays and miles of burning sand and wave after wave.

It was here that Karen was drawn. For all her northern upbringing, she was a tropical creature. She loved the sun, loved the water, loved all the things that still made Pinellas special. She found an apartment and began waiting on tables to pay the bills. She worked at the Garden, a restaurant and bar situated a few blocks from the bay in downtown St. Petersburg. The Garden was a nice enough place, with rows of dark cocoonlike booths and a beautifully battered old bar that faced a big open patio where people could sit at night and drink under the moon. At first Karen didn't mind the job—in college she'd waited on tables for her tuition money—but after awhile she grew tired of the hours and the drunks and the men who kept making passes at her.

"I'm a waitress," she'd say to Kim. "What am I doing?"

There were other adjustments as well. After Fitzwilliam, this place seemed like a metropolis, filled with strange people. Karen started locking her doors at home and in her car—something there had been no need to do in New Hampshire. One night she was at Kim's house when someone knocked on the door. It was late, but Kim got up and opened it without thinking twice. It was only a neighbor, looking for his cat. But once he was gone, Karen gave her little sister a lecture on safety. She couldn't believe Kim had opened the door before seeing who was there. "You've got to be more careful," she said. "What if somebody was to come in here and attack you?"

Kim never worried about things like that. But Karen did. Years before, the two of them had gone to see *Looking for Mr. Goodbar,* a movie about a woman who's stabbed to death in her home. Afterward, Karen and Kim went to a restaurant to talk. Karen sat with her hands wrapped around her throat.

"I never want to die like that," she said.

Even though it seemed big to her, Karen was happy in Pinellas County. During the day she'd ride her bicycle for miles in the heat as if it were nothing. At night she'd pop a tape into a little portable cassette player and pulse through the rooms of her apartment. She also was spending a lot of time with her sister and her brothers, walking along the water, soaking up the sun. By now all of them had grown into experienced storytellers who understood the fine art of embellishment. Roy was especially good, and when he came down to visit he would spin wild accounts of childhood folly, including the infamous grilled cheese episode. Sometimes he'd get rolling and Karen would laugh so hard she would have to beg him to stop.

At the same time, Karen and her mother were growing closer. Karen's parents were divorced now, and while Sophia would never agree with everything Karen did, the two of them had grown to understand each other better. Sophia even laughed when she thought back to Karen picking up her diploma in those boots. The sparring of the old days was over. In fact, Sophia was planning to move to Florida so she could be close to Karen and Kim.

"We'll have a chance to talk old ladies' talk," she said.

"Yeah," said Karen. "We'll have fun, Ma."

Karen had not cut off her ties with the past completely. At night she would engage in epic long-distance conversations with her old friends from New Hampshire, making the phone company rich. Soon after she moved to Florida her friends sent her a present: a sleek black telephone. Still, Karen wasn't hiding from the rest of the world anymore. She told Roy her days as queen of the hippies were over. She got her hair cut and began dressing stylishly. She even bent her vegetarian rules enough to eat chicken once in awhile. Roy told her not to do anything rash.

"You know," he said, "you don't have to get into an IBM business suit and drive a BMW right off the bat."

She was making new friends, too. She had moved into the apartment on Pass-a-Grille Beach with Anita Kilpatrick, a young freelance writer at the *St. Petersburg Times* who sometimes hung out at the Garden. Karen also had become close to Neverne Covington, another artist in her mid-thirties.

When Halloween rolled around, Karen, who was still waiting tables at the Garden, dressed up as a frowsy dimestore waitress. She made a little white apron and a little white cap, smeared on some red lipstick, stuffed a wad of gum in her mouth, and put on some of the strangest earrings ever to grace the planet.

"They looked like Sputnik," says Neverne.

But the best touch was the hair. Karen sprayed it with this black gunk—gunk so fierce it would stay on the walls of her bathroom for months—and piled it all into a towering beehive. On her way to work she accidentally bumped the beehive against the car, causing it to lean at a forty-five-degree angle. It stayed that way all night, and when her shift was over, she went to a restaurant where Neverne and some other friends were eating. Still in costume, she strolled up to their table, snapping her fingers, smacking her gum, asking for their orders. Her friends did a cartoon double take. They hadn't even recognized her.

That was Karen. She had this animated, exaggerated way about her. She could run rings around people just talking to them. She'd slow down, speed up, go into reverse, then bulldoze straight ahead with the punchline. Her style was so distinctive that Anita did an uncanny imitation of her. Anita, Neverne remembers, would put her hands on her hips, throw her shoulders forward and issue one of those declarations: "Now listen to *this*."

Of all her new friends in Florida, none was more important to Karen than David Mackey. They had met in March 1983, not long after she arrived in Florida. David was a striking man. He was only twenty-nine, but he seemed older, carrying himself with an understated but unmistakable sense of purpose and control; anyone who saw him knew in an instant, before he'd even said a word, that he was well educated. He was also slender and handsome, with dark, penetrating eyes and a face so regal it resembled a lion's. Once she'd met him, Karen went home and talked about him excitedly, like a schoolgirl, debating aloud whether or not to call him. Finally she decided to be brave and called, leaving a message on his answering machine. The two of them began dating regularly and quickly grew closer. They went sailing together, to movies together, and to reggae concerts together. Before long they were a certified couple.

"Have you seen David?" people were saying. "David's in love."

They were both in love. They talked about going abroad together. They talked about the possibility of marriage. That fall, as Christmas approached, Karen spent weeks making David a jacket. This was no ordinary jacket. It was reversible and had a patchwork of different colors and all sorts of zippers and pockets. Karen had no pattern; she just plowed ahead and hoped for the best. She worked on a table in her apartment. She wouldn't let David come over for fear he'd see. Often she sewed past midnight, and time and again she had to rip out the seams and start over. It gave Anita a headache just to watch.

When she wasn't working on the jacket, Karen was spending more and more time at David's house in Gulfport. It was a relaxing area to settle down. Once a bustling fishing village that lived on harvests of mullet and stone crab, Gulfport has grown into a slightly worn community of retirees and working-class families. Even so, a sense of history—of time suspended—hangs over the place. Hidden away from the interstate and the main thoroughfares of the county, the town feels as though it never left the seclusion and simplicity of the fifties. There's a shuffleboard club, and a cluster of tourist holes and beach bars that passes for a downtown, and the waterfront, which features a little park with boccie ball courts and horseshoe pits, not to mention the beach itself, a small brown stretch of sand where fat-necked pigeons coo among the squawking gulls. Beside the beach is the fabled Gulfport Casino, which was wiped out by the hurricane of 1921 and then rebuilt and then torn down and then rebuilt again and which now stands at the water's edge, a huge white hall with a parquet floor where couples go ballroom dancing on weekends.

Almost all of the city, however, is residential. The streets are lined with tiny houses—every one of them, it seems, painted orange or mustard yellow or some curious shade of green—that obviously were constructed decades ago and have not seen much improvement since. Rusted metal awnings hang over windows; plaster reliefs decorate side walls, showing faded scenes of leaping dolphins. The yards tend to be comfortably unkempt, with palmetto bushes edging their way into cactus gardens and the thick grass creeping over the curbs and onto the pavement. Rising above it all are the trees—live oaks, heavy with their tangled gray-green beards of Spanish moss, and narrow Washingtonian palms and silky Australian pines and gnarled slash pines and slender jacarandas, which cover the ground every spring with a blanket of fallen purple blossoms.

In March of 1984, when Karen's thirty-sixth birthday rolled around, David threw her a surprise birthday dinner—her sister Kim was there, and so were Anita and Neverne—and took her to see *Black Orpheus,* which was playing at a grand old theater in Tampa. It was a happy time. Karen quit her job at the Garden, and in May she started working as a graphic artist at Datacom. The job was challenging—she had always worried that she had little talent as an artist—but she loved it. Meanwhile, she was officially moving in with David. The two of them had even been out shopping for a couch. They'd spent weeks looking for the perfect one—the amount of time devoted to the search had become a standing joke—and finally had found a mauve one that cost slightly more than $700.

"Our first purchase together for a home," Karen was saying. "This is serious."

The last time Kim saw her sister was May 19. It was a Saturday, and Kim and her husband and daughter spent the day with Karen and David. They went to the beach and swam and then returned to the house for dinner. David was going out of town Monday for his conference in Providence, Rhode Island, and Karen was nervous about staying by herself. There was something else. Karen told Kim she'd been having trouble sleeping for the past few nights. Kim asked whether anything was bothering her. Karen said no. She had her new job, she felt good about moving in with David, everything was fine. She was just having trouble sleeping.

Three days later was Tuesday, May 22. By then, after weeks of trips between her beach apartment and the house, Karen had carted over almost all of her belongings. One of the few things that remained to be moved was her large collection of plants. Karen had complained that David didn't have any plants in his house, that he didn't have anything living or growing there. She was determined to fix that, straight from the start.

So after work that evening she went to the apartment and piled her plants into the Rabbit. This was to be her last load— about the only thing that remained to be moved was her bed. Before she left for the house in Gulfport and then dinner at Neverne's, she wrote a note to Anita, telling her she'd see her soon.

That night it was Kim's turn to suffer from insomnia. She lay there in bed, wide awake.

"What's the matter?" asked her husband.

"I just can't sleep," she said. "I don't know why."

It was the following evening, Wednesday evening, when Kim got the call from David. He was worried about Karen. He'd been trying to reach her at the house and had gotten no answer. Had Kim seen her?

Kim didn't know what to tell him. But the next morning she was at work—she worked as a nurse in Dunedin—when a colleague walked up and handed her a piece of paper.

"Call this number," said the woman.

Kim had no idea what she was talking about. The number was unfamiliar.

"What do you mean, call this number?"

The woman had a strange look on her face.

"Just call it."

"Well, who is it?"

"Just call this number, Kim. Go in the office, and call this number."

Three

Do you have a sister Karen Gregory?"

"Yes, I do."

"I'm sorry to tell you that she's passed away."

"What?"

"She's passed away."

Kim was having trouble registering what she was hearing. "What hospital is she in?" she said.

On the other end of the line, the detective who'd been given the task of breaking the news to the family tried now to help Kim understand. He told her that her sister was not in a hospital, that Kim needed to come to the house in Gulfport to identify the body.

"Are you all right?" he asked. "Do you need a ride?"

Kim said she did not need a ride. She hung up and called her husband, who drove her to Gulfport. The trip, which normally takes forty-five minutes, seemed to last six hours. Kim felt as if they were moving in slow motion. She could not stop thinking about what the detective had said. She was bewildered. The man had told her only that Karen had passed away. Why was her body still at the house?

When they arrived in Gulfport, there were people standing

on the front lawn. Around the yard was a yellow tape with some words written on it in black: POLICE LINE—DO NOT CROSS.

Kim stepped out of the car. As she walked toward the yellow tape, she could hear birds singing, could feel the sun on her skin. Two police officers met her, and in a flat, emotionless voice she told them she was Karen Gregory's sister.

"The best thing you can do," said one of the officers, "is to go home and wait to hear from us."

Kim told the officer she had been asked to identify Karen's body.

"The best thing you can do," the officer repeated, "is to go home and wait to hear from us."

So Kim turned around and got back inside the car. She does not remember how she found out that her sister had not simply died but had been murdered. She thinks maybe her husband told her on the long drive home.

Anita Kilpatrick was standing there watching when Kim drove away. Anita had been outside the house for some time, waiting to learn whatever she could about what had happened. She'd overheard one of the officers say that Karen's sister was coming to identify the body. Knowing that Kim lived all the way up in Dunedin, Anita had volunteered to make the identification herself. But she'd been told no, the sister was already on the way. And now Kim had been sent home.

That morning, after David Mackey had called looking for Karen, Anita had waited anxiously by the phone. It finally rang at around 9:00 A.M. It was David. His voice didn't sound right. He was struggling to speak. He said Anita's name. He said it again.

"Karen is dead," he told her.

Anita began screaming at David, demanding to know why he would say such a thing. David tried to calm her. He asked her—and years later, she would remember these words and their kindness—if there was someone who could be with her. There was someone, a neighbor named Michaela Jarvis, another free-lance writer from the *Times* who happened to be a friend of Anita's and an acquaintance of Karen's. Anita called her, and Michaela came over to the apartment. They phoned the police station to find out whatever they could, but the dispatcher said that if they wanted any information on the case they would have to go to Karen's house, where the investigating officers were working. So

Anita and Michaela went to Gulfport. As they drove, Anita, too, had the sense that time had begun to play tricks on her.

"God," she said as they waited for a stoplight. "Haven't we been on this road for hours?"

When they pulled up to David and Karen's house they saw the police officers and the yellow tape. Anita walked over toward the driveway, where one of the officers was standing, and asked what had happened. This officer was Cheryl Falkenstein, the rookie who had been the first to witness the scene inside the house. Now, Falkenstein told Anita and Michaela what she'd seen.

Anita didn't know what to do. She and Michaela sat on the curb, got up, walked around, cried in each other's arms.

"Pssssst."

It was an older woman, standing in a nearby yard. She motioned Anita over. She wanted to know what was going on.

"Don't you know?" said Anita.

The woman said she'd heard there had been a murder, but she wanted more information. Other neighbors were trying to learn more details too. They were milling about the street in front of the house, observing the police, listening to conversations, soaking up as much as possible. Anita saw one of them—a man with a dog—and asked if he'd heard anything the night of the murder. The man said yes, he'd heard a scream.

"And you called the police, right?" said Anita.

"No," said the man.

"Why not?"

The man said he had heard only the one scream and had not known what to make of it. What was he supposed to do, he said, call the police and report a single cry in the night? He didn't want to look foolish.

The morning wore on. Standing in the street, Anita had a partial view of the interior of the house. The front door was open, and inside she could see the investigators moving around. It occurred to Anita that everyone in the house with Karen was a stranger. These people had never met her, and yet they were there with her, walking around her body in the hallway. Anita and Michaela, meanwhile, were restricted to the other side of the yellow tape. They were the ones who had been close to Karen, they were the ones who'd known her, and yet they were being kept the farthest away from her, on the outside of the circle.

Suddenly an outburst of laughter exploded inside the house.

Someone—several people, actually—were laughing in there, laughing so hard that to Anita it seemed the walls must be shaking. Anita was not a naive person. She knew that people who deal regularly with tragedy sometimes insulate themselves in odd ways; after all, she worked at a newspaper and had heard the kind of jokes that reporters and editors sometimes make about horrible events. But on that morning, when she heard the people laughing uproariously as they stood so close to Karen's body, she could not help but wonder. What could be so funny?

Looking back, it would be difficult to say whether the laughter that rang in Anita's ears had sprung from nervousness or anxiety or simple insensitivity. But to the officers who were moving through the house that morning, taking notes and searching for at least the beginnings of some answers, there was nothing humorous in the scene before them. Later several of them would describe it as the most disturbing sight of their lives.

From the moment Officer Falkenstein had climbed through the window and made the discovery in the hall, things had happened quickly. The house and yard had been closed off, David Mackey had been asked to return from Rhode Island as soon as possible, and a virtual parade of law enforcement officials had started to arrive. There were uniformed officers and detectives and the chief of the Gulfport police and a couple of people from the state attorney's office and a couple more from the county medical examiner's office.

One of these people was Dr. Joan Wood, the medical examiner herself. Dr. Wood was what many people would call a coroner. A stout woman with glasses and short graying hair, she had the imperturbable air of someone who has long since grown accustomed to seeing the harm that can be wreaked upon the human body. Her job had not rendered her incapable of enjoying diversion—late one night she had been sighted alone inside a crowded bar, pumping quarters into a game of Ms. Pac-Man—but when she was on duty she exuded an unbending commitment to professionalism.

Now, as she stood inside the hallway on Twenty-seventh Avenue South and observed all of the blood, she decided that the officers of the Gulfport Police Department needed help. As far as she was concerned, they did not have the experience to handle this case alone.

The medical examiner knew Gulfport pretty well. She had once lived in this very neighborhood; in fact, she'd lived on Upton Street, about ten houses away from David and Karen's. She knew it had been many years since the city's police department had been faced with a murder like this one, where the killer was unknown and still at large. She told the chief of police, Herman Golliner, that as far as she could remember, the last time Gulfport had dealt with such a case was back in 1961. Chief Golliner, who had been with the department for almost twenty-five years, said yes, he remembered that case. He'd been a patrol officer then.

Dr. Wood said she wanted to call in the FDLE, the Florida Department of Law Enforcement. This request was directed to Lieutenant Frank Hanson, the officer in charge of the investigation. Hanson, a tall man with wavy brown hair and a slight rasp in his voice, had been with the Gulfport police for more than two decades. Now, just as he and his officers were about to begin processing the scene—they'd already brought their evidence bags, video gear, and other equipment—he was being asked to relinquish the job to some outsiders. It was not a prospect he found thrilling.

"Call somebody else if you want to," he said. "But, hell, I can take fingerprints just like anybody else can."

The fact was, though, that this crime scene would require a great deal more than simply dusting for fingerprints. For one thing, Dr. Wood wondered if the bloody handprints on Karen's body might contain enough ridge detail to identify the hands that had left them. If that were possible, Wood was sure it would require expertise beyond that of the Gulfport police. Wood also wanted someone who was trained to examine the body for other prints, some of which might not be visible to the naked eye.

Then there was the large amount of blood throughout the house. Obviously there had been a protracted struggle from one end of the house to the other, and Wood believed that the blood might reveal important clues as to how that struggle had taken place. The doctor knew that at their Tampa crime lab, just across the bay, the FDLE had a veteran crime scene analyst who was trained in bloodstain pattern analysis, the technical process of studying the shapes and patterns of bloodstains left behind in an attack, then using those clues to try to reconstruct the sequence of events. Where did the attack begin? In what direction was the victim moving at this point or that point? From what direction was the attacker moving? These were the kinds of questions that the FDLE's specialist—a blood spatter expert, Wood called him— might be able to answer.

Realistically, even Hanson could not ignore the fact that Gulfport had a small police force, with only a few detectives and scarcely more than a dozen patrol officers. They would be busy enough starting the door-to-door interviews with the neighbors, not to mention the normal duties of the department. So he gave in, and the FDLE was called, and in a short time the blood pattern expert was on his way, along with another crime scene analyst from Tampa.

While she waited for them, Dr. Wood went outside the house and stood under the big oak. Someone sent one of the officers to buy some soft drinks, and before long she and several others were gathered in the shade of the tree, talking and sipping their sodas and trying to escape the summer heat. When Hanson saw them he was not pleased—it didn't look good outside a murder scene, he thought—but he kept his opinion to himself.

Soon the FDLE team pulled up in its van, which served as a mobile crime lab. Dr. Wood took them inside the house and showed them the scene inside the hall. So that they would be as diplomatic as possible, she also warned them of Hanson's ruffled feelings. With that in mind, the two analysts began their work, taking photographs, dusting for fingerprints, examining the bloody handprints and footprints, searching for anything that might reveal who had killed Karen.

Outside the house, the Gulfport police had begun moving from door to door down the streets. It was not taking long for them—or anyone else—to realize how many people had heard Karen cry out and then failed to dial 911. The list of justifications and rationalizations was already growing.

"The scream was so close and so blood-curdling, and then it just stopped cold, just like that," one woman told a reporter that day. Why hadn't anyone in her house called the police? "I think we were half afraid to," she said. "Another thought that went through our minds was that maybe it wasn't a woman's voice, but maybe a cat surprised by a raccoon."

"Wouldn't have done any good," another woman would say later, defending her and her husband's decision to mind their own business. "There was a scream, and it stopped, and she died right there . . . I don't know what we could have done."

As word of the murder spread, some people were shocked to learn that so many neighbors had heard Karen scream and done nothing. That sort of thing simply was not supposed to happen in a place like Gulfport. New York, yes, or Detroit. Maybe even across the bay in Tampa. But not here.

To the police, however, it came as no surprise that all of the neighborhood's crime watch signs had not saved Karen. Veteran officers at Gulfport—and at other departments around Pinellas County as well as the rest of the country—struggled against this kind of apathy all the time. Just a few years before, in the north part of Pinellas County, a young Clearwater woman had screamed inside her apartment as she was raped and beaten so severely that bones in her face were broken. Her cries and the commotion of the attack had gone on for more than five minutes, waking neighbors in other apartments as well as some who lived down the street. None of them had called the police.

Karen's case was as frustrating as any. Even if someone had reported the scream, there was no guarantee that a patrol car could have reached the house in time to save her life. But the Gulfport police station was less than a mile away, and if someone had called, at least there would have been a chance. Furthermore, if officers had been summoned immediately, the killer either still would have been at the house or would have just escaped. Given the number and nature of the wounds he had inflicted, he almost certainly would have been covered with blood and probably left some kind of trail. Still, it had been raining off and on all night. And because no one had called, Karen's body had not been discovered for almost a day and a half. By now it would be difficult if not impossible to find any traces of the killer's trail.

Still, Hanson and his detectives already were pursuing some leads, several of which had been given to them by George Lewis, the St. Petersburg firefighter across the street who had heard the scream while working in his garage. As it happened, Hanson already knew Lewis; most of the police officers did, because George had worked as a volunteer firefighter for Gulfport for years, and the city's firehouse was next door to the police station. George was on duty in St. Pete on the morning Karen's body was discovered, but one of the detectives had called George and asked if he'd mind putting his recollections of the night of the murder down on paper, to help them keep track of what everyone had seen and heard. George had said no problem and had gone to the police station immediately and written a two-page statement.

When Hanson and the others read the statement, they were thankful that George had been among those who'd heard the scream. He was the only neighbor who had ventured outside after the scream. Others had peered out their windows or doorways, but he had actually stepped outside his garage—where he'd been working on a motorcycle and listening to the radio, when he heard the cry—then walked out onto Twenty-seventh and looked around, trying to find out where the sound had come from. At first he hadn't seen anything, he said, but a little while later, after returning to his garage to continue working, he had noticed a man ride past on a bike. George couldn't be sure, but he thought maybe he'd seen the same man earlier that evening, accompanied by another man, both of them white and around middle age, cruising through the neighborhood on ten-speeds.

There was more. In his statement George also mentioned the man who had stopped by the house the evening after the murder. George told how he'd seen the man pull up in a van and go into the porch, and then put a note on David's car before driving away. By now the detectives had found and read this note and were eager to know more about the person named Peter who had left it. They did not yet know his full name, or how he was connected to Karen, or why he had visited the house that evening, or why he had referred in the note to finding no life at the house while Karen's body lay inside only a few feet away. Nor were they sure how he could have stepped into the porch without seeing the broken glass on the walk, the hole in the jalousie door, or the smears of blood on the inner door.

George's statement listed a couple more observations that the detectives thought were worth pursuing. First, he mentioned that David Mackey, whose name he did not know, sometimes practiced martial arts. Second, he said that he'd noticed two men—two black men, he made a point of noting—mowing the lawn at David and Karen's house and that one of them had suffered a seizure at the house a month or so before. Paramedics, he added, had been summoned to the scene, which meant there ought to be a record of the incident somewhere. As he said in the statement:

Rescue 1 ran on it, they should have a report with <u>his</u> <u>name</u>.

The FDLE team had found something promising as well.

For several hours the two analysts had been hard at work, dusting for fingerprints, collecting hairs, gathering the sheets and pillowcases from the blood-stained bed, taking photographs both inside and outside the house. Working in the bedroom, one of them had found fingerprints on the sill of the bedroom window through which Officer Falkenstein had crawled. Given the dried blood that had been left on the window sill and curtain, it was obvious that this was probably the place where the killer had climbed out after the attack. Now, they'd lifted these prints from that same window. Later Hanson would remember one of the analysts—the assistant to the blood pattern expert—telling him ecstatically that she was sure these were the killer's prints. Even better, she said, the prints were sharp and clear, perfect for nailing an identification.

"They're beautiful," she said.

Not everything was going so well, however. The blood pattern expert had studied the bloody handprints on Karen's body under a magnifying glass and concluded that they would not be of much use. Karen had lain in the hall for too long. The blood in the handprints had dried and seeped into the pores of her skin, obliterating their lines and ridges. The senior analyst also had examined the bloody partial bare footprint on the bathroom floor and decided that it was just a smear, without enough detail to make an ID. But just in case, he photographed it along with the handprints and the other stains. In addition, an assistant to Dr. Wood had walked carefully through the different rooms with a video camera, scanning it all so that a visual record of the entire scene would be preserved on tape.

At the same time, the senior analyst and the other investigators were beginning to develop some theories as to the sequence of events surrounding Karen's scream. They already were fairly sure where the killer had slipped out of the house, but how had he gotten in? The detectives thought the blood-stained window was an unlikely candidate. After all, the screen had been found in place, latched at the top, and it would have been awkward to crawl through there with the screen dragging along his back. Besides, there were no obvious signs of forced entry, either around the window or anywhere else in the house. It was possible that the killer was someone Karen knew or at least recognized and that she had gone to the front door and let him in, then tried to escape once the attack began. Or maybe the person had entered the house somehow earlier on, when she was still at Neverne's, and was waiting for her when she came home that night.

And the path of the struggle? There were several scenarios, none of which satisfied every question or met with everyone's agreement. But the one that seemed most probable—the one that would last—held that Karen probably had been stabbed first in the bedroom, then had broken free and run for the front door, making it as far as the porch before she fell or was pushed against the jalousie door, knocking her head through the glass. Judging from how many neighbors had heard her, it was probably there on the porch that she screamed. Then, according to this theory, her attacker had dragged her off the porch and forced her into the hallway where she broke free and ran again, this time toward the bathroom, before he caught her once more and finished killing her.

One thing didn't make sense. There had been a terrible struggle, late at night, with two people moving from one end of the house to the other, and yet the police had found nothing knocked over. In the back bedroom there was the telephone on the magazines and the fan on the floor, and a nightstand beside the bed, and a lamp and an answering machine on top of the stand. In the living room there were stacks of records beside the stereo. None of it appeared to have been disturbed. And in the bathroom, where one might have expected the killer to try to wash up, the sink and the toilet and the tub were all clean. In fact, other than the trail of blood from the bedroom to the porch, the rest of the house seemed remarkably neat. To Hanson, that was what made the scene so eerie—finding such fury surrounded by so much perfect order.

Yet when Falkenstein and the paramedics entered the house, they had found all of the lights turned off. How could that be? If the struggle had taken place in total darkness, wouldn't something inside these rooms have been broken or bumped to the floor? And even if there had been some kind of illumination—even if Karen and her killer had fought through the house with every light blazing—wouldn't there still be at least one thing out of place?

At some point in the long and desolate hours of that day, two men drove up in a gray station wagon and rolled a gurney into the house.

Anita and Michaela, still watching and waiting on the street, saw the men and recognized them at once with a sickening feeling. The night before, a Piper Tomahawk flying at sunset had suddenly taken a nosedive into the warm shallow water just off St. Petersburg Beach, not far from where the two women lived. The pilot and a passenger had been killed, and Anita and Michaela had been walking along the water when they saw two men taking away the bodies. These were the same men. Only now, they had come to take away Karen.

A few minutes later they wheeled out the body. It was in a bag, and as the gurney rolled, Anita saw movement inside the bag, and suddenly she was seized with the notion that if she could just wrap her arms around Karen, if she could just hold her and take her away from there, everything would be all right.

Not long after that, one of the FDLE crime scene analysts—the woman who was the assistant—walked out of the house and began putting her equipment back into the van. Anita and Michaela were standing nearby, obviously enveloped in the first waves of shock and grief, and when the analyst saw them she tried to be kind. She asked if they had known Karen. When they said yes, she told them that after spending time inside the house and seeing how it was decorated, she had been able to get a sense of what kind of person Karen had been. She told them that even though their friend had been murdered, she'd looked as though she were only sleeping there on the carpet. As she said these things, tears welled in the woman's eyes.

Anita had a question. She wanted to know who was going to clean up the house. The analyst explained that she and her partner were done, and they would not be doing it. Neither would the police. The job probably would be left, the woman said, to whomever owned the house. Cruel as it may have sounded, this was standard procedure. Most police departments do not consider it their job to clean murder scenes. Instead that task is left to the victim's family or friends.

Anita was stunned. She knew David was flying back that afternoon from Rhode Island. She also knew that she did not want him to have to walk into his house and see the things that now awaited him. So she decided to do the cleaning herself. She and Michaela drove to Anita's apartment, gathered some paper towels and spray cleaner, and headed back to Gulfport.

By the time Anita and Michaela returned to the house it was

midafternoon, and the police were taking down the yellow tape and preparing to leave. Hanson was standing in the front doorway when Anita approached and asked if they could go inside and clean. Later the lieutenant would look back and wish he had said no. But it had been a tiring, trying day, and now that the FDLE team had finished and released the scene, Hanson could see no reason not to allow them to begin the scrubbing. Someone would have to do it.

He swept his hand toward the inside of the house. "Go ahead," he said.

Anita and Michaela stepped into the empty house and looked around. They knew, as did all of the onlookers gathered outside, that Karen had been murdered. But until that moment they had not realized how prolonged and violent the attack had been. Now, as they saw what remained of that struggle and understood some of what Karen had endured, they began to sob. With tears running down their cheeks, they picked up the paper towels and started to clean their friend's blood from the walls of the hallway. As she worked, Anita thought of Karen—of how hard she must have fought, how frightened she must have been in those last terrible moments, and how alone she had been through all those hours afterward, lying there in the darkness of the hallway.

Now that the police had left and taken away the yellow tape, children were running up to the house and trying to peer inside. Cars were slowly cruising past the yard, their tires rumbling on the red bricks. Every time Anita and Michaela heard the rumbling, they stopped to look up. With no one else inside the house, they were afraid. Karen's murderer was still out there. How could they be sure he wouldn't come back? They closed all of the windows, locked the front door, and went back to work.

They were still cleaning when some police officers arrived. Anita got the impression these officers had come not on business but to gawk. As they walked through the house they speculated about the murder, talking about how the attacker probably had "finished her off" in the hallway and looking through photos of Karen and her friends. All the while they said nothing to Anita or Michaela, as if the two women were not even there. And, like almost everyone else that day, these officers kept referring to "the body" or "the victim." Anita heard them and told herself that Karen was neither one of those things. She was Karen.

After the officers left, Michaela had to stop cleaning. She was sorry, she told Anita, but she couldn't do it anymore. She went out to the porch, and in a little while she called out that a car had pulled up to the house.

It was David and his brother, who had picked David up at the airport. Anita stopped working. She had done what she could, but there had not been enough time to clean up all of the blood. She went outside and met David on the steps and hugged him. She told him what she and Michaela had been doing and tried to prepare him for what he would see inside. He thanked her and said he was glad she was there.

David went into the house and looked around without saying a word. Wrapped in solitude, he walked through the rooms, taking in every terrible detail. Finally it became too much. He wandered out to the living room, dropped to his knees, and began to weep. The others came to him and wrapped their arms around him and tried to comfort him. A few minutes later, after he'd collected some clean clothes, he and his brother left for the police station, where the detectives wanted to talk with him.

Anita and Michaela left too. They went back to Anita's apartment on the beach, the apartment that also had been Karen's until only a few days before. They were still afraid, and when the sun went down, their fear grew. They pulled a foldout bed from the couch and spent the night awake, crying some more, holding each other tight, and listening for noises outside.

Four

As darkness fell that Thursday night the investigation hurtled forward.

Up at the medical examiner's midcounty office the senior analyst on the FDLE team had tried again to find some sort of usable print on Karen's body. This time he searched with iodine fuming, an old technique sometimes used for locating fingerprints on skin. He took a glass tube containing iodine crystals at one end, kept in place with cotton, and then held it close to Karen's body as he blew through the other end. The heat of his breath activated the crystals, causing them to release their poisonous fumes. As he blew into the tube and sent the fumes floating outward, the nearest area of skin turned a yellowish brown. All the while he watched closely. If the technique were going to work, any prints on the skin might reveal themselves by turning an even darker brown.

It didn't happen. The analyst tried the fumes on Karen's ankles, thighs, shoulders, and other parts of her body that might have been touched, including the areas around the bloody handprints. But no prints showed themselves.

Early that evening, Dr. Wood began the autopsy—and

quickly learned just how brutal the murder had been. Karen, she determined, had been stabbed in the neck at least thirteen times, probably with some sort of buck knife. One of the wounds had grooved a bone in her spine; two others had punctured the entire width of her larynx. In addition, her head had been repeatedly beaten with or shoved against a blunt object. Her hands had been cut and bruised, apparently from trying to fend off the killer's weapon, and the index finger of her left hand had been broken. Furthermore, there were traces of semen inside her vagina, confirming the investigators' suspicions that this was not only a murder but a rape.

Wood also had made an unexpected discovery. Inside the house, where the body was shrouded in the dried blood and the darkness of the hall, the doctor had been able to see only the stab wounds. But when the body was cleaned and examined under the light at her office, she found something else. Across the midline of the neck was a superficial cut, with hemorrhaging in the tissue underneath, which meant that the weapon had been pressed very hard against the skin. The killer had not been satisfied with stabbing Karen over and over. He also had tried to slit her throat.

Other than Lt. Hanson, the Gulfport Police Department had a grand total of three detectives—William Brinkworth, Allen Reed, and their direct supervisor, Sergeant Larry Tosi. That night they were all working late, running down whatever information they could about their first two suspects.

After some preliminary interviews they had learned that the man who left the no-signs-of-life note was Peter Kumble, an acquaintance of Karen's who in his spare time hosted a weekly bluegrass show on WMNF-FM, a local radio station. But they still hadn't had a chance to speak with him or find out why he had visited the house that evening.

They were more eager, on that first evening, to talk to the lawn man who had suffered the seizure at the house. Acting on the tip from George Lewis, they had checked him out and learned that he was Lawrence Sanders, a Vietnam veteran whom David Mackey knew and had hired to mow his lawn. The fact that Sanders worked at the house and had been inside suggested to them that he probably was familiar with the layout of the rooms and might even have known a way to get inside when no one was home. Furthermore, Sanders and another man had been seen mowing the lawn there early on Tuesday, Karen's last day alive.

All of this raised some critical questions. Had something happened that day? Had Sanders talked to Karen? Had she mentioned to him that David was out of town? Was it possible that he had seen her getting dressed and decided to come back later to make a pass?

Putting it all together, the detectives thought there was a fair chance Sanders might be their man. So when it was decided to interview him that very night, all three of them—Tosi, Brinkworth, and Reed—went together to his house.

Sanders and his wife were already in bed when they got there. They told him they were investigating the homicide of Karen Gregory, read him his rights, and asked if he would be willing to answer some questions.

"No problem," he said.

They drove him over to Gulfport's claustrophobic little police station and led him into a small, barren room within the building's cinder block walls. They questioned him for close to two hours, asking him about his background and about Karen and David and the house and the lawn. Through it all Sanders was relaxed and cooperative, making it clear he had nothing to hide. The only thing that seemed to shake him was the fact that David's girlfriend was dead.

"I can't believe it happened," he said. "They were nice people."

Sanders confirmed that he had cut the lawn the morning of the murder. It had taken a little longer than usual that day, he said, because some trimming had been needed and because his lawn mower had broken down, which meant he'd had to stop and go get a part so it could be fixed. The detectives wanted to know about the other man who'd been seen working with him. Sanders said he did not know the man's name. He said it was just some guy he'd picked up that morning in St. Pete, at a place along Eighteenth Avenue South where unemployed laborers would gather and wait for odd jobs. What about David? Had Sanders known that David was out of town? No, he said. And Karen? Had he seen her that day? Yes. Early that morning, when she was leaving for work, she'd stopped for a moment to tell him she'd left a check for him in the mailbox. She'd given him checks in the past, when David wasn't home. Was she dressed when she paid him? Always, he said.

They asked where he had been later that Tuesday, on the night of the murder. He said he had been at home all evening—something his wife had already confirmed. Was he willing to let them take his fingerprints? Yes. What about blood samples and samples of his hairs? Yes. He was more than willing, he said, to do whatever he could to help them find whoever had committed this crime.

That same evening, the detectives conducted a little experiment.

They were still thinking about the house and how unbelievably tidy it was, even though all of the lights had been found turned off. So that night Tosi and Reed went back—the department had been given a key to the house—and staged a reenactment. They turned off all of the lights, gave their eyes a few moments to adjust to the dark, then looked around to see if there was enough visibility to move around without bumping into things. The house, it turned out, was extremely dark. A streetlight stood on the corner across the street, but it was partially blocked by the huge oak tree and didn't shine much light inside. In those conditions it would have been virtually impossible for such a struggle to take place without anything being knocked over.

A light must have been on somewhere, they decided. But that didn't add up, either. This was not some rich area, filled with secluded mansions. This was a middle-class neighborhood where the yards were small and the houses were practically on top of one another. If someone were going to commit a murder in such a place, why would he risk giving the neighbors a view of what was happening?

There was another possibility, however, something that had occurred to one of the detectives. Something that made the other discoveries of that day all the more chilling.

On Wednesday, when Karen's body was still lying in the hallway, Martha Borkowski had noticed that the front jalousie door of the house was open. An hour or so later, after Peter Kumble stopped by, walked inside the porch, and then drove away, it was still open. But the next morning, when Falkenstein pulled up in her cruiser, the door was closed and locked.

The murderer, it appeared, had returned.

*   *   *

Detective Brinkworth was at the house that night too, searching Karen's belongings for names, addresses, any kind of lead. He had just been outside for a moment, talking to one of the neighbors, when the phone rang.

Not sure what to do, Brinkworth let it ring a couple of times, then picked it up.

"Hello?"

"Could I speak to Karen, please?" said a male voice.

"Who's calling?"

"Peter Kumble."

Brinkworth knew none of them had found the time yet to interview Kumble. Now, suddenly finding himself talking with the man, he was careful.

"Karen's not here."

"Then could I speak to David?"

"David's not here either."

"Who's this?"

"Detective Brinkworth with the Gulfport police. I'm here investigating the death of Ms. Gregory."

Kumble paused and said he was shocked. He said he was sorry to learn such a thing. Brinkworth asked Kumble how he had known Karen. He knew her socially, Kumble said, and with that he told the whole story of how he'd visited the house the evening before and walked inside the porch. The reason he'd stopped by, he said, was to return a cassette tape he'd borrowed and to have dinner with Karen.

Brinkworth listened, making mental notes. He took down Kumble's address and number, then hung up and went back to his search.

On the other end of the line, Kumble was shaken. He picked up the phone again and called an old girlfriend.

"Make sure your doors are locked," he said.

Five

Is this Karen Gregory?"
Anita Kilpatrick looked at the face before her. She knew she was expected to give an answer. That was why she'd been led down this corridor, to this large picture window. So she could confirm that the body lying on the stretcher on the other side of the glass was indeed that of her friend. But now Anita could not speak. She had not been prepared for this. She had not known what to expect. She stood there with her hands pressed against the glass, staring. Finally she said yes and began to cry.

Standing beside her, Peter Kumble said yes as well.

It was Friday, May 25, the day after Karen's body had been discovered. Anita had not slept all night and had spent much of the day trying, with no luck, to make arrangements for traveling to Albany, New York, where the funeral was to be held. This was the beginning of Memorial Day weekend, and after checking with the airlines she had not been able to find any plane tickets within her limited budget. She wasn't sure how she was going to make the trip.

Then Peter had called.

Kumble was not particularly close to Anita. He was more of

an acquaintance than a friend, just as he had been with Karen. Both he and Anita had been regulars at the Garden, and they'd talked there with Karen. She and Karen also used to run into him at reggae concerts out on the beach, some of which were sponsored by the radio station where Peter worked.

Now, on this Friday, as Anita searched for a way to reach the funeral, Peter phoned her at the apartment to say how badly he felt about Karen's murder. He was going to be out of touch for a couple of weeks, he told her; that very afternoon he was leaving town in his van, driving north on a long-planned vacation to Boston and other parts of the Northeast. When Peter said this, Anita had no idea the police already considered him a suspect who had some explaining to do. All she knew was that she needed to get to New York for the funeral, and when she heard that on this very afternoon he would be driving in that direction, she asked if she could ride with him. Peter said all right.

Before they left, though, she asked if they could stop at the medical examiner's office. In order for the funeral to proceed, two people were needed to identify Karen's body. Anita had already volunteered to do it, and when Peter was asked to be the second person, he reluctantly agreed.

"Well," he said, "if I have to, I have to."

He and Anita were not the only ones at the office that afternoon. Sgt. Tosi stood nearby, watching. Tosi had come to the identification because he had been told that Kumble would be there and because he wanted to study Peter's face at the emotional moment when the sheet came down and Peter found himself staring into Karen's face. Later Peter would say how much it disturbed him to make the ID; until that instant, he would say, he did not know that Karen had been stabbed. A few feet away, though, Tosi was struck by how calm Peter appeared.

But the thing that really caught Tosi's attention—the thing he would talk about most when he returned to the station—was what happened next. Once the identification was over, he asked Peter and Anita to join him in a conference room so he could ask a few preliminary questions. He knew they did not have much time to talk, but he said it would help if they could just tell him a little about Karen and how they had come to know her. As Anita began to answer, Tosi looked over at Kumble's hands, which were resting on the table, and noticed that the right one was marked with a scratch. It was a rather large scratch; it also was relatively fresh, as if it might have been made within the past several days.

Trying not to be too obvious, Tosi returned his gaze to Anita for a few seconds and then glanced back at the hand for another quick look. He could not swear that Peter knew he was being studied, but as he listened to Anita, Tosi saw out of the corner of his eye that Peter was watching him. A few seconds later, when Tosi glanced at the hand again, Peter moved it off the table for a moment, then moved it back.

When the interview was over, Tosi said goodbye, and Peter and Anita left for the ride north. They drove together for one and a half days, alone in the van except for Peter's dog, a pit bull named Lady, who kept insisting on laying her head in Anita's lap. It was a strange, distinctly uncomfortable trip. To Anita it seemed like almost every song that came over the radio revolved around death. Peter, as it happened, was a Grateful Dead fan, and as they drove he played one of their tapes, which included a song called "Dire Wolf," in which the singer repeatedly pleads "please don't murder me." Anita was at the wheel somewhere in the Carolinas when some idiot who apparently thought she was going too slow cut directly in front of her, forcing her to swerve off the road and hit the brakes. All of the tools Peter was storing in back came hurtling forward with a crash.

Peter, who had been sleeping, jerked awake. "What is it?"

"Some guy just practically ran me off the road. I'm sorry."

Anita was already a nervous wreck. She couldn't sleep. She was afraid. Every time she closed her eyes, she saw someone hurting Karen. They'd pull off the highway to eat or get some gas, and she'd find herself sitting there, shaking. Anita did not know who had killed her friend. But she was looking at the men around her in a way she never had before.

"I'm a little jumpy," she told Peter.

"I understand," he said.

Peter didn't seem quite himself either. Karen's murder and the identification of her body had left him nervous and uneasy as well. Sitting beside him, Anita thought he was acting rather distant, and she noticed that he was smoking cigarettes one after the other. That wasn't like him; if she remembered right, he usually smoked a pipe.

That night, Anita asked if they could stop briefly in Washington, D.C. She wanted to talk to some friends there who might give her a little support and make her feel better. But Peter said no, he wanted to drive straight through. They didn't drive straight through, though. A little while later, not far north of D.C., Peter pulled over at a rest stop and slept for a few hours. Anita sat awake beside him, still shaking as she watched the people move outside the van.

At first Karen's family had not been sure whether the funeral should be in Florida or New York. But Sophia insisted that her daughter be brought back to Albany.

"I want Karen to come home," she said.

As they learned a few details of what had happened, Sophia and the others searched for ways to believe that it was not true. Mark told himself that his sister was in intensive care somewhere and was going to recover. Roy told himself she had been kidnapped and that eventually they would find her. He invented other impossible scenarios that brought her back to life. He pictured Karen alone in the hallway of the house, with the phone ringing and the curtains blowing in the wind. She would be all right, he told himself, if he could pick her up and wash her off and put her into bed.

Reality kept intruding on these inventions. In the haze of that weekend, they had to buy Karen a burial dress. There had been no time to send her clothes from Florida, and so Kim and Roy and their mother went out to buy a dress.

"Make sure it has a high neck," the funeral director told Roy.

There was no need to say why. Roy tried to repeat the instruction gently to his sister and mother. They went to Marshalls, the discount outlet. Karen had loved that place. It carried nice clothes at low prices, and it had the name she'd been raised with. They used to joke that it was Karen's store. So now her family went there, searching for a purple dress with a high neck. They found it, too. There was only one, and it was Karen's size. It was as if it had been waiting for them.

The wake was that night. Both Anita and David were there, as was the family. Karen's body lay before them in an open casket. Roy walked up to it, hearing a roaring in his ears. This is what skydiving must be like, he thought. This is what it must be like to jump out of a plane.

The first thing he saw was the purple dress. Then he noticed that Karen didn't look right. The family had lent some photos of her to the people at the funeral home to assist them, but still she appeared different. Her hair was shorter than Roy remembered—she'd had it cut since he last saw her—and she was wearing a light pink shade of lipstick that she had hated. Their mother had placed a rosary in her hands, and as he looked at the hands, Roy realized there was something wrong with them, too. They looked stiff and unnatural, and one of them was partially hidden.

Suddenly Roy remembered what the attacker had done to Karen's hands. Roy knew she had suffered other, more terrible injuries. But those wounds were almost too much to contemplate. What overwhelmed him now was that someone had broken his sister's finger. He remembered how tough her fingers had been when the two of them wrestled as children. He remembered her squeezing those fingers on the back of his neck. He began to sob.

Kim stood there with her husband and said that seeing Karen's body was like looking at a seashell. It was beautiful, but it was empty inside. Kim stroked her sister's hair.

"Give me a sign," Kim said. "Tell me who did this."

The funeral was the next day. Their mother wanted a mass, so it was held at Sacred Heart, the church Karen had joked about never entering again. In his eulogy the pastor talked about how Karen had gone to a Catholic high school and a Catholic college and about how she had been a talented artist. Roy imagined Karen standing beside him, making faces and giggling about the oak doors slamming shut in their faces. It also occurred to him that Karen was still the trailblazer, even in death.

It rained that day and was still raining that night when the family finally went to sleep. Roy dreamed about Karen. He dreamed that he went to the funeral home and took her body from the casket and carried her out of the home and deep into some woods. It was raining, and Roy placed Karen's body in the mud and lay there with it and tried to push his way into the ground so they could be buried together.

When he woke from the dream, Roy got out of bed and went outside. A house was being built across the street, and he went over to the construction site and lay down in the mud, just as he had in his dream, and let the rain wash over him. He wanted to die. He wanted to be with Karen.

Anita was still in Albany, at the house of one of Karen's brothers, when Sgt. Tosi called. He wanted to know if Peter was there. She said no. He asked where Peter was. Boston, she told him. Then he asked if she had noticed the scratch on his hand.

Anita was confused. She did not understand why Tosi was asking these questions.

"Is Peter a suspect?"

Tosi sort of mumbled an answer.

Anita pressed him. *"Is Peter a suspect?"*

"Yes."

Anita felt as if she'd been slapped. She had just made a long trip, alone, with a murder suspect. And as she reflected back on that trip, now and in the days that followed, different moments from that day and a half on the road began to take on a new significance. She thought about how remote Peter had seemed and about his chain-smoking the cigarettes when she'd never seen him smoke cigarettes before. She thought about how impatient he had seemed when she wanted to contact her friends in Washington, about how he'd said he wanted to keep going and then had stopped for several hours. She thought about the two of them at the rest stop on Saturday night and how she'd sat there, shaking in the dark while Peter slept a few feet away. Suddenly she felt more afraid than ever.

Six

I t was becoming increasingly clear that the Gulfport police were facing a case unlike any they had faced before.

Over the years, the city's law officers had chased their share of bicycle thieves and burglars. But as Dr. Wood had reminded them at the crime scene, asking them to step aside in deference to the FDLE, they could hardly be considered experts when it came to tracking down murderers. On the day Karen's body was found, Bill Brinkworth had been working as a detective for only slightly more than a month. He had never investigated a murder; in that short time there had been no other murders to investigate. Even a veteran officer such as Tosi, who had served as a Gulfport detective for a dozen years, had handled only two homicides—possibly three, if he counted another case in which he'd suspected foul play but had never been able to prove it. The two confirmed cases had both been stabbings, and both had been solved quickly.

Solving Karen's case would not be so easy. It wasn't just that her attacker had escaped the house undetected, his trail washed away by the neighbors' silence and the rain and the passage of time. The nature of the murder itself defied easy explanation. None of the usual motives seemed to apply. As far as Tosi, Brinkworth, and the others could tell, money seemed to have played no part in it. Karen had hardly been wealthy.

As for someone breaking in to rob her, that seemed unlikely too. Tosi had been in the neighborhood earlier that night, only a few blocks away, checking out a domestic complaint. He had seen how hard it was raining, and he doubted that anyone would have been out prowling in the middle of such a downpour.

Moreover, little, if anything, appeared to have been stolen from the house. Not that it was easy to tell. After all, Karen had been moving in at the time, and when David returned from Rhode Island he found many of her belongings—belongings that had not been there when he left—scattered in boxes around various rooms. Nothing obvious seemed to be missing, but it was impossible for him to say for sure. As for his own things, David did report that he could not find a certain vase. But he couldn't say for sure whether it had been taken the night of the murder; for all he knew it might have been lost or broken earlier.

Like Dr. Wood, the detectives were working on the assumption that Karen had been raped. But the evidence suggested strongly that this had been more than a simple sexual assault and stabbing. Wood, for instance, had noticed that there was something odd about the clothing found on Karen—the white T-shirt, pulled up near her breasts, and a black teddy bunched around her waist. Some women wear teddies to bed, others wear T-shirts. They usually don't wear both, unless it's cold, and the murder had taken place on a warm night. A woman might sometimes wear a teddy as an undergarment during the day. But Neverne Covington had told the police what Karen had been wearing earlier that evening at dinner. She'd had on the T-shirt, but not the teddy. In addition, the placement of the clothing on the body suggested that Karen had been wearing the teddy over the T-shirt. It appeared, in other words, that the murderer might have forced Karen to put on the lingerie.

The evidence raised other disturbing possibilities as well. The most obvious ones concerned the nature of the attack. In most stabbings, as Dr. Wood would explain later, the assailant strikes the knife in a general direction, hitting different parts of the victim's body. But Karen's wounds suggested a more methodical assault in which one section of her body might have held some special significance. Each time Karen's murderer had stabbed her, he had directed the blade to her neck—and not just to her neck, but to both the left and right sides of the neck. Furthermore, the bloody handprints on the body had not been particularly smeared, which meant that Karen probably had not been struggling when they were left on her skin; the attack, in other words, apparently had continued after she was down on the ground, no longer moving. Given the location of the handprints, Wood thought it likely that the killer had made them as he rolled Karen over, either from her back or from her right side onto her left, so that he could stab the other side of her neck.

Something else had struck Wood as strange, too, and that was how the killer had both stabbed Karen and tried to cut her throat. "Usually when people stab people, they stab them," the doctor would later explain. "They don't usually attempt to cut their throat."

Wood couldn't say for sure whether her observations added up to anything. But among all of the scenarios, she thought they should consider the possibility that Karen might have died in some kind of ritualistic slaying.

There also remained the question of why the killer had apparently slipped back into the house the night after the murder. It was possible he'd gone back to straighten the house, or to wipe away his fingerprints, or to retrieve something that might identify him and that he accidentally had left behind. But there was another, perhaps even more frightening, possibility. Returning to the scene of the crime is one of the patterns of behavior commonly found in cases where the murderer is a deranged individual, someone wrestling with severe psychological problems. In such cases the killer often returns so that he can relive or fantasize about the murder. Sometimes he even takes and keeps an object, such as a piece of clothing or a driver's license, to remind him of the victim.

All of these elements—the teddy over the T-shirt, the neck wounds, and the probable return to the scene—indicated that Karen's murderer was someone deeply disturbed. And though the police had no reason to believe he was after anyone else, they could not ignore the fact that such a person certainly was capable of killing again.

A week or so after the investigation began, its most veteran detective—Sgt. Tosi—left on a month's vacation that had been scheduled long before. Knowing that his colleagues already were pursuing at least a couple of promising leads, he drove with his family to the Smokey Mountains in Tennessee and tried to get his mind off the murder. In Tosi's absence Lt. Hanson left the case largely in the hands of Bill Brinkworth.

Brinkworth, an amiable man whose bright red hair and moustache made him look like the stereotype of an Irish cop, had no illusions about his lack of experience in investigating homicides. He was continuing with the work that had begun under Tosi—interviewing Karen's friends and family, checking out Kumble and Sanders. But through it all, he could not rid himself of the feeling that he couldn't handle the case alone. He thought he needed help with this murder.

"It was my first one, and I was kind of stumbling through it," he would say later. "But I was trying the best I could."

Brinkworth was reluctant to ask Hanson for guidance with the investigation. To Brinkworth, the lieutenant seemed wrapped up in other cases and duties and didn't have either the time or the desire to give too much advice. Nor did Chief Golliner, an old-fashioned man who was known around the county as "Hap" and who had devoted much of his life to umpiring Little League baseball. The chief was a nice enough man, but as far as Brinkworth could tell, he had already withdrawn into a sort of early retirement, holing up in his office, a grim box of a room that he had converted into a showcase for his personal collection of baseball figurines. He had hundreds of them—pitchers, catchers, bat boys, fathers showing sons how to stand at the plate and swing—crowded on shelves around the room. The Ceramic Palace, Brinkworth called it, and to him it seemed almost impossible to break the room's spell on the chief.

Not knowing where else to turn, he sought the expertise of two homicide detectives he knew with the St. Petersburg police. They walked with him through Karen Gregory's house, theorizing on what could be learned from the evidence, helping him search for the murder weapon—it had never been found—and even sitting in on at least one interview to assist with the questioning.

Through it all there was never any shortage of suspects. As Brinkworth was quickly learning, Karen had been a striking, charismatic woman who had managed in her relatively short time in Florida to make a remarkable number of friends and acquaintances. Also, her days at the Garden undoubtedly had exposed her to a number of customers who had found her desirable. This only increased the number of people who might have formed some sort of attraction or obsession for her and who conceivably could have wanted to harm her. In the weeks that followed her death, Brinkworth and the others collected fingerprints—and sometimes palm prints and hair samples—from at least ten men.

The list of suspects seemed to grow longer every day. There was a man who'd known Karen from the Garden and had expressed a romantic interest in her, and another regular at the Garden who'd been overheard describing in detail how she'd been killed, and a man who'd been hired to clean the carpets at David and Karen's house one day when Karen was there alone, and a Vietnam veteran—not Lawrence Sanders—who knew David and had recently threatened a security guard with a knife, and a man who'd been accused of abducting a woman not far from Gulfport and stabbing her repeatedly, including several times in the neck. Brinkworth checked them all out and came up with nothing connecting them to the murder. He also tried, without success, to track down the middle-aged man who'd been seen after the scream riding down the street on the ten-speed bike. As for Sanders, he had a solid alibi for that night. Plus the detectives had been impressed by how calm and cooperative he'd been during his questioning. To them he simply had not acted like a cornered killer.

Inevitably, David Mackey had to be checked out as well. Though he had explained that he was at his conference when Karen was killed, they needed to be sure. Brinkworth called the airlines and found that on the day before the murder David had done as he'd said, first taking a Delta Airlines flight to John F. Kennedy International Airport in New York, then catching a flight to Providence, where the conference was to be held. Brinkworth also checked with David's hotel, a Marriott, where an assistant comptroller confirmed that a Mr. David Mackey had been registered there during the week of the murder.

Out of all these people, though, none attracted as much attention as did Peter Kumble. From the start there had been a multitude of reasons to put him at the top of the list. After seeing him at the house that Wednesday evening, walking inside the porch while Karen's body lay inside, George Lewis kept telling the detectives that Kumble needed to be investigated. Something about him hadn't been right, Lewis said.

"That guy gave me the creeps," he told them.

It was true that Kumble had left his name and number at the house that night, something no killer would do, unless he was exceedingly stupid or compulsively eager to be caught. But the unnerving wording of his note was not easy to dismiss as mere coincidence. Nor did the police find his explanation for the visit entirely convincing. On the first night of the investigation, when Brinkworth had unexpectedly spoken with him on the phone, Kumble had said that he and Karen had scheduled a dinner date. But why would she have asked him over, Brinkworth wondered, on a night when David was out of town?

Other questions nagged at Brinkworth as well. Where had Kumble gotten the scratch on his hand? Why would he have agreed to identify the murdered body of a woman who was only an acquaintance? Why accept such an unpleasant responsibility? And was it just another coincidence that Kumble had left town on the very day after the police had discovered Karen's body?

In those first weeks of June, as he took over the investigation Brinkworth spent much of his time searching for some answers. He couldn't interview Kumble face to face, because he was still out of town. But other people were available, and what they told Brinkworth only deepened his suspicions. To begin with, it seemed increasingly improbable that Karen would have had a dinner date that Wednesday evening. Neverne Covington, a close friend in whom Karen often had confided, told Brinkworth that Karen had never shown a shred of interest in getting involved with anyone other than David. In fact, Neverne remembered a time when Karen had been frustrated with the relationship—she and David were having an argument that had soon blown over—and Neverne had suggested that she might want to date other men. But Karen had said no. She certainly had had plenty of opportunities, with all of the men who'd asked her out when she was working at the Garden. But once she'd met David, Karen had said, that was it, end of chapter.

When Brinkworth interviewed David, he confirmed how close he and Karen had been. David also pointed out that his job had required him to travel out of town frequently, and that whenever he was away Karen had routinely told him where she was going at night and with whom she was going. Yet she had never mentioned anything about dinner with Peter Kumble. As far as David had been able to tell, Karen had never expressed much interest at all in Kumble, even as a friend. But he apparently had been interested in Karen; she'd noticed it herself and commented on it, and so had David and Anita, who had compared notes while they were together up north for the funeral. To the two of them, it seemed that Kumble had shown an avid interest in Karen, asking Anita to relay messages to her, repeatedly dropping her name in conversation, going on about how much both of them enjoyed bicycling and how they were both from New England and how they planned to do this or that together.

Anita and David were particularly struck by an invitation Kumble had made to Karen at a party Anita threw the previous March. At the time, Karen and David were having the disagreement Neverne had mentioned. It wasn't a big deal—it had to do with how much time David was spending with his work, and it was over in a day or so—but Karen went to the party without David. That evening, while she was still upset about the argument, she and Kumble left the other guests and took a walk on the beach. Karen confided in Kumble, telling him how depressed she was and how much she'd like to see her family in New York. Hearing this, Kumble mentioned that he would be leaving soon for a vacation in the Northeast and asked her if she wanted to drive up with him. They'd ride in the van, sharing expenses, and he would drop her off outside Boston so she could visit her family. Later, however, Karen had declined the offer.

Now, looking back, it seemed to Anita and David that Kumble had shown a keen sense of timing that night on the beach, finding Karen in an emotionally vulnerable moment, then asking her to join him on an extended journey. So they told Brinkworth about Kumble's apparent interest in Karen, about his invitation, and about his strange behavior on the trip north with Anita.

Brinkworth was already checking on Kumble, talking to his friends and coworkers, trying to find out more about him, trying to piece together his whereabouts during the week of the murder. Again, these interviews only raised more questions. Brinkworth learned, for instance, that Kumble had taught a yoga class on Tuesday evenings at a center in St. Petersburg. But a counselor there informed Brinkworth that Kumble had not been at his class on May 22, the night Karen was killed. He hadn't called to let them know the class was cancelled; he just hadn't shown up.

Kumble did have an alibi for that evening, though. At the time he shared a house with a man who worked as a draftsman at the same surveying company where Peter was employed. The housemate's name was Kenneth Kuhar, and when Brinkworth interviewed him, along with one of the St. Pete detectives who had been assisting in the investigation, Kuhar confirmed—as did others—that Kumble had been planning his vacation for some time. In fact, Kuhar said, on the night Karen was killed Kumble had spent the evening at their house, working on his van in preparation for the trip. He knew this, he said, because he had been there too. The detective asked if Kumble could have left late that night without his housemate knowing it. Kuhar said he doubted it. He would have heard the van drive away, he said.

Brinkworth also spoke with Maureen Byrnes, a former girlfriend of Kumble's. The two of them had dated steadily for about six months, but recently their relationship had cooled. They remained friends, however; in fact, they had gone out to dinner on the night of May 24, the day Karen's body was found. Later that night, after they parted, Byrnes was the one whom Kumble had called, saying that he'd just spoken to a detective at Karen's house and that Karen had been killed. Now Byrnes related these details to Brinkworth, also telling him that Peter was a kind and gentle man without a mean bone in his body.

On this point—Kumble's temperament—Brinkworth and the other detectives probed repeatedly, asking Byrnes and others if they had ever known him to be violent. All of them said no. Had they seen him intoxicated? No. Had they noticed the scratch on his hand? No.

To those close to Kumble, it seemed the detectives were taking this line of inquiry to a ridiculous extreme, throwing loaded questions at them and then watching for their reactions.

"Does he ever get mad?" they asked Kuhar.

"Well, yes," he said. "Doesn't everybody?"

In mid-June, when Kumble returned to town, he quickly learned that the Gulfport police had been scrutinizing him and his character with a rather ominous interest. So he called the detectives' office and told them he was back and offered to come down and answer anything they might want to know.

The session began at 5:30 P.M. on June 12, in the same room where Lawrence Sanders had been interviewed. It wasn't much more than a glorified broom closet, with a couple of chairs and a big desk that hugged the walls and made everything all the more uncomfortable. Brinkworth and Allen Reed sat Kumble down behind the desk, and then Brinkworth settled on top of the desk, right in Kumble's face. Now that the detectives finally sat within a few inches of the man who had so aroused their suspicions, they launched into a torrent of questions.

"How did you meet Ms. Gregory?" Reed asked him.

"At the Garden," he said. "I used to stop there after work."

"Did you see her anywhere else?"

"At some reggae concerts. And at Anita Kilpatrick's party."

Kumble made no secret of the fact that he and Karen had spoken that night. She'd seemed depressed, he said. She'd wanted someone to talk to, and so the two of them had walked to the beach.

"Wasn't that the night," Reed said, "that you asked her to go with you on your trip up north?"

"Yes."

"Was she going to go?"

"She considered it. . . . But then I called her at the house, and she told me she couldn't go because she'd just started her new job at Datacom."

They wanted to know what Kumble was doing on the night Karen was killed.

"I'd worked all day," he said, "and then I went to the grocery and to another store and bought some things for my van. Then I went home and stayed there all night."

Here Brinkworth stopped him.

"What about your yoga class?" he said. "We know you teach yoga on Tuesday nights. Why didn't you go that night?"

"I was too busy. I was getting ready for my vacation."

Brinkworth and Reed were taking turns. First one of them would quiz Kumble, then the other would take over. Their questions were moving around, too. They wanted to know about the evening after the murder, that Wednesday when Kumble had stopped by the house and walked on the porch and left the note. Why did he go there that night?

"Karen had lent me a tape at Anita's party," he said. "A reggae tape. Peter Tosh's *Bush Doctor*. I was returning it."

They listened to this answer and then repeated the question. "Why did you stop by the house that night?"

Kumble repeated his answer.

"To return the tape."

"Wait a minute," Brinkworth said. "When we talked over

the phone a couple weeks ago, didn't you tell me that Karen had asked you over for dinner?"

Suddenly Kumble remembered. "You're right," he said. "I forgot."

He had called her the Sunday before, he said. That was the day he checked back with her to see if she had decided whether to join him on the trip north. During the conversation, he said, he mentioned that he still had her tape, and she said she wanted it back. She suggested that he come over to the house the following Wednesday and bring the tape and have some dinner.

Here again, the detectives applied pressure.

"What about Mr. Mackey?" said Brinkworth. "Was he going to be at this dinner?"

"Yes. I thought so. I was looking forward to seeing him."

"What about the broken glass?" said Reed. "When you went there that night, didn't you notice the broken glass on the walk?"

"I did notice it. I thought it was strange, because the rest of the house seemed so well-kept."

"Did you notice any blood or hair on the screen of the jalousie door?"

"No, I didn't."

"Did you see the floor of the porch?"

"No."

The detectives also wanted to talk about the following evening, Thursday. What had Kumble done that night?

"I worked till 3:00, and then I went to WMNF and hosted my show until 6:00. Then I stopped at the grocery and went home and stayed there all evening."

Brinkworth stopped him again.

"You're leaving something out, aren't you? You went to Maureen Byrnes that night and had dinner with her, didn't you? Why didn't you tell us about that?"

"I forgot."

"And later that night, after you and I talked at the house, didn't you call Ms. Byrnes and tell her Karen was dead?"

"Yes."

"Did you forget that, too?"

"Yes."

Reed moved on. "You had a scratch on your right hand a few days after the murder. Where did it come from?"

"My hands are always scratched up. Sometimes it's from all

the work I do on my van. Sometimes it's from playing with my dog."

The interview ground on like this for hours. Brinkworth and Reed kept going over Kumble's story. They led him through it over and over, covering the same territory backward, forward, and backward again.

As Kumble sat there, listening and trying to answer, it seemed to him, as it had to his friends, that the detectives were firing off loaded questions and then watching as each one hit, just to gauge his reaction. Besides, they were asking him for details about things that had happened several weeks before and that had not seemed, at the time, particularly important. By now, it was hard for him to remember all the specifics.

"Am I a suspect?" he said.

"Everyone is a suspect," they told him.

The questions just kept coming. Reed wanted to go back to how Karen had been considering catching a ride in Kumble's van on this trip up north. Did Karen ever say where she was thinking of going once they arrived? She wanted to see her family, Kumble said. He also took it for granted, he said, that she might meet David somewhere around Providence and return home with him.

But why, Brinkworth said, would Kumble think that? Why would he think David was up in Rhode Island? Hadn't he just told them that he had assumed, when Karen asked him for this alleged dinner date, that David was here in Florida? As Brinkworth now pointed out, Karen certainly had been aware of David's travel plans. Had she passed those along to Kumble? Had she told him when David was going to be out of town?

Kumble said no. He had been totally under the impression, he said, that David would be at the house in Gulfport for Wednesday night's dinner.

Brinkworth didn't buy it.

"Peter, you're bullshitting me here, bud," he said. "We're both men in this room. Let's be honest."

By now they could see the anger rising in Kumble. His face was becoming rigid; his answers were getting shorter. But he insisted he was telling the truth.

They were at a standoff. Brinkworth and Reed could not say for sure whether Kumble had harbored any romantic desires for Karen. But to them it seemed he certainly had acted as if he wanted to be more than friends. And even though he was still describing

Maureen Byrnes as his girlfriend, Byrnes had told them otherwise, which meant that Kumble might well have been looking for someone new in his life. As they listened to Peter that night, it seemed to both Brinkworth and Reed that the two-week vacation had given him an awful lot of time to prepare a convincing story. Even so, he had forgotten to mention certain facts.

Still, their doubts did not prove anything. At approximately 9:30 P.M., four hours after the interview had begun, they told Kumble he could go. Before he left, though, he gave them his fingerprints and palm prints. He had told them that he wouldn't be surprised if his prints had been found on the porch. But there was no way, he said, that they would match any of the evidence inside the house. He had never been inside that house, he said. Never.

Now they would see.

Even after the hours of grilling, Kumble wasn't sure what to think. He told Maureen Byrnes the kinds of questions they had asked. Surely, he said, they didn't really think he had killed Karen?

"Stop being so naive," she told him. "Get a lawyer."

Seven

One week after Karen's body was found, the *Gulfport Gabber,* a free newspaper distributed weekly around the city, briefly mentioned the case in a roundup of local crime news. Like so many small-town weeklies, the *Gabber* tends to be relentlessly upbeat—its motto, displayed prominently on the front page, is REMEMBER: TODAY IS THE FIRST DAY OF THE REST OF YOUR LIFE!—and it typically is filled with health columns, horoscopes, gardening tips, poetry, fun facts, thoughts for the day, and old jokes that revolve around such stock characters as brain surgeons, priests, and large talking bears.

Not surprisingly, the paper did not devote much space to the disturbing details of the murder that had taken place in the paper's own backyard. The May 31 issue merely pointed out that indeed there had been a homicide, gave a few preliminary details of the investigation, and said that the police were working on the case. Anyone with a tip was asked to call the station.

Appearing in the same issue was the latest "Gulfport Gabs," one of those columns in which a question is posed to several people on the street and then their answers are published beside their photos. The question in this "Gulfport Gabs" was: "Do you think

Neighborhood Crime Watch is effective?" The answer from the people on the street was: yes.

"People watch their neighbors' homes and will contact the police if anything is wrong," said one woman. "I know I would and expect others to do it for me."

If the irony of this answer occurred to the members of the *Gabber* staff—if they realized that Karen had cried out for her life in a neighborhood filled with crime watch signs, including the one across the street from her house—they made no mention of it in the pages of the issue. Others, however, found it hard to contain their outrage. Neverne Covington, for one, wrote a letter to the *St. Petersburg Times* explaining how Karen had screamed and no one had answered. Neverne said she was screaming now for Karen, who no longer had a voice. Neverne said she was screaming at the apathy of the neighbors, at the injustice of what had happened.

The letter was never published, though. With the killer still at large, she was afraid of having her name in print.

Neverne had been in Boston when the police discovered the murder, and several days had passed before she learned what had happened. David Mackey had waited until after the wedding to tell her, calling her on that following Sunday, when she was at a brunch at the house of the bride's parents. When she heard that her friend was dead, she fell to the floor, her body collapsing, as she later would describe it, like an empty paper bag.

In the weeks that followed, Neverne found that she was afraid of many things. At night she refused to drive by herself and would not go alone into her backyard to carry out the garbage. After going to bed she got up repeatedly to make sure the doors were locked. She even enrolled in a self-defense class.

Neverne, a striking woman with shoulder-length blond hair, intense green eyes, and an almost startling commitment to candor, was not the type to scare easily. But Karen had come to her house the night she was killed, and since then Neverne had been forced to think in ways she had never thought before. No longer did she assume that the people around her meant no harm. No longer did she take it for granted that she would survive to see the end of the day.

One night she had a dream about Karen. In the dream, Karen was alive. Neverne saw her outside the pier in Gulfport and could not believe it. She told Karen she was supposed to be dead. Karen said no, she had gone to Texas to get better. She said she'd had to leave Gulfport, had to get away from everyone and everything, or she never would have recovered. She showed where the wounds on her neck had started to heal. Then she began walking away. Neverne said she wanted to go with her, but Karen said that was impossible.

"I'm sorry," she said. "But you can't come with me. You can't come here."

In her waking hours Neverne was frustrated because she could not describe the feelings of fear and grief inside her. It was as if such words were part of another language. That summer she painted a picture of an empty red chair. She didn't think about it at the time, but weeks later she realized that the chair in the picture was Karen's. Karen should have been sitting there.

Neverne also painted a picture of David Mackey, who was then staying with her and her boyfriend. The picture showed David sitting in front of a window. He was surrounded by bright, vibrant colors—sunshine was pouring through the blinds on the window—but his face had the weary look of someone in prolonged pain.

David, too, was dreaming about Karen. Many times the same thing happened. He and Karen would be near each other but would not be able to communicate. Something—one time it was a wall of glass—kept coming between them.

Since the murder David had become extremely concerned, sometimes obsessive, about the safety of his friends. He had trouble eating. He had trouble sleeping. At times he doubted he would ever recover the ability to enjoy life. He had lost Karen, lost their future together, lost the home they had planned to share. That Thursday afternoon when he had returned from Rhode Island and seen how Karen had died, he had been overwhelmed by a sense of violation. To him it felt as if his house had ceased to be his home and instead had become a place that merely contained some of his belongings. Occasionally he would return to do some chores, to see if he could grow accustomed to being there. But it was no good. He lived with friends for awhile, then rented an apartment in St. Petersburg. Eventually he sold the house in Gulfport.

Then there was Anita Kilpatrick. Anita, twenty-nine, was afraid of the dark because Karen had died at night. She was afraid that the murderer might be hunting her. The police had told her that the man might have been someone who knew Karen, and if he'd known Karen, Anita thought, then maybe he knew her as well. For weeks after the murder she stayed out of town, moving from Albany, New York, to Providence, Rhode Island, to Montreal, hoping the detectives would find the killer. One day, staying at someone's house in Providence, she heard footsteps in the hall—heavy footsteps, as if the person was wearing boots. Anita dropped to her hands and knees and peered through the crack at the bottom of the door. Outside, she could see somone's feet. She moved away from the door, crawled under a bed, and waited until the person left. Later she learned that it probably had been a woman who lived downstairs. The woman, she was told, wore clogs. That did not end her fears, though. The police still had not arrested Karen's murderer.

Eventually Anita returned to Pinellas County. But the day she returned, something happened to upset her all over again. She had gone to the newsroom of the *St. Petersburg Times,* when one of the reporters approached her. The reporter said she was working on an article on the Gregory murder case and that the police had arrested a man but had not yet released his identity. She had the man's initials, she said; she wanted to know if Anita could tell her the full name. Anita was stunned. She had heard nothing about an arrest. When she called the Gulfport police and asked if it was true, she was told no. The reporter, Anita realized, probably had been bluffing in order to get information.

That night Anita did not stay in her apartment. She called some friends who lived on the eighteenth floor of the Bayfront Tower, a high-rise in downtown St. Petersburg, and asked if she could stay with them. The building had a guard at the front door, so she felt safer there. But as the days passed, Anita remained terrified. She felt as if she were sinking. She called a friend who was living in Costa Rica and told him about her fear and paranoia. She asked if he thought she was crazy. The friend reassured her and suggested that she visit him in Costa Rica, where she would be safe and could relax.

She stayed there for more than a month, living with her friend in a remote cabin. She knew there was almost no way anyone could have followed her, yet that did not stop the fear. At night she awoke screaming from dreams in which she saw Karen being killed, over and over.

It went on like that for weeks. Then, one night, Anita had a different dream, one similar to Neverne's. Karen came to Anita in this dream and assured her she was all right. Karen called her "honey," just as she had in real life. She said she wanted Anita to see that she'd healed, to stop worrying about her. Karen said she couldn't stay. Someone was with her. They had to go.

In early June, when Sgt. Tosi left for his month-long vacation in the mountains of Tennessee, he had thought Karen Gregory's murder would be solved by the time he came back to work. Then the weeks rolled by, and June turned into July, and Tosi returned to Gulfport to find there had been no arrest.

When Brinkworth briefed him on what had been accomplished so far, Tosi was not pleased. To him the investigation seemed disorganized, veering off in too many directions. Peter Kumble had been a suspect before; he was still a suspect. Meanwhile, the detectives had been out chasing all of these other suspects. There didn't seem to be any system to it. They hadn't even thoroughly eliminated David Mackey from the list. Yes, they had confirmed David's flights and hotel reservation, but Tosi didn't think that was enough. Instead of just working the phones, he said, someone should have flown up to Providence and checked out David's alibi in person.

Nor did Tosi keep these opinions to himself. He passed them along to Hanson and Golliner. Whatever he said must have made an impression, because one day in early July the lieutenant summoned Brinkworth into his office.

When Brinkworth walked in, Hanson looked up from his desk.

"I'm reassigning this whole case to Tosi," he said. "You are officially off the case."

Brinkworth was flabbergasted. For weeks now he had been logging twelve to fourteen hours a day on the case. He recognized that he was inexperienced and lacked training in homicide investigation, but that was why he had sought the guidance of the two St. Petersburg detectives. Through it all, he had been working under the scrutiny of David and Neverne and Karen's other friends, who were regularly checking in for updates, asking questions, making sure Karen was not forgotten. As it happened, David and Neverne both felt that Brinkworth had worked hard on the case and was dedicated to finding the killer. They also felt he had treated them like human beings, showing compassion and sensitivity to their pain. Inside the department, meanwhile, no one had told him he was doing poorly. So now, as he was being ordered to hand over the case, he wanted to know why.

"Don't ask questions," Hanson told him.

That was the end of the discussion. The case was Tosi's.

At the time, Lawrence C. Tosi was thirty-nine and had been with the Gulfport police for thirteen years. He and Brinkworth and Reed all shared a cramped little office with fake wood paneling on the walls and no windows and some strange shade of fluorescent lighting that made everything look like it hadn't been dusted since the fifties. Officially the place was referred to as the Detective Bureau, but Brinkworth called it the Room of Doom. The thing was, Tosi seemed to belong there. He was a rumpled figure, with brown eyes, a brown moustache, and huge brown bangs that defied gravity as they swept across his forehead. He had a habit of mumbling—his voice seemed to emanate from somewhere far away—and people were always asking him to speak up. His desk, covered with a maelstrom of files and reports, was a study in chaos, and he was always jotting notes to himself on scraps of paper and then losing them. He chain-smoked Marlboros, drove a beat-up yellow 1973 Barracuda, and was married to a woman who adored Elvis Presley, whose pictures were mounted all around their house. Larry's favorite singer was Roy Orbison, who was hitting the high notes in "Only the Lonely" back when Larry was still a teenager. In his spare time he collected tropical fish and served as treasurer of the home and school association at his Catholic church. His middle name was Constant.

Around the station Tosi was known for his talent at creating minor mayhem. He'd walk up some stairs and the banister would come off in his hand. He'd lean back in a chair and fold his arms behind his head and both sleeves would rip away from his shirt. One time he was in the office, shredding documents, when he felt a tugging at his neck. He looked down and saw that his tie, a brand new silk Pierre Cardin from his wife, was partway through the shredder.

"Now, Larry," the other detectives would say as he headed out the door, "don't break anything."

They called him Inspector Clouseau, not just for his klutziness but also because he was a fanatic about the Pink Panther movies.

He had them on tape at home and watched them repeatedly. Sometimes he'd phone the station, ask for one of the detectives, then start talking in the inspector's voice.

"This is Clouseau," he'd say.

Tosi had wanted to be a police officer since he was a kid. His father had been a private investigator and a fingerprint examiner, and Larry used to read the detective magazines and watch "The Untouchables." The problem was, he was too short to be a cop. Back then many police departments had a minimum height requirement of five feet eight inches; Tosi barely reached about five seven, even in shoes. When he graduated from high school he figured he never would get hired as a police officer, so he didn't bother applying anywhere. He went into the U.S. Army, then he sold lumber, and then he worked on an assembly line. He hated it—hated the boredom and hated knowing that the only thing between him and a police badge was one lousy inch. So he tried to correct the situation. He bought a book on how to make yourself grow taller and began to perform a series of exercises—stretching, hanging from a bar like a bat, that kind of thing—designed to extend his spinal column. Within a few months he thought he had made enough progress to apply to the St. Petersburg Police Department.

He made sure the physical was scheduled in the morning, because he had read that people are tallest early in the day, before they've walked around. The night before the appointment he stretched and hung upside down for hours. The next morning he did everything he could to keep his weight off his spine. He lay down until it was time to leave, then he ran to the car and lay down in the backseat while his mother drove him. When he arrived for the physical, he did not sit in his chair. He lay back against it, stretching his legs rigidly in front of him and keeping his back as horizontal as possible.

Then a nurse measured him. "You're not tall enough," she said.

He was five feet seven and three-quarters inches, a quarter of an inch too short. He left the physical believing he'd never be a police officer. Then, a month or so later, a friend suggested he apply to the Gulfport Police Department. They had openings— and no height requirement.

When he joined the department, in 1971, he was a uniformed officer. He wasn't thrilled with patrolling the streets, though.

Instead of writing tickets, he wanted a chance to solve some of the crimes he encountered. A few months later, when his superiors promoted him to detective, he finally was happy.

It was a couple of years later, in 1973, when a fire burned down a house one night in the northern section of the city. A boarder, a fifty-two-year-old man named Frank Sweet, was found dead on the floor of his room, as if he had been crawling toward a closet to escape the flames. When Tosi arrived and looked around, he saw signs that suggested the fire had been set intentionally. It already had been confirmed that Sweet had been a heavy smoker, but when Tosi studied the burn patterns left on the floor, it appeared to him that someone had poured a flammable liquid around the room and ignited it. The woman who owned the house had been with Sweet that night and had been seen leaving his room not long before the fire started; furthermore, she kept insisting that his car, a 1965 Cadillac parked out on the lawn, rightfully belonged to her. One day Tosi was up at the house, digging through the ashes with a shovel, when he got this feeling someone was watching him. He looked up, and there in the doorway was the woman, staring at him.

Though he had never investigated a murder before, Tosi was sure this was his first. But Hanson and Golliner, his superiors even in those early days, did not agree. They told him to shelve the case.

"You're wasting your time," Hanson told him. "The guy died smoking in bed."

Tosi was angry, but he had no choice. He was a young detective, still fairly new to the job, and orders were orders. But he never forgot that not long after the case was dropped, the woman who owned the house was driving in the dead man's Cadillac.

It was eleven years later when Tosi returned from vacation and took over the Karen Gregory case. That July, as he reviewed the evidence, he realized he was inheriting an investigation that had been handicapped from the start.

The problems went beyond those created by the neighbors' silence or by the scattershot efforts of his own department. Tosi also was dissatisfied with the job the FDLE analysts had done processing the crime scene. He knew that they had been called in because of their superior training and expertise, but now, looking back, it seemed clear to him that the experts had not been very thorough. For one thing, they had not vacuumed the house for hairs, fibers, or other evidence. Hanson, thinking back to that first day of the investigation, said that the analysts had seemed to slack off once they found the promising prints on the windowsill in the back bedroom. As it turned out, those prints had been left not by the murderer but by either Falkenstein or one of the paramedics when they removed the screen and she climbed in through the window. Plus, once the FDLE team had finished up and driven away in their mobile crime lab, Hanson had assumed it was all right to let Anita Kilpatrick and Michaela Jarvis into the house to clean. The crime scene, in other words, had been repeatedly disturbed, and at this point it was impossible to return it to its original state.

Still, Tosi did have the next best thing—the photos and the videotape of the scene that had been shot before the cleaning—and now he studied them carefully, looking for anything that might hold some clue to the killer's identity. He was curious about the bloody handprints on Karen's body. He knew the FDLE's expert already had examined them and determined that they were useless for identification purposes. But he wanted to be sure, so he had photos of the handprints blown up to life size and showed them to a print specialist at the Pinellas County Sheriff's Department. Unfortunately, the specialist confirmed the FDLE's call. The handprints were of no help.

Something else in the photos caught Tosi's eye, however, and that was the bloody partial bare footprint in the bathroom. Other footprints had been found in the hallway; however, they had been left in the soft, absorbable surface of the carpet, which meant that they were no good for making an ID either. But the partial footprint had been made on the smooth, hard floor of the bathroom. The tile with the partial print had not been collected, but it had been photographed, with a ruler placed in the frame for proportion. If that photo was enlarged, Tosi figured, maybe it would contain enough detail for an ID or at least allow someone to figure out the size of the foot that had left the print. So he called the FDLE laboratory in Tampa and asked if it was possible to give it a try.

There is some disagreement over what happened at this point. Tosi says he spoke with a serologist at the lab that day. But the serologist says she does not remember the conversation. Further, she says, she would not have been the one to consider this particular request. In any case, Tosi spoke with someone at the lab and asked her to examine the photo. She did so, Tosi says, then called him back and told him to forget it.

"It's just a blotch of blood," she said. "There's nothing there. There's no point in making a photograph any larger."

On top of all this, the semen found during the autopsy had been tested to see if it was possible to determine the blood type of her attacker. But that was no good either; the test results were inconclusive.

Tosi pushed on, conducting more interviews, talking again to Karen's neighbors, checking out everything he could think of. Despite the cleaning that had taken place, he repeatedly returned to the empty house on Twenty-seventh Avenue South to dust for new prints and to look for anything that might have been used as the murder weapon. They already had asked David to check in the kitchen to see whether any knives appeared to be missing, but he hadn't found any. At one point, though, while looking around the kitchen himself, Tosi noticed some shears. Not realizing that they were kitchen shears, he thought it was a strange place to find them, and so he dusted them for prints and took them to Dr. Wood to see if their dimensions and blades were consistent with the weapon that had caused Karen's wounds. She said no.

Dr. Wood was still wondering if it was possible that the murder might have been some kind of ritualistic slaying. To find out, she asked for the help of an agent in the FBI's Tampa office who was trained in psychological profiling—trained to study the scenes of unsolved murders, then use the characteristics of a scene, if possible, to put together a profile of what kind of person the killer might be. Is he (or she) young? Old? White? Black? Does he live nearby? Does he live alone? In some cases FBI profiling experts have answered such questions with what turned out to be startling accuracy. So one day this agent met with Dr. Wood and Sgt. Tosi at the medical examiner's office to look at the photos and videotape that had been shot at the house.

But it was no good. From what he saw, the agent said he did not think this particular scene lent itself to profiling. And even though Wood pointed out her observations about Karen's neck wounds, the agent also said he did not see anything that made him believe that the attack had been ritualistic. So another lead—or more accurately, a theory that had been tested in the hope of generating some hint of a lead—had evaporated.

Not to be deterred, Tosi already was checking out something else—something that gave him and the other detectives even more reason to believe that the killer might be looking for another victim. After some investigation, Tosi had discovered that David and Karen's neighborhood had a history of peeping incidents. They had been going on for some time now. A young couple that had once lived next to David's house had seen a man looking through one of their windows; so had an elderly woman who lived a block over. And in the days immediately after the murder there had been a flurry of prowling calls at a house just to the south of David's, around the corner on Forty-eighth Street. Two women lived there, one thirty-two and the other nineteen; both were black. In fact, other than David, they were the only blacks living in the immediate area, which made the incidents even more disturbing.

The first of them had occurred at about 3:00 A.M. on Thursday, May 24, only a few hours before Karen's body was to be discovered in the next block. The thirty-two-year-old woman had called the police—she had had to wait until the day, as there was no phone in her home—after someone tried to break into the back of her house by prying open a window.

Five days later, at 4:00 A.M. on May 29, the nineteen-year-old had awakened to another noise outside the house. She then had roused her roommate, who looked out her bedroom and bathroom windows and saw the shadow of a man crouching near the house. She couldn't see what he looked like, but as she watched, he moved around the back of the house—near the northeast corner, where the younger woman's bedroom was located—and then disappeared.

Two days later, just after 2:00 A.M., the nineteen-year-old had heard another noise outside her bedroom window. Again she had alerted the other woman, who looked out and saw a man fleeing from the yard, heading toward the northeast.

The police had done all they could. They had repeatedly searched the yard; they also had stepped up patrols in the neighborhood and advised people to take special precautions, such as keeping their outdoor lights on all night. Tosi, meanwhile, had interviewed some of the neighbors, trying to put together a description of the prowler. None of them, however, had gotten a good enough look at the man to say much about him—other than that he was white—or to even confirm that the same person was involved in every case. There wasn't even any proof that the incidents had any connection to the murder.

Still, Tosi thought it was possible. From early on, he and the other detectives had wondered if the murder might have been linked to the fact that Karen was living with a black man. Now, with someone preying upon the only other two blacks in the area, Tosi was placing more credence in this theory. Maybe, he thought, the killer was some bigot who had killed one woman who'd offended his racial sensibilities and who had made at least a couple of attempts to kill two others. Maybe, he thought, this person was on a campaign to rid his streets of those he saw as undesirable.

Talking about the incidents with Neverne one day, Tosi made a map of the houses around David's, showing her all of the surrounding places where a prowler had been sighted.

"Something is going on in this neighborhood," he said.

In the meantime, another question had arisen. It was the blood-stained Hawaiian shirt that had been found on the bed in the back bedroom. Nobody seemed to know where it had come from.

Tosi had noticed it while looking through the crime scene photos and had retrieved it from evidence for further study. It was a blue-patterned shirt and it appeared to be handmade, because there were no labels. Still, it obviously was a woman's shirt; it was too small for a man, and the buttons ran down the left side instead of the right. But what had caught Tosi's attention was that it had been found in a place where it did not belong. The back bedroom was where David's clothes were kept; virtually all of Karen's clothes, except for the shorts and shoes she'd been wearing in the hours before the murder, were in the next bedroom. So now Tosi couldn't help but wonder. If the Hawaiian shirt was Karen's, why wouldn't it have been down the hall with the rest of her things?

The answer, Tosi learned, was that the shirt might have belonged to someone else. When he asked around, he found that no one could remember her having worn it, either at home or at work, in the days before the murder. In fact, no one seemed to be able to confirm that she'd ever worn it. He showed it to David and to Karen's other friends and to her sister, and sent a picture of it to her former boyfriend in New Hampshire. None of them could say for sure that it had been Karen's. Although it wasn't hard to picture Karen wearing this particular shirt—it would not have been completely out of character for her—Neverne said that she knew most of Karen's wardrobe and could not remember ever having seen it. Besides, she pointed out, Karen usually had worn solid colors, not prints.

"Look at her closet," she said. "Look at her clothes. This doesn't belong."

So where had this shirt come from? To Tosi it seemed there was only one other logical choice. If Karen hadn't brought it into the house, then the murderer had. Maybe he'd used it to conceal his weapon, keeping the knife wrapped inside it as he knocked on the door. Or, if he'd entered the house some other way, he might have wrapped it around his head to hide his face. Maybe, Tosi thought, that shirt was what had led to the final struggle. Maybe Karen had ripped it off him and he'd decided he had no choice but to kill her.

Either way, the shirt might be the key they'd been searching for. If they could find out where it had come from, they might just find the killer.

They had not forgotten Peter Kumble.

He had been questioned once already, at great length. But shortly after Tosi took over the case, he asked if Peter would sit down with them again.

"We're just trying to clear suspects," Tosi said.

Kumble was hardly overjoyed to be hearing from the police again. From the start, his involvement with the case had been a distinctly disquieting experience. It wasn't enough that someone he knew and respected had been murdered. Or that he'd unknowingly visited the scene while Karen's body lay inside. Or that by coincidence he'd chosen words in his note that would later haunt and horrify him. Ever since he'd returned from his vacation, he had found himself uncomfortably at the center of the investigation. He did not like the kinds of questions the Gulfport detectives had been asking about him. Nor did he appreciate being considered a suspect, even for a second, in a brutal rape and homicide. He'd tried to explain why he had stopped by the house that one evening. He'd told them that he had expected both Karen and David to be there. When no one answered his knock, hadn't he addressed his note to both of them? But the detectives had obviously not been convinced. To Kumble, it felt as though he had been presumed guilty until proven innocent.

Still, he wanted to clear his name. So when Tosi called, asking for a second interview, Peter agreed. But this time he brought a lawyer.

The interview was conducted by Tosi and Brinkworth, who was still assisting in the investigation from time to time. For the most part, they wanted to go over much of the same territory that already had been covered. But as the interview unfolded, Peter sensed that his days as a suspect were drawing to a close. Tosi didn't try to grill him; he calmly asked what needed to be asked and then moved on. The purpose of the session, it seemed, was exactly what Tosi had promised—simply to eliminate one more name from their list. In any case, it would probably be the last such session they would have. Kumble's attorney said that his client had tried to be cooperative but that enough was enough. Whatever they needed to ask him, the attorney said, they'd better ask it now.

So Tosi and Brinkworth asked their questions and collected samples of Kumble's head, chest, and pubic hairs—they'd taken his fingerprints earlier—and then finally they told him once again that he could go.

They sent his hair samples, as they had already done with his prints, to the FDLE laboratory. But as the weeks went by, the lab was not matching Kumble—or any of the other suspects who had given their fingerprints and hairs—to the evidence found at the scene. Eventually, the detectives would conclude that Kumble had nothing to do with the murder.

They were getting nowhere, and around Gulfport, people were noticing it.

"You guys can write speeding tickets and arrest drunks," someone told one of them. "But you can't solve a murder."

Neverne Covington was not surprised when Kumble's prints did not match those inside the house. As far as she was concerned, the police had been chasing down the wrong track with Kumble. From the beginning it had seemed to her that the killer had to be someone in the neighborhood. Whoever the attacker was, it was almost certain that he had been covered with blood when he left the house. Knowing this, Neverne had concluded that only someone who did not have far to go could have escaped undetected.

It troubled Neverne when the detectives told her that one of the neighbors had seen Kumble stopping by the house and passed that fact along to the police. Neverne had a question. Who was paying such close attention to the house, she wondered, that he had noticed Peter? And if this neighbor was so attentive, why hadn't he called the police the night before, when Karen had screamed in vain for her life?

Eight

As that summer turned into fall and still there had been no arrest, those close to Karen Gregory found themselves lost in a strange and unsettling new world.

David Mackey struggled to understand. He needed to make sense of Karen's death, even if it had been an inherently senseless act. The murder had forced him to come to grips, in a way he never had before, with the fact that there were people around him, more people than he cared to consider, who were capable of terrible, unthinkable violence. Even worse, it forced him to realize that he could not simply look at these people and see that capacity in their faces. David often thought about Karen's murderer. He tried to imagine how the man could live with himself; he tried to comprehend what this person carried within him that allowed him to get through a single day after what he had done inside that house.

By now Anita Kilpatrick had moved back to her apartment on the beach and had installed a chain on the door. She was still afraid, though, especially when the sun went down. She was trying to get past her terror, but she still worried that the same man who had killed Karen might come for her too. She felt helpless; she felt as if the man had taken Karen's life and was now controlling hers.

Neverne was still afraid as well. Like David, she was frustrated that she could not tell which people around her were capable of such violence. It bothered her, as she put it, that her radar was broken. She felt as if she were suffocating.

The members of Karen's family, meanwhile, were struggling with their own grief and fear. In the days after the murder, Roy, the older of Karen's two brothers, had clung to the hope that it was all some horrible misunderstanding, that Karen was not really dead. Before she died, Karen had made it known that she wanted to be cremated, and an urn containing her ashes had been given to the family. Roy peered inside the urn, sifting through the ashes with his fingers, wondering whether they were really all that was left of his sister. Then he found a small piece of chain from the rosary their mother had placed in Karen's hands in the casket, and he knew she was gone.

Karen's mother, Sophia, told herself she'd been a failure as a parent. Looking back over the years, she wished she had not been so strict with Karen. She couldn't believe she had been so stubborn that she had missed her daughter's wedding. For hours she would sit in a rocking chair and stare out the window at the branches of the trees swaying in the wind. If only Karen could see this, she'd say to herself. If only Karen were here, sitting beside me.

Sophia remembered something Karen had said once. If she were ever raped, she'd said, she would try not to struggle, so her attacker might not hurt her any further. It wasn't worth getting killed for, she'd said. Now Sophia could not stop thinking about such things. At night she imagined that someone was climbing into her own bedroom to attack her. The possibility so unnerved her that she insisted that bars be placed over the windows.

It was the same with Karen's sister Kim. After Karen's death, Kim waited to be murdered next. For months she carried a can of Mace in her purse. Not knowing who had murdered Karen plagued her and the rest of the family. They did not understand who could have done it or how it could have happened to Karen. One day Kim's father called her from New York, where he lived.

"What is going on?" he said. "What is going on?"

The detectives, Kim had heard, were considering the possibility that the killer had been a stranger. Perhaps some drifter who had wandered into the neighborhood. This theory made no sense to her. She drove by the house in Gulfport a couple of times, circling the block, trying to imagine what had happened. Why, she asked herself, would a drifter have been out on a night when it was raining? She remembered that both David's and Karen's cars had been there in the yard. Why would a drifter risk approaching a house that appeared to be full of people?

Kim found herself wondering about everyone around her. She'd stop at a traffic light and look over at the man in the car beside her and ask if he could be the one. She could not get it out of her head that the murderer was out there, going on with his life. What did he do for a living? Did he have a family?

As the weeks passed with no visible progress in the case, Karen's friends and family began to ask themselves if the killer would ever be found. Desperate for answers, some of them went to psychics, knowing that detectives themselves sometimes turn to such people for help. The psychics pointed the finger in different directions and at different people. David found one woman whose son had died in a traffic accident and who said she had managed to contact his spirit and had taken solace from the contact. David asked her to join him and Kim one night at Neverne's house. Neverne felt a little self-conscious about it. She had never dealt with a psychic before. But after the murder, she did not know what she believed in anymore. Her mind was open to anything that might help. She wanted to find a way, she said, to make the illogical logical and the incomprehensible comprehensible.

They sat in a circle of chairs in Neverne's living room. They turned off the lights and turned on a tape recorder. The psychic asked them to join hands, close their eyes, and think about Karen. Kim thought about their last day together, when they were at the beach, dunking each other in the waves. Neverne thought about the crystalline quality of Karen's eyes. Soon the psychic spoke of sensing Karen's presence in the room. Neverne felt a pricking sensation at the back of her neck. Slowly she and the others began to speak.

David said he saw an image of Karen stroking a cat she'd once owned, a cat that had died . . . Neverne said she could see Karen looking at them. Karen was crying. She missed them. It was painful for her to look at them . . . The psychic said she was picking up something about Karen and plants . . . She asked Karen to tell them anything she could . . . She said she sensed surprise . . . perhaps an initial blow so horrendous that it had sapped much of Karen's strength . . . David said he felt a numbness that started in his left cheek and spread downward. He said he had an image of Karen going into a tunnel or a cavern . . . He saw a bridge made of rope that sloped steeply downward into deep space, then sloped back up . . . like a roller coaster, he said . . .

Then he began talking about something else.

"I just got this image of a wrench being used to turn a bolt of some sort . . . It seems to be kind of a rusty wrench on some kind of old machinery."

"What kind of machinery?" asked the psychic.

"Some kind of engine, it seems."

"Look at it. Is it big?"

"It's not really big. It could be a car engine. Part of a transmission, perhaps. I just have this image of a man, a man's hands turning, working on this, this automobile."

"It seems," the psychic said, "like Karen wants us to know as much as she could know about her assailant . . . I see a man putting all his tools back in a green oblong toolbox and driving off . . . I also get a dark green or dark blue outfit on this man. Not—it's not a uniform, but it's one of those work clothes like a mechanic or a, someone who works with machines might wear . . ."

The murder was changing other lives as well.

Around the neighborhood where Karen had died, one man now kept a gun close to his side. Although she never really had known Karen, a woman who lived up the street turned around her sense of priorities. She decided to treat each day as if it might be her last. She sold her fast sports car; she bought a piece of island property she had always wanted. And in the house across from David and Karen's, Martha Borkowski wrestled with her conscience.

Borkowski, forty-eight, was the woman who had been lying awake in bed when she heard the scream and then a door slam. Afterward she had asked herself if she could have saved Karen's life by calling the police. The answer, she had decided, was no. The scream had sounded to her like it came from behind her house, so if she had called the police she would have sent the officers in the wrong direction. But she could not help thinking about how

Karen must have looked across the street during the struggle and seen the lights of her house.

The murder had left Borkowski afraid, too. She had new locks installed. She had a burglar alarm installed and acquired a 38-caliber revolver. At one point her fear and guilt were so strong that she moved out of her home and stayed with her sister-in-law for a few days. Even after she came back, though, she avoided looking at the small white house across the street. Every time she stepped out her front door, she said, she saw that house staring her in the face.

Still, in a strange way, she began to feel close to Karen. Borkowski had never really known the young woman across the street, but now she found herself wondering what Karen had been like. She wondered if Karen had ever married or had children. She wondered if Karen had been happy.

Sgt. Tosi was still trying to figure out what had happened that night in the dark. As the months went by he returned repeatedly to the neighborhood, talking to people about what they had seen or heard, picking their memories for stray details, looking for anything that might yield a lead.

One of the people he interviewed was Martha Borkowski, who told him how she'd heard the scream and then the door slam. It had sounded like a car door, she said, but she didn't remember hearing any car start up or drive away. Tosi thought maybe the slam had occurred when Karen escaped to the front porch and the murderer dragged her back inside. One night, to test this theory, he asked Borkowski to go into the bedroom where she'd been when she heard the scream. Then he went across the street to Karen's house and slammed the inner door on the porch, then went back to Mrs. Borkowski.

"Did you hear anything?"

"I heard a door slam."

"Did it sound like what you heard that night?"

"It could be."

Another neighbor Tosi interviewed was George Lewis, the firefighter who had heard the scream. It had not surprised Tosi to learn that Lewis was working late that night in the garage. He already knew that Lewis liked to burn the midnight oil out there. He knew because he and George were friends. Larry's wife Debbie

and George's girlfriend, Glenda Harness, had been working together for about five years, first as cashiers at a Publix supermarket
and then as tellers at the drive-through window of a First Florida
Bank branch. The two couples had gone out and had barbecues
together. George, who had a real knack for mechanical things,
had even worked on Larry's Barracuda when it blew a valve.
George and Glenda were expecting a child and were engaged to
be married that coming December; Larry, who happened to be a
notary, was to perform the ceremony.

That summer the murder had become part of all their lives.
That night in May, when the scream had awakened Glenda along
with the other neighbors, she did not know what she had heard.
But when Karen Gregory's body was found two days later it was
Debbie Tosi who called and told Glenda that a woman had been
killed across the street.

"Oh my God," Glenda said. "I have to call George."

A day or so later she was over at the Tosi house, talking about
that night, about how she had looked out the back window toward
the garage and seen that George was not there, and about how
scared she had been while she waited for him to come back. She
said that he had been gone for the longest time—about half an
hour, she said—and that while she waited, a silhouette had appeared in one of the back windows. At first she'd thought it might
be a black man, because the hair appeared frizzy. But she wasn't
sure. Maybe the person's hair had simply been mussed up.
Whoever it was, though, had soon disappeared.

Later Tosi tried to learn more about the silhouette.

"Did Glenda talk to you about that?" he asked George.

"Yeah, she mentioned it," George said. "But it wasn't me."

Tosi often chatted with George about the murder. By coincidence, his friend had turned out to be one of the case's most
important witnesses. So Larry would stop by the house sometimes
when George was off duty, and they'd go over what had happened
that night—how George had heard the cry and then looked up
and down the street, trying to find out what was wrong. One
day, while they stood outside and went over it again, George
pointed across the street to David and Karen's house and said that
he had even gone over on their lawn that night, looking between
their cars. Tosi noted this new detail and filed it away in his mind,
as he was filing everything he learned.

At the same time, Tosi was speaking frequently with David

Mackey. He didn't have much choice, since David was determined to do everything in his power to keep the investigation moving forward. To David, it seemed like the only thing he could do. He couldn't reverse time or bring Karen back to life. But now that she had been silenced, he could take every step possible to see that her murderer was caught and brought to justice. So he kept in close contact with Tosi, as he had with Brinkworth, and told him any detail he thought might be relevant. He tried to think of things that might have been forgotten or missed. He removed the front jalousie door and saved it in case the police might need it later. He had the blood-stained section of hallway carpet rolled up and saved as well. He searched through the house for items that might have been the murder weapon. He collected a poker from the fireplace and an iron and gave them to the police for analysis. He walked up and down the streets of the neighborhood, combing through the gutters and the bushes. One day he climbed up on the roof of the house, wondering if the killer might have thrown the weapon there.

The search produced nothing. But as he looked through Karen's clothes one day, David did find that something else, something other than the vase, did appear to be missing from the house. A couple of months before the murder, when Karen's thirty-sixth birthday arrived, she had gone on a little spree and bought some clothes for herself. Among the items she'd bought was a white teddy. Now David could not find the teddy. It was possible Karen had returned it—David remembered her wearing it only once, when she tried it on along with the other new clothes—but as far as he knew, that hadn't happened. In any case, he reported to Tosi that the white teddy was gone.

As the case wore on without an arrest, David grew more and more frustrated. He thought the FDLE had done a poor job of collecting evidence and that the department's labs had wasted time in studying the evidence that had been collected. He told Tosi he didn't understand why the FDLE hadn't at least tried to make an identification from the partial footprint on the bathroom floor. Tosi told him he had tried and had been assured the footprint was useless. David didn't believe it. He knew Tosi was putting in long hours and was dedicated to tracking down the killer. But it seemed to him, as it had to Brinkworth, that not everyone else—especially those who issued orders from the upper echelons of the Gulfport police—shared the same depth of commitment. He sensed that

Tosi was being pressured to take time out from the investigation for other cases. So up the line he went, making his presence felt with Lt. Hanson and the Gulfport city manager and the prosecutors in the state attorney's office. He told them he was not going to allow the system to forget Karen or to treat her murder as just another case. He said he did not want them to just number the pieces of evidence and put them into little bags and then send them away to linger forever in some crime lab. He asked them to imagine how they would feel if Karen had been their girlfriend, or their wife, or their mother.

Hanson considered David a pest. He thought he was getting too close to the investigation, asking too many questions, taking up unreasonable chunks of their time.

"He's in here too much," the lieutenant would say. "Get him out of here."

Such edicts did not dissuade David. One day he went to the station and expressed his concerns directly to Chief Golliner. As David would remember it later, Golliner tried to mollify him, assuring him that they were still following up leads and weren't about to let the case drop. David was not moved. He told Golliner that he was not going to allow the chief or anyone else to rest until Karen's murderer was caught. He said that he had already lost everything he had to lose and that he was ready to do whatever it took to make sure that the investigation did not falter. If that meant destroying someone's career, he said, then he would be happy to oblige.

Surrounded by his beloved figurines, Golliner responded as if he'd been ejected from a double-header. He could hardly believe what he was hearing. He was furious.

"You're threatening me?" he shouted.

David looked straight back at him. "You take it any way you want to take it."

There was no question that David was a handful. Even Tosi thought so. But the sergeant couldn't deny that David was saving things that the FDLE had not bothered to take into evidence. So Tosi accepted the jalousie door and the carpet and the other items and stored them away for future reference. To him it was all worth saving. Besides, he understood how important the case was to David and to the others who cared about Karen. It was important to him as well. Even after a decade, the Frank Sweet case was fresh in his memory. He still thought about how laziness and apathy had allowed the woman to drive away in that Cadillac, scot free. He did not intend to let such a thing happen again.

As the months rolled by, Tosi went on studying the photos and video that had been taken that first day inside the house. He kept the photos in a black notebook, and every day he pulled out the book and searched for some detail he might have missed. He peered at the pages with a magnifying glass. He muttered to himself. For hours he sat there at his desk, staring at Karen as she lay there in the hall.

"Nobody deserves to die like that," he said.

Another detective had once told Tosi that when he investigated a murder, he liked to be alone at the murder scene. The detective would ask everyone to leave, and he'd stay there and try to get a feel for what had happened. So Tosi would take a key and go alone to the house. He'd sit down and try to picture the struggle and how it had unfolded. He would try to imagine what the killer had been thinking. He said he wanted to let the house talk to him.

Tosi was not the only one returning to the house for answers. In the midst of everything else, David was still going to psychics, and he had found one, a woman who lived in Pasco County, just north of Pinellas County, who was willing to visit the scene of the murder and share whatever it told her. David wanted Tosi to be there, and Tosi agreed.

On the appointed day, the three of them met at the house. The psychic walked through the rooms and stood in the hallway, in the place on the floor where Karen had been found, and then began to speak. The person they were looking for, she said, had been stalking Karen for some time. That night, when she was alone, he had stood outside and watched her through the windows, following her from room to room. Actually, she said, there may have been two of them watching her. Or maybe it was one person with two personalities. She wasn't sure . . .

Nine

In the middle of that barren time, when the investigation was languishing in a void of dead-end leads and almost hopeless inertia, David walked into the police station and handed Tosi a startling new piece of evidence.

David had been back at the house, moving some of his belongings, and had picked up some technical papers sitting on the dining room table. There were two sets of papers, actually. One was a section from a book on computers; the other was a section from a maintenance manual on cockpit voice recorders. What had attracted David's attention was that he didn't remember having seen them before he left for Rhode Island. He didn't know how they'd gotten into the house; all he knew was that when he returned after the discovery of Karen's body, the papers had been there on the table and he'd collected them with everything else in the house. Later, he said, when he finally had a chance to look through them, he'd noticed a name on the papers, typewritten at the top of one of the pages. "Fischler," it said.

Tosi already knew who that was. There was a technical writer named Fischler—a Steven Fischler—who had worked with Karen at Datacom. Tosi had already checked him out, as he had checked out other men from Datacom. Now here were these papers, which had found their way into the house at almost exactly the same time as the murder. And when Tosi glanced through them he saw that on one page there was a fingerprint that appeared to have been left in blood.

Clearly it was time to interview Mr. Fischler. When Tosi tracked him down, Fischler said he didn't have much to tell. He knew where the papers had come from. Both he and Karen had been working on the cockpit recorder manual for Datacom; as for the section on computers, it came from a book he was writing in his spare time. Karen had talked about illustrating it. But he could not say for sure how or when the documents had ended up in Karen's house. He insisted that he had not brought them there; he'd barely known Karen, he said, and had never been to the house. She probably had brought them home herself.

Tosi wasn't satisfied. He didn't know whether to believe Fischler or not. But he was growing tired of chasing after so many suspects; it was time, he thought, to see if some of them could be eliminated. He asked Fischler to take a polygraph test.

Fischler, not surprisingly, did not take kindly to the suggestion that he might have murdered one of his colleagues. But if it would help clear him, he was willing to take the test. So one evening he went down to the station and sat alone in the Room of Doom with a polygraph examiner from a private firm that was rather hopefully known as ESP Investigators, or Executive Security Professionals. The examiner was Mike Brentnell, a harmless-looking young man with green eyes and a moustache and an amazing ability to ask the most awful questions in the friendliest of voices. Brentnell remained calm when his questions made people angry; in fact, he took it as a sign of exoneration when they stood up and cursed him out. It was usually the guilty ones, he had found, who were impossible to offend.

By that rule of thumb, Fischler was fervently innocent. Brentnell opened the gold-colored case that held his instrument—a five-pin UltraScribe, the top of which was covered with an intimidating collection of knobs and switches and needle-thin pens that recorded the breathing patterns and heart rates and sweat production as though they were seismic tremors of the soul—and connected it with tubes and wires and Velcro straps to Fischler's chest, upper arm, and fingers. Then he proceeded to ask his subject, repeatedly, if he had stabbed Karen Gregory. Fischler denied it every time.

But when Brentnell studied the charts on the instrument, he could not determine whether Fischler was answering truthfully. So Brentnell unhooked him and interrogated him further, trying to push him and see which way he would go. He told him he hadn't done well on the test. He said there was a reason for that, and that he believed it was because Fischler had something more to tell and was not telling it.

Hearing such accusations fired in his direction, Fischler grew flustered and increasingly hostile. It wasn't true, he said. He hadn't done anything, he said. When Tosi came in and began grilling him anew, he continued his denials, getting madder and madder, until finally he had had enough.

"Okay, I did it," he said, completely exasperated. "What are you going to do about it?"*

Eventually he stood up and stormed from the office, yelling and swearing and calling all of them names as he made his way out of the station and into the Florida night.

Tosi knew that Fischler's confession was probably not a confession at all. Just to be sure, though, he did as he had with all of the earlier suspects and sent the man's fingerprints and hairs off to the FDLE, along with the papers and the apparently bloody print. Weeks later the report came back saying that Fischler had matched up with none of the evidence originally found inside the house. Furthermore, the lab had determined that the reddish substance on the one page was not blood at all but some kind of food coloring. As for the print itself, it had been left not by Fischler but by David.

Tosi was not surprised. Even as Fischler was cleared, the sergeant was already working on another theory as to who had killed Karen. As far as he was concerned, David was the prime suspect.

It was highly distasteful to suggest that the man Karen had loved, and who by all accounts had loved her back, might have ended up brutally killing her. Yet it seemed almost inevitable that

---

*Years later, when asked about this conversation, Fischler would say he remembered almost nothing about it. But he insists that he never would have made this statement. However, four people—Brentnell, Tosi, Hanson, and Scott Barnes, another detective at the station that night—all agree they heard him say it.

this possibility would be considered. One of the most terrible things about an unsolved murder is the taint of uncertainty it casts on everyone around it. If one person in our midst is capable of violently taking someone's life, then any of us may be capable—and may be scrutinized with that possibility in mind. Suddenly, the most innocent actions may be viewed in the most sinister light. Lawrence Sanders had suffered a seizure, and it had brought three detectives to his door after dark. Kumble had agreed to give someone a ride to a funeral and had accepted the unenviable task of identifying a body, and both favors had been held against him as indications of possible guilt. Fischler had labored over some documents with a coworker, and suddenly he'd found himself strapped to a machine, denying that he had committed a capital crime.

Now David's close involvement with the case—his repeated phone calls and visits to the station, his attempts to uncover new leads, his overwhelming insistence that he be kept informed of every development—was precisely what had placed him at the top of Tosi's list. Maybe David truly was trying to see to it that Karen's murderer was brought to justice. Or maybe, Tosi thought, he was really the killer, engaged in some elaborate game of cat and mouse.

Certainly Tosi had not been the first to wonder about David. From day one, George Lewis had made a point of letting the detectives know that his neighbor practiced some kind of martial arts. Just as he had with Peter Kumble, George had told them that David made him uneasy and should be checked out. These "martial arts" turned out to be t'ai chi ch'uan—the ancient Chinese system of exercises where the practitioner stands alone, swirling and moving in a kind of intense slow motion—which David used to relax and meditate. Even so, from the time Tosi returned from his vacation he'd been investigating David thoroughly.

In his hours of studying the crime scene photos, Tosi had found himself staring repeatedly at the black umbrella sitting on the floor of the northwest bedroom, where the blood had been found on the bed. Tosi knew this was David's umbrella; by now he had asked. But he couldn't understand how it had ended up in that room. Before David left for Rhode Island he'd bought a Providence newspaper so he could learn more about the town and read the weather forecast and know what to pack for his conference. But the forecast that week had been for rain. Why, then, hadn't David taken his umbrella? When Tosi had asked, David had told him he'd forgotten it. But Tosi found that somewhat hard to believe. After talking to him repeatedly over the past weeks, Tosi was well aware that David was a remarkably careful, well-organized person. It seemed unlikely that he would have gone to the trouble of checking the weather and then neglected such an important detail. The only other explanation, then, was that he had brought it back to the house on the night of the murder—it had been raining in Gulfport, too, after all—and had left it there, either accidentally or on purpose, after killing Karen.

No longer did Tosi believe that such a thing was logistically impossible. By now Tosi had flown up to Rhode Island and interviewed employees at David's hotel as well as several of his colleagues who had attended the conference with him. One person who'd had dinner with him that night remembered being with him until about 8:45; the next morning someone had seen him at around 8:30, just after he'd been informed of Karen's death over the phone. But when Tosi had checked the airline schedules, he discovered that there had been flights available that would have allowed David just enough time to make it down to Gulfport late that night and then return to Rhode Island by early morning.

It would have been extremely difficult. After all, the killer had had to find a way not just to enter the house without being seen and murder Karen but to get rid of all of the blood on his clothes and body and escape without being seen. For David it would have required careful planning and ruthless efficiency. That was just it, though. David had already shown, again and again, that he was extremely methodical and efficient. To Tosi it was easy to picture David charting it all out, preparing for both the murder and an almost unbeatable alibi. If true, it certainly would explain why no other suspect's fingerprints had been found in the house.

As for motive, Tosi thought the most likely was jealousy. Karen, he'd learned, used to have a boyfriend in Jamaica. She had visited there several times over the years, soaking up the sun and the reggae shows. She also had dated a man who lived in Montego Bay. After some investigating, Tosi had learned that before the murder Karen had been considering another trip to the island. It was possible, Tosi thought, that David had found out and become angry and decided to make sure Karen never went near Montego Bay again.

When asked about it, David said he didn't know what Tosi was talking about. As far as he remembered, he said, Karen hadn't been planning any trip to Jamaica. Even if she had been, he said, long ago she had made it clear to the old boyfriend that any romance between them was over. As he talked about this, David grew irritated, but he remained calm and controlled. The fact was, David always seemed calm and controlled, even when he clearly was angry or upset. He was always rational, always logical, always careful to not let his emotions get the better of him. What would happen, Tosi wondered, if something were to make David finally lose it? What would happen if that controlled exterior were shattered and all of the emotion came bursting forth?

Now Tosi found himself suspecting everything David did. He began to believe that David was in fact the killer and that all of his vaunted efforts to help were merely smokescreens designed to confuse and taunt them. Yes, he had saved the carpet and other items for the investigation. But they were all from his house. David knew—he had to know, Tosi thought—that even if his prints or hair were identified on any of these items, it would prove nothing.

The Fischler documents only made Tosi wonder more. David had handed Tosi these papers—papers with another man's name on them—without uttering a word about the fingerprint. The print had been almost impossible to miss; it was marked prominently on one of the outside pages. And yet David had said nothing. Later, when Tosi asked him why, David said he'd assumed Tosi would see it and check it out. But that wasn't like him, Tosi thought. David seemed too thorough, too careful, too meticulous to have left something like that to chance. Had David wanted to send him chasing after Fischler? Or had he deliberately placed the print there, using some substance that looked like blood, knowing that Tosi would have it tested and find out the print was his? Was he teasing Tosi, daring him to try and catch him?

Finally, after weeks of debating with himself, Tosi had his fill of guessing. It was time, he decided, to tell David what he thought. "I'm going to confront him point blank," Tosi told Brinkworth.

That was exactly what happened. David came to the station one night, as he often did, and Tosi laid it all out for him, accusing him of the murder to his face. He told David how he thought he'd done it and why he thought he'd done it and how it seemed increasingly likely that he'd done nothing since the murder but toy with him and the other detectives.

David had been expecting this. He knew that Tosi had been asking about him up in Providence—word had filtered down from VA headquarters—and it had been obvious from the questions he was being asked that he was now considered a prime suspect. He'd wondered when Tosi would get around to confronting him directly. He'd been waiting for it. Still, now that the moment had come, now that the words had actually been spoken, it was hard not to feel an overwhelming outrage. For a second it looked as if he might explode at last. He got up and walked over to a far corner and stood there for a few minutes with his arms crossed, fixing a fearful glare in Tosi's direction. Then, through some monumental act of will, he reined it in. He brought down his temperature and regained his composure and then sat back in the chair and started talking. He couldn't believe it, he said. He could not believe that Larry actually thought he would do such a thing. What did he have to do to make Larry see how wrong he was?

A polygraph, Tosi said. He wanted David to take a polygraph, just like Fischler.

Fine, David said.

"I have nothing to hide," he said. "Let's go for it."

So they called harmless-looking Mike Brentnell back in, and he brought in the UltraScribe and asked the same awful questions he'd asked before. This time, though, nothing clouded the responses.

There was no doubt about it, Brentnell said. David was telling the truth.

David had not relished the idea of being hooked up to a machine. But he'd been more than willing to do it; in fact, he had offered to take a polygraph several weeks before, when he had realized suspicion was shifting in his direction. David did not want Tosi wasting any more time worrying about him instead of the real killer. Now that he'd taken the test and had passed, he hoped the police would begin moving forward again. David was still conducting an investigation of his own, searching for whatever answers he could find, wherever he could find them. As rational and logical as he tried to be, he was still talking to psychics, hoping they might lead him to some truth that could not be charted on any scientific instrument.

One day he and Neverne attended a service at a small church in St. Petersburg where messages were carried to and from the dead. When they entered the church, it struck Neverne that somehow the place belonged in the past. They were in a large, dusty room, all colored with purple, with an assortment of chairs for the members of the congregation, several dozen of whom were gathered around them. Neverne and David took their seats, and a reverend of some sort came out and greeted everyone and gave a sermon about the need to respect all living things. The people in the audience wrote down their messages to their loved ones on pieces of paper and placed them in a basket passed around by ushers. In their message, David and Neverne asked Karen to tell them what she could reveal about what had happened to her.

The reverend, a heavy, middle-aged man with a soothing voice, put on a blindfold. When the basket was brought to him, he picked up the messages one by one and rubbed them on top of his head, and then spoke to those who had written them. Most of the time David and Neverne did not understand what the man was talking about. Without knowing the original messages, it was impossible to fathom the responses. Still, what he was saying clearly meant something to others in the audience, who were nodding and crying. And it was obvious when he picked up the piece of paper from David and Neverne.

The man said he did not know who the two of them were or why they had come to his temple. But he said that the person to whom the message was addressed—he did not say Karen's name—had joined the spirit world only recently in a terrible and violent way and was having trouble traveling through the tunnel. He said the person wanted them to know that they should not worry, that it did not hurt as much anymore. He also wanted them to know that justice would be served. Ultimately, he said, justice would prevail.

Neverne wanted to believe what the minister had said, but as the months went by it grew harder. Thanksgiving arrived, and she found herself thinking about the murderer—wondering what he was eating for his holiday dinner, trying to imagine whether he was having sweet potatoes with his turkey. Christmas arrived, and she wondered what kinds of presents he was getting. Was he opening them in front of a family? Did he ever think about what he had done to Karen?

Someone else close to David, meanwhile, had received another message for him. This one came from a friend of his in Atlanta, another counselor who also worked with Vietnam veterans and who was concerned about David and the uncertainties around him.

This friend happened to be a Navajo, and one day, while visiting the reservation in Arizona where he'd grown up, he asked a medicine man if there was any way to establish the identity of whoever had killed Karen. The friend meditated on this with the medicine man for a time, but eventually he gave up in frustration. Images were coming to him, he would later tell David, but he couldn't make sense of them. There was one dominant image, however, that kept returning.

Fire. He kept seeing fire.

Part Two

Breakthrough

Ten

The first glimmering of progress—the first hint of all of the revelations that were to come—did not look like much. It appeared to be just another lead, and not nearly as promising a lead as so many of the others that had melted away into nothing long ago. And when it surfaced, late in December 1984, the discovery was purely accidental.

For Larry Tosi, it had been a busy month. Along with all of the hours he was logging on the investigation, he'd taken time out on December 15 to perform his duties as a notary and preside at the wedding of George Lewis and Glenda Harness. In keeping with his firefighting background, George wanted to exchange the vows on a ladder truck. So they gathered with their friends at St. Pete Fire Station No. 4, George's station, and then the three of them—George in a black tux, Glenda in her gown and veil, and Larry in a suit and carrying his book with the appropriate passages—stepped into the basket of one of the department's trucks and went through the ceremony in midair. Larry wouldn't let them go too high, though. He didn't like heights and insisted that they put no more than five or six feet between themselves and the ground. When the vows were over, the basket was lowered, Tosi stepped out, and the newlyweds were raised high so they could kiss above the wedding party and commemorate the occasion by signing the top of a nearby streetlight.

It was a week or so later, right around Christmas, when the Gulfport police received a new tip. There was a farewell party for the city manager, who was resigning to take another job, and Marie Messervey, a Gulfport bus driver, was at this party, chatting with an off-duty officer, when she happened to mention that she had heard the scream that night back in May.

By itself, the fact that she'd heard it was not so striking. But when the officer passed on this information, Hanson checked Messervey's address and was amazed to learn that she lived on Forty-sixth Street South, three blocks east and one block south of the murder scene.

Hanson called Tosi into his office immediately.

"You gotta hear this," he said.

Until that moment, they'd had no idea Karen's scream had carried that far. In those early days of the investigation, when the officers were going door to door, they had not bothered to interview people more than a couple of blocks away. Now, knowing how loud the cry had been, Tosi and Hanson began reviewing everything they'd gathered over the months. When they came to the original handwritten statement from Lewis, the detectives stopped. George, the statement reminded them, had been out in the garage when Karen screamed. George had been the only neighbor outside his house that night. And if someone who lived as far away as Marie Messervey did had heard Karen scream, they thought, then maybe George had heard something from his garage across the street that he hadn't thought to mention before.

They thought it would be a good idea for someone to talk to him again. But there was a slight problem. Tosi didn't think he should do the interview. After all, he was close to George— too close, perhaps, to be objective. So the job went to Hanson. Arranging the interview, however, did not turn out to be easy. Hanson spoke to George over the phone and they set up a couple of times for him to come to the station.

George didn't show up.

New Year's Day of 1985 came and went. Then, late one afternoon in mid-January, there was a house fire in Gulfport. Hanson and a new detective, Scott Barnes—Detective Reed had been transferred back to patrol—went to check it out in case it was an arson. The street was crowded with fire trucks, and thick hoses were splayed across the ground, and when Hanson and Barnes approached the scene, they saw George working the fire. He was an easy person to pick out. He was a young guy, with a thick crop of red hair, a respectable red moustache, and a smattering of freckles. When they spotted him he was leaning over, hooking up a hose. Hanson called out to him and George stood up and saw them, and suddenly this peculiar look washed over his face.

"Hi, George," said the lieutenant.

Hanson went to talk to the chief in charge of the scene. A few minutes later, when he'd finished his work, George apologized for not making it to the interviews. He said he'd had to lay some carpet, but that he could come to the station to talk the following week. No problem, said Hanson.

A few minutes later, when George had gone back to working the scene, Barnes was still thinking about that look on George's face. It was one of sheer fright. It was the same cornered, desperate expression—Barnes had seen it many times before—that comes over people when a cop suddenly walks up to them with a piece of paper and they know their name is on that paper and they're about to be hauled off to jail.

"If you're not looking at him as a suspect," Barnes told Hanson as they drove away, "you should be."

This time George showed up for his interview. As he had so many times in the past, he went over again what he had seen and heard the night of the murder, how he had been working on his motorcycle and listening to the radio in the garage when he heard the scream, then checked around outside to see what was wrong. He also brought up again that on the following evening he had seen Peter Kumble drive up in his van.

Hanson listened, comparing what George was saying now to his original handwritten statement. Something didn't sound quite right. Before George had said that he heard the scream, checked up and down the street, then went back to the garage and continued working before seeing the man ride past on the bike. Now, he was saying that he checked along the street, then turned off his garage light, closed the door, and went inside the house. In addition he was saying he hadn't heard any glass breaking. Hanson couldn't understand that. A woman several blocks away had heard

Karen scream, and George had been right across the street—in his garage, with the door open—and not heard the glass breaking when Karen rammed into the jalousie door?

At this point Hanson was thinking. He was an acquaintance of George's himself. Shouldn't the Gulfport police get somebody who didn't know George at all to go over this? "George," he said, "would you mind taking a polygraph test?"

George wasn't thrilled with the idea. But if that was what they needed him to do, he said, he would do it.

A few days later, on the evening of February 7, he found himself sitting alone in the detective bureau with Mike Brentnell and the UltraScribe. George gave his name and address and date of birth and stated that he was in good health, that he had completed the twelfth grade, that he did not gamble or use drugs, and that he had never been arrested. Before the test began, Brentnell went over the questions he intended to ask. That way, he said, George would not be surprised. George said he was nervous. Brentnell told him not to worry. He attached him to the instrument and told him to close his eyes.

"Is your name George?"

"Yes."

"Regarding Karen Gregory, do you intend to answer each question truthfully?"

"Yes."

"Do you believe I will only ask you the questions we talked about?"

"No."

"Before this year did you ever hit anyone from behind?"

This was a control question, designed to start the needles jumping so Brentnell could see what kind of reading George gave when he lied about something unrelated to the subject at hand. Almost everybody has hit somebody at some point in his life, even if it was only in some faraway moment on a school playground. But when asked that during a polygraph, almost everyone denies it.

George was no different.

"No," he said.

Brentnell looked at the chart, where the needles had gone up into a little jagged hill.

"Did you stab Karen?"

"No."

"Before this year did you ever intentionally want to hurt anyone?"

Another control question.

"No."

Another hill.

"Did you stab Karen in her home?"

"No."

"Is there anything else you are afraid I will ask you a question about even though I have told you I would not?"

"No."

"Prior to this did you ever do anything else you could go to jail for?"

"No."

"Were you present when Karen was stabbed?"

"No."

George was still nervous—the smell of his sweat filled the room now—so Brentnell gave him a little demonstration to assure him that the instrument truly worked. He said he was going to write down some numbers on a piece of paper and that he wanted George to pick one. Then, when Brentnell asked him what number he'd picked, he wanted George to lie to him.

"I want to make sure the instrument is reacting to you," Brentnell said. "I want to make sure everything is getting a good pattern here."

They did the number test. When George did as he was told and lied about his choice, Brentnell told him the deception had shown up on the chart. That seemed to relieve George, and so they continued. Brentnell asked the same questions as before, plus several more that they had already discussed.

"Do you suspect anyone else of stabbing Karen?"

"No."

"Do you know for sure who stabbed Karen?"

"No."

They went through the questions, then Brentnell unhooked George from the instrument and gathered up the chart.

"Relax," he said. "I'll be back in just a minute."

He stepped outside and went to another room. Alone, he studied the readings. What he saw were clear indications of deception. Every time George had denied committing the murder or having knowledge of the murder, the needles had jumped, reaching upward into a series of peaks that dwarfed the hills that had followed the control questions.

Brentnell stepped back into the interview room and sat down and looked George in the eye.

"You're not telling me the truth," he said. "You know it. I know it. God knows it."

Brentnell loved to throw God at his subjects. If God knew they were lying, then everyone knew, and what was the point of denying it?

George began to cry.

"You stabbed Karen," Brentnell said.

"No, I didn't."

"Either you did, or you know who did."

A few minutes later, Brentnell walked out and asked Tosi and Hanson to come inside. Tosi looked at his friend and saw the tears in his eyes.

"George has something else to tell you," Brentnell said. "He saw somebody that night."

That's when George told them about the man on the lawn. After hearing the scream that night, he said, he stepped outside, turned out the garage light, and waited a few moments for his eyes to adjust to the dark. He looked around, trying to see where the scream had come from. When he found nothing wrong, he said, he went back to the garage and collected some metal filings and other trash from the work he'd been doing and then walked across the driveway to throw the trash into his garbage can. Just as he closed the lid, he said, he looked over toward David and Karen's lawn and saw a man walking under the big oak tree toward the back of the property. The man saw him and stopped, and both of them froze for a moment as they gazed across the street at each other.

"I got scared," George said, "because this guy looked right at me and stared."

"What did the guy look like?" asked Tosi.

He was big, George said. He was white, middle-aged, about six four, with a trim light-red beard and red collar-length hair. He had stocky shoulders and what looked like weight lifter's arms. He wore a loose-fitting green shirt with short sleeves and gray or black dress pants. He wasn't carrying anything.

"Did the shirt have a collar on it?" said Tosi.

No collar, George said. It was open in front, with no buttons. It looked like one of those surgical scrub shirts.

"Did you notice his shoes?"

No, George said. He hadn't really looked at the man's feet. He said that he and the man stood there for a moment, looking at each other, before George went back inside the house, watching as the man walked away. The man was walking toward the driveway, where David and Karen's cars were parked. But George said he didn't hear a car start up. He didn't actually see the man leave, he said. Afterward, he said, he didn't tell Glenda about the man because he didn't want her to worry. And he didn't tell the police, he said, because the man had seen him and seen where he lived, and he was afraid for his wife and baby.

This last comment sounded odd to Tosi. At the time of the murder, George and Glenda weren't married yet. And even though she had already become pregnant, that night the baby's birth was still months away. In fact, as George sat there giving the detectives this new account, Glenda was still expecting, due to deliver shortly. As far as Tosi was concerned, George's vivid description of the intruder did not make a lot of sense either. The murder had happened at about 1:15 A.M. It had been raining. George had been standing by his garage; the man had been standing all the way over in David and Karen's yard. How could George have seen him in such detail?

Obviously George had lied to them before. Was he still lying now? Tosi knew a way to find out. They would stage a reenactment.

They did it about 9:30 one night. Beforehand, Tosi had checked around the two houses and found that since the murder some of the neighbors, including George, had installed spotlights for security. Because these lights would not have been shining that night, Tosi now made sure that they would be turned off on the night of the reenactment.

That evening he picked up Brinkworth—who had red hair and had been told to wear a green jacket—and dropped him off with a radio about a block away from the two houses. Then Tosi went to George's house and waited for Lt. Hanson to arrive.

When Hanson got there, the three of them stood outside the garage by the garbage can. Tosi told George they had positioned a man not far from David and Karen's house, that they were going to have him walk onto their lawn, and that George should let them know when the man reached the point where the intruder had been.

Tosi picked up his radio and, without mentioning a name, told Brinkworth to start moving. When George said stop, Tosi told Brinkworth to hold it and then turned back to George and asked him to describe who was over there.

"Well," said George, "he's wearing some kind of a jacket."

"Okay. Can you tell me what color it is?"

"No."

Tosi asked George if he could describe the man any further—the color of his hair or anything else. George said no.

"Do you know who that is over there?"

"No."

This was not encouraging. George had known Brinkworth for years. But now, as he stood in the same exact place from where he supposedly had seen the intruder in such detail, George could not tell it was Brinkworth across the street. Try as he might, Tosi could not make him out, either. Nor could Hanson, even though he was wearing his glasses. It was too dark and too far.

Hanson asked how that could be.

"Frank," George said, "something is wrong with the lighting."

It had been different on the night of the murder, he said. That night it had been raining; now they stood there under clear skies. George pointed to a streetlight that stood on the corner of his lawn, the corner closest to David and Karen's house. Maybe, he said, the light had reflected off the wet street that night and had cast more light onto the lawn. Or maybe the moon had been brighter.

Tosi didn't buy this explanation. He knew it had been overcast the night of the murder. He also knew that the street had been darker that night than it was now, despite his efforts to duplicate the lighting. Martha Borkowski, whose house was directly across from David and Karen's, had told Tosi that she might have had a small porch light on during the night of the murder. But there had also been three tall evergreens in her yard that night, cutting down on the light from the house. Since then she had gotten rid of the bushes.

Obviously, Tosi thought, George could not have stood outside his garage and seen the intruder so clearly. He must have been closer to David and Karen's house. They asked him if that was possible. George said yes, maybe a little closer. Maybe over in his yard.

"But I know I didn't go off of my property," he said. "I know I never left my property."

Tosi didn't think that sounded right either. In his original statement George had talked about walking into the street after the scream and looking around. And there were more contradictions as well. Earlier George had told them that he never saw Karen on the day or night of the murder. Now they asked again if he had seen her, and this time he said yes. He saw her in the window at around 7:30 that evening, he said. She was in the kitchen washing dishes.

"How do you know she was doing dishes?"

"I could tell," George said. "Because her arms were moving."

To Tosi and Hanson it was clear George was still lying. Obviously he was hiding something, and whatever it was, they thought maybe he was keeping it to himself because he was afraid for his own and his family's safety. For the moment, though, they couldn't prove that. They called it a night and went home.

In the days that followed, Tosi checked with the weather service and confirmed that there had been no moon visible that night. Still, he continued going to George's house so he could review his account with him, over and over. One night, as they went through it again, George brought up some more new details. This time he said that he not only had seen Karen doing the dishes that night, but had heard the dishes rattling.

That was the way it was going. As the weeks passed, George was giving them one story after another. Hanson was sick of it. He reminded George that he was a firefighter and told him he was obstructing the investigation. He told George that if he was holding back because he was afraid of somebody on the loose out there, not to worry, because they would catch the man. He wanted the truth, he said. All of it.

George insisted he was telling the truth. He said he wasn't holding anything back. Again he began to cry.

"I didn't do it," he said.

Eleven

That February, as he sorted through the startling new disclosures George Lewis had so reluctantly divulged, Tosi was forced to stare into the face of some undeniably ugly facts.

There was no way around it. Larry had trusted George, and George had repaid that trust with an astonishing pattern of deceit. He had been lying to them from the start, from that first morning when he came to the station and wrote out the statement. And in the long months afterward, when the detectives were working nights and weekends to find the slightest clue that might put them on the killer's track, George had kept on lying. He had sent them chasing after Sanders and Kumble and Mackey and some stranger on a ten-speed. But in all the times he and Tosi had spent together—all the times when Larry stopped by the house to chat, when they'd gone out with Glenda and Debbie, when they'd stood together on the fire truck at the wedding—George had never mentioned seeing this red-haired man on the lawn.

The funny thing was, George had been under suspicion all along, at least in one person's mind. It was Chief Golliner. From day one, when he'd heard George's original story, the chief had been insisting that it was a bunch of garbage. He'd actually emerged from the windowless realm of the Ceramic Palace and walked down the hall to the detectives' office and announced, repeatedly, that George was their man.

"I think that guy did it," he'd said.

At their desks, the detectives who'd heard him barely looked up. They never knew when old Hap was serious; he was always telling wild stories, trying to impress them. This time, though, he clearly had gone off the deep end. Did he actually expect them to believe George was a murderer? "Right, chief," they'd say, shaking their heads after he'd walked away.

Now, so many months later, it appeared that Golliner might have been on to something. Hanson felt there was no choice but to consider George a suspect. As far as the lieutenant was concerned, all of the contradictions and changing stories had catapulted George to the top of the list. "He's the one," Hanson said.

Tosi, however, was not ready to accept that his friend might be capable of the brutality that had been committed inside that house. Yes, George had hidden the truth from them, and might still be hiding it. But that did not necessarily make him a murderer. Despite all of the lies, Tosi wanted to go on trusting him. He wanted to believe that George had witnessed something that night that had cowed him into silence. Whatever it was, it had to have been terrifying. George was not exactly the type to be easily intimidated. The man was a firefighter, wasn't he? Part of his job was risking his life. Besides, as far as Tosi knew, he had never been violent in the past.

George Lewis was the kind of person who inspired trust. He was a good-looking man, with a slightly muscular build and dark chocolate-brown eyes and large white teeth that occasionally broke free into a disarmingly goofy grin. Only twenty-three, he was already a well-liked and respected figure around Gulfport. He had lived there since he was a boy and had graduated from Boca Ciega High School, the same public school Debbie Tosi had attended. He was from a big Catholic family that belonged to Most Holy Name of Jesus, the same church Larry Tosi attended. Carl Lewis, Sr., George's father, worked for the postal department in St. Petersburg; Evelyn Lewis, his mother, was a secretary for the local Roman Catholic diocese. They had seven children, and George was the youngest. Sometimes they called him Georgie.

Among his friends he was considered easy-going, earnest, and a little shy at times. He was like a big overgrown boy, with a weakness for chocolate chip cookies—sometimes he'd sneak into the kitchen and bake them himself—and an avid affection for water-skiing and racing model cars and driving his pickup truck through the mud. Back in school he had been called Big Red, which was appropriate not just because of his hair but because he loved chasing fires. From the time he was a little kid, that was what he'd always wanted to do. As a teenager he used to hang out at the fire station, listening to the veterans trade stories, taking in everything he could. Whenever possible, he followed the trucks. He'd hear the high-pitched call of the sirens and jump on his bike and race after them. Finally, when he turned eighteen, he became a volunteer with the Gulfport Fire Department; then, at twenty-one, the city of St. Pete hired him full time.

George's devotion to his job ran through almost everything he did. A certified emergency medical technician, he kept a first-aid kit in his pickup truck and would stop if he saw an accident. He watched reruns of "Emergency" on TV. And in May 1980, when a freighter hit the Sunshine Skyway Bridge at the mouth of Tampa Bay and sent its center span—along with a Greyhound bus and several cars—tumbling fifteen stories into the dark water below, he'd volunteered to assist with the rescue. That was the kind of guy he was. Whenever he heard sirens, even if he was on vacation in another state, he would wonder aloud if he should be helping.

Around the streets where he lived, he was known as an exceptionally good neighbor. He often did favors for people, watching their yards when they were away, helping them fix things, occasionally even mowing their grass for them. At the same time, he was always willing to investigate anything suspicious going on in the neighborhood. In fact, he enjoyed playing amateur detective almost as much as he loved firefighting. If he saw some kids he didn't recognize riding by on their bikes, he'd check them out. If people drove by wildly, he'd jump into his truck and chase after them. And if he heard or saw anything that didn't set right with him, he would pick up the phone and call the police.

"Justice is never done," he would complain. "People get away with murder."

The house where George lived was owned by his parents, who lived up the street. It was a small house, nothing fancy, with light-yellow cinder block walls and big metal awnings and, on one of the sidewalls, a plaster relief of what appeared to be an ancient Spanish galleon, sailing with the wind. The garage was a little separate building, with a weather vane on the roof—the vane was topped by a silhouetted figure of a man fishing—and was far enough away from the house that he could weld and solder and hammer late into the night.

George and his first wife, Denise, had lived in the house as newlyweds. But the marriage had not lasted long, and as they divorced, Glenda had moved in. She was a slender woman, rather pale, with a careful smile and wavy light-brown hair that sometimes meandered toward blond. By May 1984, when the murder took place, she and George had been living together for a couple of years. That summer was a rocky period for the two of them. Glenda had found out she was pregnant, and while some of the couple's friends would insist later that George had been happy to marry her, others would say that he'd had no intention of getting married again, baby or no baby.

Either way, there was a great deal of friction in the house. Mike Blank, a friend of George's who used to chase after the fire trucks with him when they were kids, was living there too. Then one of George's sisters moved in, and things grew complicated. Quarters were cramped, and George's sister, Mary Lewis, had squabbled with the others. She'd wanted George and Glenda and Mike to sign contracts over the payment of the bills. The pressures were too much for Blank, who moved out only a few days before the murder. Glenda stayed a little longer—long enough to hear the scream that night. But a short time later, she left as well, leaving the house to George and his sister.

The murder was the talk of the town that summer. As the rumors and theories and tidbits of information were bantered back and forth, some observers couldn't help thinking that it was a little odd that George, of all people, had not reported the scream. One Monday night, when the Gulfport firefighters were having their regular weekly meeting, another volunteer cornered him outside the station and asked him to his face why he hadn't called the police that night. George explained how he'd searched up and down the street and hadn't seen anything—this was before the ground beneath his story began to disintegrate—and said he'd done what he felt was necessary. The other firefighter wasn't convinced. He said he didn't think it was right that George hadn't picked up the phone. It stunk, he said.

The police didn't look at it that way. Hanson, for one, had

been thankful that George had done as much as he had. At least he'd gone outside and tried to check it out. Besides, in those early months the detectives were up to their eyeballs in prime suspects. There wasn't much time, and didn't seem to be much point, to chewing out George.

Meanwhile, Glenda's absence from the house did not last long. By that fall they'd patched things up and agreed to set a wedding date. Whatever reservations George may have had about settling down, he seemed to have worked them out. It was none too soon, either; they were about to become a family. That December, when Tosi married them on the fire truck, Glenda was at least six months along in her pregnancy. The baby, a seven-pound twelve-ounce girl named Tiffany, was born on February 24, 1985.

It was right around then, just as his daughter was entering the world, that George failed the polygraph and failed the reenactment and was forced, after so many months of lies, to admit tearfully that he knew something more about the killing across the street.

Tosi and Hanson wanted him to sit for another polygraph. They were sure he was still holding back, but they'd had no success in pulling anything more from him. So they asked him to meet again with Mike Brentnell.

George wasn't exactly eager to comply. He missed one appointment, and when he showed up for the next, on the evening of March 7, he was in a hurry to leave, saying he hadn't eaten any dinner and was hungry. Brentnell didn't like the sound of that—whenever a subject tried to rush through an examination, it raised a flag in his mind—but he did his best to get George to relax.

"So how's being a new father?" he said.

"I wouldn't give it up for the world," said George, pulling out a photo of Tiffany for him to see.

But much of the session—most of which was tape-recorded—simmered with tension. Before the test had even begun, Brentnell demanded to know why George was still lying to them. He said he knew the reenactment had been a bust and that George still hadn't come clean. He said he wanted the truth. "I don't have time for this," he said. "What the hell happened?"

With that, George changed his story again. This time the news was that he and the man on the lawn had spoken that night.

He had heard the scream, he said, then walked down both Twenty-seventh Avenue and Upton Street—he was back in the street now, after having insisted before that he'd never left his property—and was just rounding the corner of David and Karen's lawn when he looked over and saw this man standing under the tree, only a few feet away. When George asked him what was the matter, the man told him that he should get lost. He said that George better not say "a goddamned word" to anyone about seeing him or he'd come back and kill him.

Brentnell listened, taking notes. He said he wanted to try out this account with the polygraph. So he hooked George up again and went through the new details, one by one.

Again the charts showed that George was lying.

Brentnell told George he wanted to believe him. He said he was trying to help him. He asked if there was anything else that George might have left out. Because if there was, he said, it would show up on the test. George thought for a moment, then added that the man also had told him not to be a "smart ass." And when the man threatened him, he said, he'd promised to keep his mouth shut.

"Is that everything?" said Brentnell.

"Yes."

During the test, Hanson had been waiting outside. Now Brentnell called him in to inform him of the new development in George's account. Hanson grew angry. He said he was tired of all the changing stories. First George had told them he was on the driveway. Then he was on the lawn. Now he was telling them he'd been in the street, beside David and Karen's yard.

"The next thing that's going to happen," Hanson said, "is you're going to be in the house."

"No. I wasn't in the house."

Hanson said he didn't buy it. There were so many conflicting stories, he said, that he didn't believe any of them. He said he would have to advise George of his Miranda rights.

George looked disgusted. "Go ahead," he said.

Hanson did it and then he stepped out, and Brentnell put George under the polygraph again. This time they returned to the questions from the very first test back in February, the questions that focused directly on whether George had been involved in the murder.

"Did you stab Karen?"

"No."

"Were you present when Karen was stabbed?"

"No."

"Do you suspect anyone else of stabbing Karen?"

"No."

Again Brentnell looked at the charts. Again he told George that he had failed.

The room was quiet for a moment. Brentnell pulled up his chair and leaned in close, planting one of his feet on the floor between George's shoes, so that George could no longer close his legs, so that he would feel as vulnerable and exposed as possible when he heard what Brentnell was about to say.

"I know why you're failing the test, George," said Brentnell, speaking more softly than he had all evening. "I need to know the reason why. What did that girl do to upset you?"

"What do you mean?" asked George.

"Because I think you killed her."

"What?"

"I do. I think you killed her. But there has to be a reason why."

George said he didn't do it. He said that he'd already told them everything he knew.

"I'm scared shitless," he said, "that that guy is going to come back and kill me."

Brentnell pressed for details on the man. "Did he have blood all over him?"

"No."

"Then that guy did not kill her."

It was possible, George said, that the man had been waiting out there for someone else inside the house.

Brentnell scoffed. He said he didn't believe there was any man on the lawn. The man, he said, was George. George was the one who had killed Karen. Now, he said, he just wanted to find out why. Was it possible that George was drunk that night? George said no. Did Karen say something to him? No, he said. He said he never even knew her. Well, did he want to sleep with her? No.

"We all fall down," Brentnell said. "We all make mistakes. We're all human . . . Now, George, why don't you be honest. Did you make a mistake?"

"No."

"If you didn't kill her, then you had to be in that house. Did you go in there and look and then you were scared and you ran out and didn't want to call the cops? . . . Be honest with me. Because if that's the case, it would frig the whole test up."

"I never went in there."

"If you can't come up with anything else like that, George, then I can only still say that you killed her."

"I didn't kill her, and I never saw anything else."

Brentnell didn't believe it. He said George had done so badly on the tests that he was winging all over the chart.

"By jumping around like all this, you're obstructing justice. You know that."

"I know."

"What is the real truth?"

George pointed to a written copy of his new statement.

"That right there."

"No, it's not."

"Yes, it is."

"No, it's not, George. It can't be . . . Did you go in there and stab her?"

"No."

"Why would you do something like that?"

"*I didn't do it.*"

"Then help me. Because I'm not in here just trying to get someone. You know that."

"Sometimes people just don't take good polygraphs."

"You've had three polygraphs . . . You're bombing it, George."

Brentnell said he knew George was a good person. He knew George wasn't normally violent. But maybe, he said, something had happened.

"Do you know how many times she was stabbed?"

"No."

"She was stabbed a lot . . . That person who killed her had to be really upset at something. That's a person who just snapped, just like that. The person in front of me I don't think could do that."

"I didn't do it."

"Well who the hell did?"

"I don't know . . . All I can say is, I don't believe that you're actually trying to say that I killed her."

"I don't have to *try* it. I'm telling you, George: you killed her. See my lips?"

George stood his ground. "I am telling the truth."

"You can't be."

"I am."

"You can't be."

"I don't care what the machine says. I am telling the truth."

They went around in circles for more than an hour. Brentnell attacked from every angle he could think of. Again he told George that God knew what he had done. He reminded him that Tosi and Hanson were his friends and said that they wanted to help him. He said that until George confessed, the guilt would tear away at him.

"You got a bear on your back, buddy," he said, "and it's going to eat you alive. It's going to be staring at you tonight."

Through it all, George held his ground. He kept denying it. He kept saying he had never hurt Karen.

Brentnell heard this and paused.

"Wait a minute, George . . . I'm not asking if you hurt her. I'm telling you, you killed her. Not hurt her. Killed her. Okay? Not hurt, killed . . . Is that what you wish? That all you did was hurt her?"

George said no. He said he didn't like the way Brentnell was trying to put words in his mouth.

Brentnell ignored him and kept pushing. "You were there inside that house. You took that knife, and you killed her."

"No, I didn't."

"What did you do with the knife?"

"I never had the knife."

"What type of knife was it? Was it a little knife? A big knife?"

"I don't know, because I didn't do it."

Then why, Brentnell said, didn't he call the police? If he was such a good citizen, why did he not tell anyone about this man on the lawn? Why did he wait seven months before telling anyone—and then only after a polygraph?

"This son-of-a-bitch is out running around, and he may get away because of your holding that information."

"I know, and I feel bad about that."

"Bad? That's bullshit . . . You just told me you were brought up in a Catholic school. You have a lot of morals, buddy. You would have turned that person in. You wouldn't have waited."

But George wouldn't budge. He said he'd told them everything he knew. He said he was innocent.

Finally Brentnell asked him what he thought should happen to the person who'd killed Karen.

"I hope the guy is locked up forever."

"What would you do if you found him?"

"I don't know."

By the end of the night, George was officially considered a suspect. But his changing stories still did not prove he was the killer. The detectives typed up a written summary of his new statement, had him sign it, and told him he could go.

Now even Tosi was having trouble trusting George. There were too many inconsistencies. Before, he had told them that he hadn't paid attention to what the man on the lawn was wearing on his feet. Now he was saying the man had worn dress sandals. He was also saying that he hadn't noticed any blood on the man. How could that be? And why would this person have allowed George to stand a few feet away and look at him so thoroughly? There had been a scream. Glass had shattered. For all the killer knew, a neighbor had called 911. The police could have been coming around the corner any second. Why would this stranger have stood there waiting to be caught? Why wouldn't he have killed George?

Tosi didn't know what to think. He was still trying to believe in George, but it was getting harder with every contradiction.

Their friendship, not surprisingly, was growing strained. The two of them would be together with their wives and Larry would ask George some questions, and George would insist on talking in a whisper, off to the side. He said he didn't want Glenda to know about what he'd seen that night. He didn't want to upset her. At the same time, Glenda was worried about how upset George was becoming. Seeing him and Larry going through it all, she'd turn unhappily to Debbie Tosi.

"I wish they wouldn't talk about that," Glenda would tell Debbie. "George does not like to talk about the murder."

But Larry needed George to talk about it. If they were going to eliminate him from the list of suspects, they needed to track down the man on the lawn. So they went over it and over it. One day they sat down together with an identikit set and made a composite drawing of the man based on George's description, and then Larry began showing the drawing to people who'd known Karen. All of them said they didn't know anyone who looked like that.

Larry did, though. To him, the drawing looked like George, who years before had worn a trim red beard.

Twelve

On the night of March 15, one week after the second polygraph session, a possible break-in was reported at the white house on the corner. Details were sketchy, but it appeared that the murderer might have returned again.

By this time a family of renters was living in the house. All of them were gone that evening and the house was dark. A neighbor had phoned the police after noticing that the front door was wide open. The investigating officer was Ted Heffelfinger, and when he arrived, he found that the door from the porch into the living room also was wide open, along with a side door. Heffelfinger, an old friend of Tosi's, knew Larry would want to be informed, so he gave him a call. Tosi drove over immediately.

The first thing they did was have a K-9 officer search the premises with his dog. The officer happened to be Tommy Polletta, a friend of both Tosi's and Lewis's; sometimes he and George would watch stock car races together at a local speedway. Polletta was not yet aware that George was a suspect in the murder. All he knew was that he and his dog, a German shepherd named Marshall, were supposed to make sure no one was hiding in the house. So Polletta unfastened his gun holster and put a leather attack collar on Marshall and called out at the front door, warning anyone within that they were about to enter.

He let Marshall off his lead, and the dog began trotting through the house, sniffing for a fresh scent. He went through the living room and into the kitchen, with Polletta quickly following and Tosi and Heffelfinger bringing up the rear, and then back into the hallway. He didn't find anything, however, until he went into the northwest bedroom, where Karen was believed to have been raped and first stabbed. Marshall seemed to sense that something horrible had happened here. He walked through the door, and suddenly he stopped and froze.

"Something isn't right," Polletta whispered to the others.

They could feel it too. As Heffelfinger would later describe it, the room seemed to be filled with a kind of aura. They were standing there in the dark, not saying anything, watching the dog, who had begun to whimper and bark and sniff the air. This was his "alert," the signal that he had found a fresh scent. But this was different. Polletta knew this dog. He worked with him, lived with him, let him sleep at the foot of his bed every night. And now he realized that Marshall was signaling with an enthusiasm usually reserved for those moments when the owner of the scent is still present. In fact, he was insisting that another person was in the room with them.

"There's gotta be someone in here," said Polletta.

They looked around, but they couldn't see anyone. Yet the dog went on barking and scratching at the wall by the door, trying to find whoever it was. Polletta had never seen anything so spooky.

"It's like there's someone standing there," he told the others, "and the dog sees him and we can't."

There was no one. They checked the closets. They knocked on the walls, making sure there weren't any concealed hiding places. Polletta looked across the room, toward the window where the killer had slipped out so many months before. It was open, and there was a breeze coming through. It was possible, Polletta thought, that someone had been in the room only moments ago and had climbed out that window just before they came in. Maybe that person's scent had blown across the room onto the wall. Maybe the person was still out there, listening to them and driving the dog crazy.

Polletta took Marshall outside, put him on a lead with a

tracking harness, and began circling the outer walls of the house. They had just reached the area near the back bedroom when the dog jerked forward—jerked with such force he almost yanked Polletta to the ground—and began moving to the north.

"That's a good boy," Polletta told him. "Track the man. Track him."

Marshall didn't need any encouragement. Straining at the harness as if someone were fleeing only a few yards ahead of him, he led them through the backyard and into the backyard of the next house to the north and then turned east toward Upton. When he reached the curb, he lost the trail. This wasn't surprising; even if the track had crossed the street, the passage of a car easily could have disturbed it.

Polletta took Marshall back to the house and let him play with an old chewed up tennis ball that had been his toy since training school and then put him back inside the car. A few minutes later, though, he decided to try the trail again. So he took the dog back out of the car and off they went one more time. When they reached Upton, Polletta walked him across the street and let him sniff around, and this time the dog found the scent and resumed the track. The dog turned right again, southward now, and went through the yard of the house on the northeast corner of Upton and Twenty-seventh Avenue, then went across Twenty-seventh all the way to the curb near the opposite corner.

It was there that Marshall lost the trail. Polletta wasn't sure what to think. He doubted that the person they were tracking had gotten into a car and driven away; when that happens, the acceleration of the car and exhaust fumes often send the person's scent swirling, which sends the dog moving in circles. But Marshall wasn't circling—he was weaving, which suggested to Polletta that whoever they were looking for had moved away fast, fast enough to leave almost no scent, without the aid of gasoline. His guess was that the person had either climbed on a bicycle or taken some huge running strides onto the lawn that stretched beyond the curb.

Of course, Polletta knew that lawn well. It was George Lewis's.

Tosi took no chances. When the family that lived in the house came home, he interviewed them and asked them to look around to see if anything appeared to have been stolen. At first they said no, but then a day or so later the wife called back and said that she had looked inside her jewelry box and could not find a pearl necklace. Tosi asked her to bring him the box, and he dusted that for prints, just as he had done on the outside of the house.

He was still studying a long list of suspects. Not just George, but several others, including Steven Fischler and David Mackey and a man who had once raked leaves at the house and another who had been caught prowling around the neighborhood one night. Fingerprints had been taken from all of these people, and now these were sent, along with some prints collected from the reported break-in, to the Pinellas County Sheriff's Department for comparison. If the killer had indeed come back once more, maybe this time he'd left behind some identifiable trace of himself.

Even as he investigated this most recent twist, Tosi had his hands full with a new bulletin from George about some mysterious phone calls. Someone, George said, was harassing him at home, calling there repeatedly during the early evening and after midnight, then hanging up without saying a word.

This claim met with more than a touch of skepticism. Lt. Hanson and Mike Brentnell both thought he was making up the calls, trying to lend credence to his purported fears that the man on the lawn might be out to get him. Brentnell had even gone so far as to suggest that if any calls truly had been placed, George might have rigged the whole thing by arranging it with one of his buddies. Tosi wasn't sure what to think. But just to be safe, he arranged for General Telephone to place a trap on the Lewis phone, so that the company's computer would keep track of every call to the house. George was instructed to write down the date and time he received the calls.

The phone company started the trap on March 8, the day after the second polygraph session. Suddenly George said he wasn't getting any more of the calls. Glenda and his sister Mary had received a couple, he said, but they hadn't marked down the times. George said he had told them to keep track, but that he would remind them. The weeks went by, and still George said he had not gotten any more of the calls. Finally, on April 12, after thirty-eight days with no results, the trap was removed. Whoever had been calling—if anyone had been calling—had shown a remarkable talent for avoiding detection.

None of this made it any easier to swallow George's stories. Still, Tosi clung to the hope that his friend might be telling the truth. Trying to give him the benefit of the doubt, he had arranged the phone trap and put together the composite drawing and done everything he could to find and identify the intruder George had described on the lawn. Tosi collected photos of dozens of different men who had been suspects and showed them to George, asking if any of them was the one. George said no.

As before, George said he didn't know who the man on the lawn was. But he looked similar, George said, to a guy he'd seen in the area a couple of weeks before the murder, going door to door and asking if anyone needed their trees trimmed.

"Did he come to your house?" asked Tosi. "Did he talk to you?"

"No," said George.

"Well, which houses did he go to?"

"I don't know."

That didn't make sense to Tosi. How could you see someone knocking on doors without noticing which houses? Nonetheless, he pursued this lead as well, asking George's neighbors if they remembered the tree trimmer. But nobody did.

Of course, the neighbors were more than familiar with George. Almost all of them spoke glowingly of the young man on the corner, telling how he was always helping them with their yards or with other favors. One woman, however, shared an anecdote that only raised more questions in Tosi's mind. This neighbor had known George for several years and thought he was a nice young man. They'd spoken together many times; he had been to her house for a New Year's Eve party.

One evening not long after the murder, the neighbor was going up her front walk, returning home from a late night out— it was after midnight—when she heard someone in her yard say hello. The sound startled her. She looked over, and there was George, walking his dog. She went over to say hi, and the two of them began chatting about the murder. He told her he had a little inside information on the case. He said that he worked with the police from time to time and that he had some friends with the department who were keeping him up to date on the murder investigation.

"I have a lot of friends," he said.

His sources, he said, had learned that Karen Gregory had liked black men and had been known to date them. They'd also told him, he said, that before she died, Karen had brought some plants home and left them on the driveway. She had planned to transplant them into larger pots, he said, but had been killed before she had the chance. The sad thing was, he said, that someone had stolen a couple of the plants.

As for the killer, he said the police believed it was a large man. "He had to be big," George said.

"Why?"

"To drag her body around the way it was dragged."

"George, she was small."

"Yeah, but she was muscular."

Now, months later, the woman remembered this conversation and passed it along to Tosi. He was surprised. As far as he knew, no one in the police department had been sharing any inside information with George. Besides, much of what he had told the neighbor was incorrect. The police were not necessarily looking for a large man. Nor had it ever been determined that Karen's body had been dragged. During the autopsy Dr. Wood had found a skin burn apparently created after Karen died, but there'd been no way to tell for sure what had caused the mark. In fact, Dr. Wood had thought it might have been made as the body was removed from the house. So why would George insist on such a thing? And how would he know that Karen had been so strong? It was true she had kept herself in good shape, working out with weights and riding her bike. But she hadn't looked particularly muscular. In fact, she had been slender.

In addition, Tosi had never heard anything about Karen transplanting her plants into larger pots. He went to David, Anita, Neverne, and Karen's sister Kim and asked if Karen had ever mentioned it to them. All of them said no. Tosi could not find anyone who knew this about Karen, or who knew anything about plants having been stolen that night.

How did George know?

When the sheriff's department's report on the new fingerprints came back, it was all negative. None of the suspects matched up with the prints that had been gathered from the recent break-in. There was no proof that the incident was connected to the murder. Tosi could not even be positive that there had been a break-in in the first place; the missing necklace, it turned out, had since been found. The whole thing was just another dead end.

Not that Tosi was giving up. He had arranged for a variety

of samples to be collected from George—not just fingerprints, but palm prints and footprints as well as head, chest, and pubic hairs—and now, as he had in the past with other suspects, he submitted these to the FDLE. The lab work would take weeks, maybe months. But it was the best shot they had.

In the meantime, while they waited for the results, Tosi was trying to understand how George could have been pushed to the point of murder. Tosi knew George had a temper; Larry had seen it himself while they were working on their cars. Something wouldn't go right, and in the space of a few seconds, George would fly off the handle and throw his tools to the ground. His other friends and fellow firefighters had noticed it too. When Tosi began interviewing them, they commented on what a hothead George could be. He liked things to go his way, they said; if they didn't, he sometimes lost it, breaking out in tears or erupting in anger.

Tosi asked one of George's friends how far he thought George might go to protect himself. If he were desperate—if he found himself, Tosi said, in a situation where his firefighting career and everything else he loved was threatened—was it possible that George would actually get violent?

"It's possible," the friend said. "Anything is possible."

There was no doubt that George had been under a lot of pressure that summer. There were the yelling matches with Glenda, the unexpected pregnancy, and the question of whether they should marry, not to mention the two of them crammed into that little house with Mike Blank and George's sister Mary. Tosi also noted that Mary's arrival—and Mike's and Glenda's departures—had coincided almost exactly with the night of the murder. Obviously the tension inside the house had reached a boiling point.

George apparently had responded with an almost unrestrained abandon. Once Glenda was gone, his friends had noticed him acting wildly, drinking more than usual, joining a singles club, regaling his pals at the fire department with wanton tales of sexual exploits. Most of his energies had been directed toward a dark-haired sixteen-year-old girl named Tonja who lived near the fire station. If George wasn't in love with her, he was certainly in lust. They dated for a few months, carrying on throughout the summer, generating new material for George's locker-room stories. Once, George had asked another Gulfport firefighter to join him at a motel for an orgy. He told his buddy he could bring his ex-girlfriend. "I don't think she'd be interested," the friend had told him, politely begging off.

Tosi tried to find this Tonja, hoping she might offer some clues as to why George had undergone such a radical change of behavior. But she had moved since that summer, and no one seemed to remember her last name. Meanwhile, George's friends were making it clear that George had not exactly been blind to the fact that he was living across the street from an attractive woman. Richard Pashkow, a volunteer Gulfport firefighter who had known George for years, told Tosi that George had once mentioned to a couple of friends how Karen was always walking around her house half-naked. This statement was never confirmed; in fact, the two friends who supposedly had heard George say this—Mike Blank and Richard McCann—both denied hearing such a thing. McCann, however, shared an illuminating story of his own.

One day in 1984, when he and George had been standing outside George's garage, they had noticed a woman walking around in a bikini over at David Mackey's house. "Look at that," George had said.

McCann wasn't sure if this woman was Karen Gregory, but he remembered that she had dark hair, and he thought she might have been unloading things from her car that day. Whoever she was, McCann said, both he and George had commented on how pretty she was.

Yet another Gulfport volunteer had once been at the Lewis house when he and George saw two women in bikinis sitting in lawn chairs at one of the houses next door. Again the identity of these women was unclear; this witness later would insist that neither of them was Karen. Either way, he remembered what George had said to him when they noticed the two women.

"I've already checked it out," he'd said.

That was the type of guy George was. In fact, the same friend told Tosi he wouldn't be surprised if George had made a pass at Karen. If he'd thought she might be receptive—if he'd thought, as the other firefighter put it, "he could go over there and get a piece of ass"—then he might well have given it a try.

Still, there was no indication that George and Karen had known much, if anything, about each other. David couldn't even remember Karen saying hello to the man. But the more Tosi learned, the more conceivable it seemed that George might have gone over there that night to try starting something with his new neighbor. Certainly the opportunity had existed. It was late, Glenda was asleep in the house, and George was alone out in the garage, where he easily could have stood gazing across the street at this woman whose boyfriend just happened to be out of town—and also happened to be black.

George, Tosi had been told, did not like blacks. Undoubtedly he took special note of them, as he'd already shown with Lawrence Sanders and with his comment about Karen's interest in black men. Around the St. Pete fire department, he'd been heard complaining that black firefighters received special treatment. These gripes might have grown from a long-standing resentment. George had often talked about how he believed a black administrator had delayed his getting hired by the city.

All of this made Tosi return to the theory that the motive for the murder might have included some sort of racial component. Was it possible, he wondered, that George had bought into the racist stereotypes? Had he figured that a white woman who lived with a black man was promiscuous? Had he thought that Karen automatically would sleep with a white man who wandered over late one night when she was by herself?

There was something else, something more that had been passed along by the neighbor woman who'd had the late-night chat with George. She said they had also spoken briefly about a black woman who lived over on Forty-eighth Street—one of the same women who'd repeatedly seen a prowler in her backyard in the days after the murder. This woman, George had told her, had been causing a problem in the neighborhood, with all sorts of cars parking at her house. He was helping the police with her, he'd said. He was making a point, he said, of keeping an eye on her house.

Tosi couldn't prove that George had been the one lurking outside that woman's house. He couldn't prove that George had anything to do with any of the other incidents around the neighborhood. But bit by bit, a scenario for the murder was shaping in his mind. A few months before, if anyone had suggested it to him, this scenario would have struck him as outlandish. Now, to both him and Lt. Hanson, it seemed increasingly plausible.

Looking at it cold, trying to imagine the worst, it was hard to deny that George would have had little trouble that night—

less than almost anybody else—escaping from Karen's house undetected, even covered with blood. Logistically, everything was
in place for him. There was a bush by the back bedroom window,
which would have offered some cover. He could have climbed
out, slipped around the rear of the property, then made his way
back home, probably circling to the east and then to the south to
avoid the streetlight on the corner. His garage, separate from the
house, would have been an ideal place to get out of his bloody
clothes without anyone seeing him. Also, Tosi and Hanson knew
that George kept old pairs of shorts and shirts in the garage to use
as rags and so forth, which would have made it easy for him to
change. As for how he would have disposed of the stained clothes,
Hanson thought the most likely candidate was the trash can right
outside. George had changed an awful lot of details from one
version of his story to the next, but he had always come back to
that trash can and how he had been throwing away metal filings
and other junk that night—perfect for covering up evidence he
didn't want anyone to see.

Still, he would have needed to wash himself off. Here, Tosi
and Hanson thought back to what Glenda had said, just after the
murder when she was at the Tosi house, talking about seeing a
silhouette in the back window. They knew there was a faucet and
hose at the rear of the house, near that window, and that George
routinely washed up out there after working in the garage. The
neighbors had seen him do it many times.

It was time to ask Glenda a few questions.

That May, as the one-year anniversary of the murder came
and went, Hanson drove over to the Lewis house. He knew that
George would not be there, because he'd checked with the St.
Pete fire department to find out when he was on duty. Hanson
wanted it that way. He wanted to talk to Glenda alone. As it
turned out, she wasn't alone at all. Young Tiffany, several months
old now, was crying in the playpen, demanding her mother's
attention. So Glenda picked her up and held her while she answered
Hanson's questions. She was rather vague, he would later recall.
She told him how she had heard the scream that night and then
gone to the kitchen and waited for George.

"Did you hear the water running outside?" said Hanson.

"No."

"Did you see anyone in the yard?"

"No."

"Anything in the window?"

"No."

"How long did you wait before George came back?"

"About five to ten minutes."

"Was he wet?"

"No," said Glenda. "He might have been sweating a little bit, though."

George had been upset, she said. He'd heard the scream, she said, and it had upset him.

Hanson asked Glenda if she knew why the detectives kept calling her husband over to the station. She said George had explained they were asking about a man he'd seen that night. When George told her this, she said, he had looked scared. He'd had tears in his eyes.

A few days later Hanson went back to the house, again making sure George would not be there, and pressed Glenda for more details. He was confused about the lights, he said. He wanted to know which ones were on and which were off when she'd sat in the kitchen. Glenda told him the garage light had been off but the utility light just outside the kitchen had been on. Again he asked if she'd seen anyone in the yard that night.

"No," she said. "Only George, walking toward the garage. I could tell it was him by the frizzy hair."

"Do you remember what he was wearing?"

"Usually he has on an old shirt and some shorts. But I can't remember if he had a shirt on that night. He was probably barefoot as usual."

"And how long did you say you waited for him to come back?"

"About ten minutes."

On this point Hanson pushed hard, reminding her that she'd originally told Debbie and Larry Tosi that George had been gone for approximately thirty minutes.

Glenda said she'd been mistaken that day at the Tosi house. "I was upset," she said. "I couldn't tell the difference between ten minutes and thirty minutes."

"What about the silhouette? Both Debbie and Larry remember hearing you talk about the silhouette at the window."

"They're wrong," she said. "The only person I saw was George."

By now Hanson was finding Glenda's account impossible to believe. Just like George, she couldn't keep her story straight. At first, when there was no reason to lie, she had vividly described the silhouette. Then, after George was forced to admit during the polygraph sessions that he had been lying, she had insisted there was no silhouette; in fact, she had told Hanson in their first interview that she saw no one in the backyard. Now, suddenly, she was saying that she saw George in the yard that night, heading for the garage.

Hanson had had enough. He wanted someone else to talk to Glenda, someone she didn't know and who might be able to nail her down. Arranging this was no problem. Shortly after their second interview, the Pinellas State Attorney's Office issued Glenda a subpoena, summoning her to the criminal justice complex for questioning.

The session took place on June 11. Glenda did not have a car that day, so Hanson himself drove her up to the midcounty complex and escorted her to the offices of the state attorney. He waited out in the lobby while she spoke to an assistant who'd been handling the case. The details of this interview are not known—a transcript has never been released—but when Glenda came out, she was crying. The prosecutor had told her that they were getting tired of her changing stories and George's changing stories and that all of the inconsistencies had left them with no choice but to consider George a suspect. Glenda said she couldn't believe it. No one had told her before that George was a suspect.

Now, just after she was handed this disturbing piece of news, she got into the car with the lieutenant and headed back to Gulfport. It was a thirty-minute drive on the interstate, with not much to look at along the way except a few palmettos and a flurry of out-of-state plates. Stuck behind the wheel, Hanson could only listen as Glenda ripped into him left and right with a stream of swear words and accusations.

"You son-of-a-bitch. You lied to me. You didn't tell me George was a suspect."

Hanson tried to defend himself, explaining that George was also their key witness. But Glenda just kept going.

"How could you do this to me? . . . Why would you make me go out there and testify against my husband? . . . You never told me he was a suspect . . . How could you suspect him of doing such a thing?''

The truth was, Hanson and Tosi couldn't believe it had taken them so long to suspect George. They looked back over the past year and kicked themselves for not seeing the signs any sooner. They should have been asking the hard questions from the start. George was a firefighter and an emergency medical technician. When that scream echoed down those streets, he would have known better than anybody how crucial it was to call the police. Didn't he always call before? If anything went wrong in that neighborhood, if someone so much as sneezed funny, didn't they know they could count on George to pick up the phone?

They had been too close to him. They had known him too well. At least, they'd thought they knew him.

A terrible thought had entered Tosi's mind. He remembered that several years before, when Debbie and Glenda were still working the check-out lines at the Publix, the store had put on some kind of promotional gimmick where all of the employees were supposed to dress up in tropical garb. Hawaiian Day, they called it, or something like that. Glenda and Debbie had both worn wild shirts that day, and when Tosi thought back, it seemed like the one Glenda had worn looked awfully familiar. Larry couldn't swear to it, but he thought the shirt bore a distinct resemblance to the flowered one that was later found, stained with blood, on Karen Gregory's bed.

By then the shirt would have been old. So old that Glenda might have tired of it and given it to George to be used as one of his rags out in the garage.

Thirteen

"Check it out."

Dutifully, Denise Lewis would turn and look at whatever woman had caught her husband's eye this time. Tiresome as it was, she'd grown accustomed to George's girl-watching. He'd been doing it openly since they were newlyweds. The two of them would be out together, and he'd see a face or figure that struck his fancy, and he'd get so excited that he'd have to tell her.

"Would you look at that."

Years later, long after she and George had divorced and she'd moved back up north, Denise still remembered it well. She'd never really figured George out. For all his interest in other women, he'd been strangely jealous. He had hated it when other men talked to her; he'd treated her like a piece of property that was off limits to even the eyes of anyone else. And yet he hadn't seemed to want anything to do with her. He had always been retreating from her, always avoiding her. Sometimes she'd wondered how much she really knew about this man she'd married.

But in that summer of 1985, when Lt. Hanson called looking for clues from George's past, Denise told him what she could.

She was a long shot. Hanson and Tosi knew that Glenda

certainly wasn't going to divulge whether there was another side to her husband's personality. But they thought maybe his ex-wife would. So Hanson tracked her down—she was living in Creighton, Pennsylvania, in the hills outside Pittsburgh—and asked her what she remembered.

Denise, it turned out, remembered a great deal. She said that George had lied to her repeatedly during their marriage. She said that one of the main reasons they'd broken up was because he was out in the garage at all hours of the day and night. But the worst, she said, had come the day he tried to strangle her.

They had met on a blind date in April 1980. Denise Kissel, nineteen, a soft-spoken woman with short blonde hair and an easy smile, was a proofreader up in Pennsylvania. That spring she went to Florida with a girlfriend for a two-week vacation, eager to bask in the rays on Pinellas County's beaches. On her first night in town she was introduced to George on a double date with her girlfriend and another man; a friend of her girlfriend's had arranged the date before they left for Florida. That evening they went to dinner and saw *Urban Cowboy*.

It wasn't exactly love at first sight. George, only eighteen at the time and still a little gawky, was shy and didn't say much. But he and Denise hit it off well enough to keep seeing each other. By the time her vacation was over and she was headed back north, they were ready to start a long-distance relationship. George called and sent her mushy cards signed "Porgie," which was short for Georgie-Porgie. The following fall, he drove to Pennsylvania to visit her. He grew a beard, clowned around in the snow, and eventually proposed. "I have something for you," he told her one day, handing her a ring.

They were married at Most Holy Name of Jesus Catholic Church in Gulfport on February 21, 1981. In the beginning the two of them lived in an apartment, but a couple of months after the wedding they moved into the house on Upton Street. At the time George was working as a welder—he was already a volunteer firefighter with Gulfport but hadn't yet joined the St. Petersburg Fire Department—and Denise took care of the house.

George was generally amiable and easy-going. Denise remembers him as caring and soft-spoken, a nice guy who loved children, took in stray cats, and once tried to rescue a baby squirrel that had fallen from a tree. But she thought he didn't pay enough attention to her. He was always out in the garage, working on his ocean blue pickup truck, which he called "Betsy," or building model cars and boats. George's mother tried to tell her not to worry about him out there. The garage, Mrs. Lewis explained, was George's way of unwinding.

Still, Denise didn't like it. Nor did she care much for George's miniature cars and boats, which she viewed as toys that he had never learned to put away. As much as she loved him, she thought George sometimes acted like a spoiled little boy who had never gotten past being the baby of the family. One of her girlfriends, who thought the same, gave Denise a hard time, kidding her about the fact that she was married to a grown man whose mother still called him "Georgie." If George knew he was a source of ridicule, he didn't show it. He was too busy welding, tinkering, water-skiing, and racing off after fires in Betsy. He was never happier than when he was speeding along in that truck, on his way to an emergency call, with a blue flashing light stuck on the roof. He loved being the first one to arrive, loved coming to the aid of injured people, and loved bragging about it later.

One thing he didn't love, Denise recalls, was when blacks came into his neighborhood. One time, she says, he saw some black men mowing yards down the street and vowed that they had better not set foot on his lawn. Furthermore, he told her, he wasn't the only one who felt that way.

"Blacks," she remembers him saying to her one time, "have to be out of Gulfport by nine o'clock."

The truth was, George was suspicious of almost any stranger who wandered into the neighborhood—or into the vicinity of Denise. He didn't want anyone touching his belongings or his wife. He told her he didn't want delivery men inside the house; he didn't even like her to stand outside on the edge of the yard and buy ice cream from the man who circled the block in his little truck. And when Denise got a job waiting on tables at a Frisch's Big Boy and men began flirting with her, he promptly forced her to quit. Possessive as he was, though, he showed almost no interest in her. On the rare occasion when he came inside the house, he'd pick up a boating magazine and flip through the pages rather than talk to her. He didn't seem to know what to say; in fact, he seemed uncomfortable talking to women in general.

He never minded looking at them, though. He collected *Play-boys* by the dozens and was so attached to them that, in the beginning, when he and Denise were just dating and he drove to Pennsylvania to see her, he actually carted along boxes filled with the magazine. After they were married he kept stacks of them back in the bedroom; he and one of his buddies liked swapping issues. Out in public, his ogling seemed to know no limits. One day he and Denise went boating with one of George's friends. With them that day was another woman, a slender young brunette named Glenda Harness. George could hardly take his eyes off her. "Boy," he said, "would you look at her in that bikini."

At home George wanted a more exotic sex life, and he was constantly pushing Denise to slip into some alluring piece of lingerie. One day he had a surprise for her. He had seen an ad in a magazine for a mail-order company and had purchased a vibrator and a collection of other sexual novelties. Now they had arrived and he wanted to show them to her. Denise was furious. She said she wanted nothing to do with the stuff. She said it made her feel cheap. That day, and on a score of others, she began to realize how little she knew about her husband. Once she caught him slipping a phone number from another woman into his wallet. Repeatedly she caught him lying to her. Even when she could prove it—even when he was cornered—George would never admit to the lie. There were other hints of trouble as well. She would send him to the grocery, and he'd be gone for an hour and a half, even though there was a Winn Dixie just a few blocks away.

Within six months after the wedding their marriage was crumbling. They seemed to be arguing all the time. According to Denise, George slapped her a couple of times. But usually when the tension got to be too much for him, he would just retreat to the safety and seclusion of the garage.

"Quit nagging me," he would say. "I don't want to hear it."

One day in August they were going at it again in the kitchen. As she had so many times before, Denise was complaining about George's late hours in the garage.

"You never have any time for me," she told him.

He didn't want to hear it. "Shut up," he said.

"Why should I? I'm part of your life too."

"Shut up."

"You shut up."

They kept at it. Denise kept pressing, George kept telling her to shut up. Finally, she says, he backed her into a corner and wrapped his hands around her throat. She was startled. She'd never seen him this way. He looked physically different. His face was growing red. His eyes were bulging. He held his hands there at her throat, talking about how he didn't want to hear her nag anymore. He was squeezing so tightly she could barely breathe.

"Go ahead and kill me," she said, struggling to speak beneath the force of his hands. "You'll be behind bars for the rest of your life."

He let go and she moved away. It was the first time she'd ever been afraid of him. But she didn't want to call the Gulfport police. They were his friends, weren't they?

A few days later, still upset over what had happened, Denise flew north to see her family. When she returned in September she could tell something was bothering George. He kept sitting on the sofa, getting up, then sitting down again.

"What's wrong?" she asked him.

"Nothing."

"I know something happened while I was gone."

George looked at her. "Why? Who told you?"

Denise didn't know what he was talking about. She said he'd better tell her what was going on.

So he did. "Did you ever hear that song," he said, " 'Torn Between Two Lovers'? Well . . ."

It was Glenda Harness. He was having an affair with her. He said he wasn't sure which one of them he loved.

Denise couldn't believe it. "If it's a matter of your own wife or another woman, you can have her," she said. "I'm packing."

The next day he drove her to the airport. What she remembers about their parting was something that happened along the way. They were stopped at a red light when George looked over at a pretty woman in a phone booth.

"Boy," he said. "Look at that."

Denise started crying.

"I can't believe you," she told him. "You cheat on me, and you're still talking about other women."

That was the last time she ever saw him. She returned to Pennsylvania and waited for the divorce to become final, while Glenda moved in with George into the house on Upton, where he wouldn't have to gaze at her from a distance anymore.

Four years later, when the detectives called, Denise Lewis told them about the lies and the arguments and George's habits.

There were two things, however, that she forgot to mention.

The first was the time George had told her about seeing a couple making love. It was a boy he knew, a longtime friend who lived nearby, and his girlfriend. George, Denise recalls, told her that he had stood in the friend's yard and watched through a window.

"I saw it with my own eyes," he told her. He was laughing and giggling. He couldn't get over it.

The second thing Denise had forgotten was the night she and George went over what she should do if someone ever broke into the house. At the time they were lying in bed. Denise had heard a noise, and that had started her off talking about how afraid she was sometimes. It seemed she was always hearing sirens in the distance. What should she do, she asked, if someone came in and attacked her some night when George was off on a fire call? George, as she remembers, told her not to worry. Gulfport, he said, was safe. But if it ever happened—if push came to shove, he said—she would need a weapon. Maybe they should buy a gun, he said. Denise told him she could never use a gun. She wouldn't know how to shoot it, she said. So George suggested a knife. He said he had one she could use. He said he kept an old one out in the garage.

The conversation went on. Denise kept talking about her fear of someone breaking into the house and killing her. She said she didn't know how anyone could get away with such a thing. But George, she remembers, had it all figured out. If the killer was stained with blood, he said, all he would have to do would be to slip away from the scene and then wash off outside. He could find a hose or a faucet, then use it to clean his clothes and his weapon. Once the blood was gone, he said, there'd be no proof.

"It's easy," he said.

Tosi was looking differently at his friend these days. They didn't see much of each other anymore; after the polygraphs, George seemed to be avoiding him. But the few times when they were together, Tosi would find himself staring at George's face, searching for hints of some stranger beneath the surface. He would study George's hands, trying to figure out if they were the same size as the bloody handprints that had been left on Karen's body.

At home, Larry began taking precautions. He told his wife she should avoid being alone with George. Sometimes George had brought Tiffany over to the house so Debbie could babysit her; Larry didn't think that was a good idea anymore. He also didn't want Debbie taking their daughter to the Lewis house for babysitting. George, he told her, was the prime suspect.

Debbie didn't believe it. She said George couldn't be the murderer.

"I'm telling you," said Larry. "I wouldn't let him in the house if I were you."

Fourteen

That fall, Karen Gregory's friends were trying to move on with their lives.

More than a year after the murder, Anita Kilpatrick was still working to overcome her fear. She still did not like to go anywhere alone after dark; every night, before she went to sleep, she made sure the chain on her door was latched.

Neverne Covington also was searching for ways to deal with fear. She was beginning to drive in the evenings by herself. She was trying to learn to trust the people around her again. She knew, though, that she would never feel as safe as she had before. It was as if she had lost a kind of innocence.

David Mackey had quit his job with the VA that summer and gone to the University of Miami to work on a doctoral degree in psychology. But David was unhappy in Miami. He could not stop thinking about Karen and how there still had been no arrest. It was too hard being so far away when the case was unresolved. After one semester at the university, he left, moved to Tampa, and took a counseling job at another vet center. There at work he would look at the veterans around him and find himself moved by the strength and resiliency they had discovered inside themselves to survive their pain. Still, David found it was not enough to deal with the murder day by day. He had to deal with it, he said, moment by moment.

One day in October 1985, Neverne was standing in line at a bank in the west end of Gulfport when she was struck by the feeling that someone was looking at her. She turned around and there, standing in line not six feet away, was Lewis. Neverne knew who he was and knew he was a suspect. She recognized him from the times she'd been through the neighborhood. She'd seen him across the street from David and Karen's house, getting into his pickup truck and roaring away. The truck had scared her.

Now he was standing there, staring at her. He was staring so hard that to her he seemed to be boring a hole through her. She turned back around. When she finished at the teller's window, she left the bank, climbed into her car, and drove toward Eckerd College, a small school in south St. Petersburg where she worked as an artist in residence. She was on her way when she looked in her rearview mirror and noticed Lewis driving behind her. She tried to tell herself that he wasn't following her. She had worked so hard for so many months to get past her fear; she did not want to be afraid all over again. Watching him in the mirror, she tried to think of logical explanations. Maybe he had already been heading in this direction. Maybe he had just happened to pick the same stretch of road.

The farther they went, though, the less likely this seemed. Neverne drove eastward through the town, past the library, past the shuffleboard club, past the casino, past block after block of houses. She turned onto another street and passed the exit for Lewis's house, and still he stayed with her. She drove out of the city—she was officially in St. Petersburg by now—and then turned onto another street, watching him make the same turn behind her. Now she was getting scared. Before they'd been driving on busy roads. But this street was not a route people typically took unless they lived in this area or were looking for a shortcut or worked at Florida Power, whose headquarters were a few blocks to the south. Neverne drove on anyway, past some sprawling apartment complexes, past a few scattered houses, into a quiet stretch of road lined with slash pines, and still he stayed behind her.

Finally, after they'd driven more than four miles together, Lewis turned around and headed back in the opposite direction.

Neverne couldn't prove that Lewis had been following her, but she thought Tosi should know what had happened. She stopped by the station several times, but he was always out. Finally, near the end of the month, she left Tosi a note. She took a small print of the painting she'd done of David—the one that showed him sitting in front of the window, framed in sunlight, while shadows of pain played across his face—and wrote a message on the back, telling about the incident on the road. But that wasn't the main reason she'd written Tosi. More than anything else, she wanted to remind him that on Halloween, two years before, she and Karen had been together, laughing. She said she knew a long time had gone by since the murder. But she was still waiting, she said, for the resolution of the case.

No one needed to remind Tosi that the case was still unsolved. The information from Denise Lewis had opened a whole new chain of possibilities in his mind. For one thing, he was thinking about Denise's neck. When George was angry with her, she'd said, that's where he'd directed his anger. Tosi wondered if that explained why that portion of Karen's body had been attacked. Had she said something that enraged George so much that he wanted to silence her, just as he'd tried to silence Denise?

As thought-provoking as such questions might have been, they did not bring Tosi any closer to an arrest. That fall, after immersing himself in the case for so long, after taking it home night after night, and after living and breathing and sleeping with it, he was still coming up empty-handed. All of his suspicions and theories and scenarios didn't matter. He still didn't have the evidence to place George inside the house that night. He had hoped that the FDLE might help on that score. But when the lab reports came back, they said George did not match up with the fingerprints or hair found at the scene. Again they'd struck out.

Hanson thought it was time to move on. For the past year and a half, his senior detective had worked on almost nothing else. But now every lead, and every hint of a lead, had been exhausted. As much as Hanson believed George was the murderer, he doubted they would ever be able to prove it. To him it seemed like they were just ramming their heads against a brick wall. There were other cases that needed attention. Tosi, he said, should put the investigation aside until something new came up.

Tosi said no. "You remember what happened in 1973?" he said. "Do you remember?"

Hanson knew he was referring to the Frank Sweet case. Over the years they had talked many times about the fire and the body on the floor and the woman driving the dead man's Cadillac. It was all moot now; the woman had since died. But Hanson knew how Tosi felt. Larry had never let go of that case and probably never would. So when the old specter was raised again, the lieutenant backed away.

Back at his desk, Tosi sat and muttered. "I'll never shelve this case," he said.

Tosi began to withdraw inside himself. Kneeling at church on Sundays, he prayed for Karen's soul and asked for God's help. At work the other detectives would watch him slowly imploding. They'd look up from their desks and see him sitting there, staring at his hands. They'd hear him talking aloud to Karen, asking her how it had happened. And every day, without fail, they'd watch as he picked up the magnifying glass and studied, one more time, the black book filled with the photos. At night he'd take the book home and study it there. He'd wait until his daughter was asleep, then slide the videotape of the crime scene into his VCR and sit in the living room, watching again and again the flickering image of Karen's body curled on the floor.

Finally they returned to the bloody partial footprint on the bathroom floor.

From the start of the case, David had believed that an ID might be made from the photo of the footprint, even though the FDLE had already said to forget it. That December, when he moved back from Miami, he still believed it. It was too important, he thought, to just take the FDLE's word for it. Tosi felt the same way. So he called the Tampa crime lab, he says, and asked again if it was possible to give the photo a try. He was given the same answer. A supervisor looked at the negatives and told him it wouldn't work.

Tosi was getting tired of hearing that. He wasn't convinced; he wanted, he said, to see that photo. With that, he drove across the bay and retrieved the negatives himself. The supervisor, he says, saw him there that day and told him he was wasting his time.

"It's just a smidgen of blood," he remembers the man telling him. "There's nothing there."

The supervisor would later remember this differently, saying that Tosi did call and ask for the negatives but did not ask him about enlarging the photo. The supervisor, however, acknowledges that at some point in the investigation the FDLE should have tried enlarging the photo.

In any case, Tosi got the negatives and drove them back to the station in Gulfport and gave them to the department's one and only technician, an old hand by the name of Charlie Brown. Using the ruler that had been placed in the photo for scale, Brown enlarged it to a life-size print. He made several copies, lightening, darkening, trying to get maximum contrast.

Tosi looked at the photo. There, curving and swirling unmistakably before him, was the sight he had waited so long to behold.

Ridges. He could see ridges in the footprint.

But were they distinct enough for an ID? Tosi wasn't sure. He took the negatives to the technicians at the Pinellas County Sheriff's Department, who had more sophisticated equipment. They made another photo of the footprint, this time with sharper definition, then gave it—along with one of the inked footprints Lewis had given months before—to one of the sheriff's print examiners, who compared the two to see if they matched.

The answer was no.

"Negative on that print," said the examiner.

Tosi still wasn't convinced. The Gulfport detectives had been sending prints to the sheriff's department for some time, asking for comparisons, and several examiners had done it for them. This particular one had been doing it for roughly a year. It seemed to Tosi and the others that the number of matches had dropped off once this person had taken over. Again and again, they had struck out with him, even in cases in which they were sure they had the right man and there had to be a match. Now here was the same guy, telling them the footprint on the floor was not from Lewis.

Tosi decided to get a second opinion. On February 10, 1986, he sent the negatives and Lewis's footprint to the FBI laboratory in Washington, D.C.

*   *   *

While they waited for the results, Gulfport got a new police chief. After a quarter century with the department, Hap Golliner had retired. His replacement was Jim Sewell, a soft-spoken thirty-five-year-old former FDLE official with a doctorate in criminology. The new chief was no stranger to homicide; a decade before, when serial killer Ted Bundy murdered two sorority women at Florida State University, Sewell—a campus police officer at the time—had been one of the first investigators at the scene.

On March 4, his first day on the job, Sewell learned that he had inherited another murder investigation. Tosi and Hanson came into the office and briefed him on the case. Though they still had not totally ruled out Mackey, they said, Lewis was their prime suspect. Any day now they expected to hear back from Washington.

One week later, on the morning of Tuesday, March 11, Hanson was sitting at his desk when the phone rang. It was someone named John Saunders. He was from the FBI.

"I've made a positive comparison," he said.

Saunders, one of the bureau's veteran print specialists, spoke with a quiet assurance. Making the match had not been easy, he said. He'd had to work at it. But eventually he had found more than thirty-one points of comparison. He said he could keep looking for more if they wanted him to, but he didn't think that was necessary. There wasn't any doubt about it. George Alan Lewis, he said, had left the bloody footprint in the bathroom.

Hanson thanked him and hung up. He called Tosi at home—his shift hadn't started yet—and told him to get down to the station right away. When he showed up, Hanson sat him down and broke the news to him.

Once he'd heard the words, Larry didn't say anything for a few seconds. He just sat there, shaking his head.

Fifteen

There were only two other detectives in the Gulfport Police Department. Both of them were bewildered.

"What the fuck is going on?" said Scott Barnes.

Sitting a few feet away at his desk, cloistered with his paperwork inside the Room of Doom, Brinkworth shook his head. It was obvious that something momentous was about to happen. Tosi and Hanson were scurrying around with an air of intense purpose, holding hushed conferences behind closed doors, slipping out for secret meetings with unnamed others. Whatever they were doing, they had decided it was best not to share with their subordinates. Barnes and Brinkworth could only guess.

The truth was that the lieutenant and sergeant were trying to figure out the best way to arrest George Lewis. If they wanted, they knew they could get a judge to sign a warrant and have him behind bars before noon that very morning. But they didn't think that was the smart approach. They didn't want him in custody, with a lawyer at his side and his mouth sealed shut, before they had a chance to confront him with the footprint. Cornered, faced with the most damning evidence yet, he might give them more details. Maybe he would even fold and admit everything. Tosi,

Hanson knew, wanted it that way. As convinced as he was that George was guilty, Larry wanted to hear him say it. It would make it easier to do what they had to do.

So they waited until they could interview him again. They didn't want to call for him at home, because they knew from past experience that he would probably give them some excuse and put them off, possibly for weeks. Nor did they want Glenda, who was no doubt still suspicious and hostile, trying to talk him out of cooperating. So they checked with the St. Pete fire department and found out that the next time he'd be on duty was the upcoming Saturday. He was scheduled to start at 8:00 that morning at Fire Station No. 9, over on the west side of town, only a few miles north of Gulfport.

Tosi and Hanson drove over in one of the unmarked detective cars first thing that morning, arriving at the start of George's shift. They didn't want to attract a lot of attention, so they asked one of the officers to get him and then waited for him in a conference room. A few minutes later he came in, already wearing his uniform. He saw them and smiled.

"Hi, Frank," he said. "Hi, Larry."

"Hi, George."

They told him something had come up in the case and asked if he'd come talk with them at the police station. George said he wasn't sure if he could. He said he was busy. Could they wait until later, when he wasn't on duty? Gently, trying not to spook him, they told him it was important. They said they had already checked with his bosses and been told it was okay for him to go with them. He asked if he could drive over in his pickup truck. No problem, they said.

On the way back to Gulfport, Tosi drove carefully, slowing down at stoplights so they wouldn't get separated. Every few seconds he kept looking in the rearview mirror, making sure the blue truck was still behind them.

"I don't think he's really going to skate out on us, Larry," Hanson said.

Tosi kept his eye on the mirror anyway.

The police station was almost deserted when they got there. It was still early on a Saturday morning; hardly anybody was on duty. They led Lewis down a dingy little hall adorned with most wanted posters, took him into the detectives' office, and gave him a seat toward the back of the room, next to a desk with a tape recorder. Hanson, who was to lead the questioning, sat a few feet away behind the desk; Tosi sat behind them, at his own desk, between George and the door.

"Okay, George," said Hanson. "We're gonna ask you a few questions now. Are you under the influence of any drugs or alcoholic beverages?"

"No."

"Do you know how to read?"

"Yes."

"Do you know how to write?"

"Yes."

The lieutenant read him his rights and asked him to sign a piece of paper waiving the presence of an attorney. Then, one more time, he asked George to tell them what had happened the night of the murder. George went through it all—how he'd been in the garage all evening, how he'd seen Karen in the kitchen and heard the clatter of the dishes. He'd seen her coming and going in the car that evening, he said. Later, after midnight, he'd heard the scream and the sound of glass breaking. He'd thought it was kids throwing bottles, he said, until he looked around and saw the man on David and Karen's lawn, standing near the big live oak.

"I asked him if everything was all right and stuff, 'cause I'd never seen him there before. I thought David and her were home, 'cause both cars were there, and I thought maybe they were having a party or somebody got restless or something and I asked him, you know, if it's okay, and he said no, you know, sure, just get lost. He said never bother about saying anything about seeing me here, otherwise I might come back."

"Did he scare you? Were you frightened of this guy?"

"Yes, I was. He threatened me verbally."

"How frightened were you?"

"Well, number one I was scared to begin with, 'cause I don't like, you know, being out by myself in an area where I know something could happen after I hear some screaming or something."

"Okay. So what did you do then, George?"

"I started walking away and stuff. I looked back over my shoulder and stood there for a minute. And when I got back in the yard, it was like he walked past the tree, down past the cars. I don't know if he stayed there or watched me go inside or what."

"What did you do when you walked back over? Did you run into the house right away?"

"No. I walked over, closed the garage door, and that's about it."

Hanson didn't like this answer. "Well," he said, "you weren't too afraid then if you closed the garage door. That's the only thing that's kinda distracting me. You stayed out there and closed the door?"

"Well, I wasn't going to leave my garage door open with some stranger in the area."

"Can you describe this guy again to me?"

"He's about five foot eight, maybe six foot something, husky guy."

The man was shrinking. Before George had described his being as tall as six four.

"Did you see anybody else?"

"Not really, I don't think. I think he was there by himself, unless he was outside waitin' for somebody."

"Okay. When you went out to look over there, were there any lights on in the house?"

"No."

"Could you see in there in any way?"

"No."

Hanson asked again what the man on the lawn had said to him.

"He just told me to get lost and never to mention to anybody that I saw him there, otherwise he'd come back."

"Did he brandish any weapon or take a weapon out?"

"No. He just sternly looked at me, and like that."

"Did he point his finger or what?"

"Yeah. Like he meant what he said."

Hanson was tired of it. He said they'd heard so many stories. He asked George if he had gone onto David and Karen's lawn that night.

"No."

"Were you ever on the sidewalk in front of the house?"

"No."

"Were you ever in the house?"

Only once, George said. When the lawn man suffered the seizures and the paramedics were called. Other than that, no.

"You've never been in that house?"

"No."

"You're sure you never been in there?"

George shook his head.

"Were you in there that night?"

"No."

Tosi sat nearby, listening to the same lie again and again. Finally, when he'd heard it enough, he spoke.

"We got a problem, George," he said. "We got a call from Washington, and they indicated that they made positive identification on your footprint from inside the house."

"There is no way," George said.

"I'll let you read it." Tosi reached into the pocket of his jacket, pulled out a letter from the FBI, and handed it to him. George looked at it for a second and gave it back.

"I don't understand this. What does it mean?"

Tosi explained that it confirmed that the FBI had received George's footprint and the negatives of the footprint from inside the house.

"I wasn't even barefoot that night," George said.

"Well, they called us and told us they have positive identification . . . So this is the FBI laboratory in Washington, and they positively made identification of your footprint in the house."

"Larry, you talked to Glenda, and there's no way."

Hanson moved in. "I've talked to Glenda, George. I've talked to you. You've given me so many stories. You told me you were never in the house."

"Right."

"You were never in that house?"

George's voice was rising. "No."

"They're sending me a teletype saying that's your footprint—the FBI. They've got more than thirty-one points of comparison on it. Now there's no doubt in their technician's mind that that's your footprint that was found inside the house, and you tell me you've never been in that house?"

"No, I haven't. You tell me how I could get into that house so quick and do all that and come back and my wife be there."

"Your wife was sleeping all night, George. She went to bed. She don't know what happened. She was in bed . . . Now how did your footprint get in the house?"

"I don't know. I did not put it there."

"Well, somebody else didn't take your foot off and put it in there, did they?"

"No."

"So then the only other conclusion I've got is that you were in the house that night. So you're saying that that technician is wrong?"

"I'm saying somethin' is wrong, Frank, because I am not that sadistic or anything to do that."

"But that might not have been the way it happened, George," Tosi said.

"Larry, I didn't do it."

Tosi looked back at him. "Well, something happened I guess, George."

There was a finality to these words, an edge of weary resignation that made it clear that Tosi was no longer swayed by a thing his friend was telling him. It was the sound of a door slamming shut.

George must have heard it, because at that moment he announced he wanted a lawyer.

"You want to end the conversation then?"

"Yes."

"Okay," Tosi said. "Now what we were doing in essence was affording you an opportunity to explain the presence of that footprint. But I'm not going to question you anymore, so we'll just have to end it."

George looked at him. *"Larry."*

"We're ending the questioning, George."

"Wait a minute . . . I still don't believe this. . . ."

"Well, I guess we've reached that point, George. I'm just going to have to place you under arrest for the murder of Karen Gregory."

"I didn't do it to her, Larry."

"I've got no choice, George. All indications are that you did."

George sat there with his head bowed. Suddenly he started talking. "I saw the guy," he said. "I went in the house."

He began to cry.

"I heard Karen scream. Okay? Oh God. I never seen anything like that before. I didn't see the guy do it, okay? I saw the guy outside. I went in after that, real quick. I still don't believe it. I didn't kill her, Larry. I saw her laying there with her throat cut open. The guy had seen me. When he left, I ran back in the house, okay? I didn't kill her. I saw her laying there in blood. I panicked. I didn't know what to do. The guy had seen me. To this day I still get bad dreams about that."

George paused for a moment, then continued in a quavering voice.

"When he left—after I walked back over to the garage, he left—I ran back over there 'cause I wanted to see. I wasn't sure if David or somebody was there, too. There wasn't any lights on in the house, and when I went in, I went in through the back window 'cause I ran around the back bedroom. I looked, and I saw her laying on the floor. That's it. I didn't do anything else. I was scared. I saw what that guy did to her. He saw *me*. He knows what I look like right now. I would never do anything like that to a human being, ever."

Tosi still wasn't swayed. "Well, by law we can't talk to you anymore about it," he said. "So we can't further discuss it, and I can't ask you any other questions."

George was begging now. "Come on." He looked over at Hanson. "Frank, I didn't kill her. I should've just told you the whole thing to begin with and worried about the guy coming back earlier . . . I can't even prove my innocence now. I was so afraid to tell you guys that I was in there. 'Cause I wasn't sure if that guy was gonna come back."

Tosi listened quietly. "This hurts me worse than it does you," he said. "Believe me."

Tosi photographed him and fingerprinted him and put him into a holding cell. Someone called Glenda and George's brother James, and they came down to the station to see him before he was taken to the county jail. Glenda cried and said he was innocent.

"How could you do this?" she said. "How could you do this to George?"

James stood inside the cell and yelled about how the detectives had framed George because they needed a scapegoat.

"Don't worry. We'll get an attorney," he told George. "We know you didn't do it."

George didn't say much. He just sat on a bench inside the cell and stared at the floor.

Meanwhile, Tosi was typing out an arrest affidavit, swearing

Thomas French

and certifying that he had just and reasonable grounds to believe that at approximately 1:15 A.M. on May 23, 1984, the defendant did:

> unlawfully, while engaged in the perpetration of, or in an attempt to perpetrate the crime of sexual battery, did strike in the head with an unknown blunt instrument and did repeatedly stab a human being, with a weapon; knife, thereby inflicting upon her mortal wounds, of such said mortal wounds, and by the means aforesaid and as a direct result thereof, the said Karen Gregory died.

The charge was listed at the top of the page:

MURDER; IN THE FIRST DEGREE

They put George into a squad car and took him to the Pinellas County Jail. A uniformed officer drove, with Tosi next to him in the front seat. Lewis sat handcuffed in the back. It was raining that morning, and as they drove, Tosi couldn't get it out of his head that it had also been raining the night of the murder. He looked back at Lewis. His head was leaning against the window. He appeared to be falling asleep. Tosi asked if he was okay.

"Yeah."

They arrived at the jail, a gray hulking complex that sat beside the criminal courthouse, surrounded by fences and guard towers. Tosi handed the paperwork on the arrest to a booking officer, then walked over to Lewis and patted him on the shoulder.

"Take care of yourself."

"Thanks, Larry."

"Are you all right?"

"Yeah. If you could just do me a favor and see to it that my wife's taken care of."

"Sure."

It was the last time they would speak.

Book
Two

His lawyer called out his name. He stood up, put his hand on a Bible, and swore to tell the truth and nothing but. He sat down in the witness box and looked toward the jurors so they could see his face and study it and decide for themselves what kind of man he was.

"Did you rape Karen Gregory?" asked his lawyer.

"No, sir, I did not."

"Did you murder Karen Gregory?"

"No, sir."

That night, he said, he waited for the man to leave. He watched him disappear into the darkness, and then he walked back across the street and went up to the house and knocked, and when no one answered, he found an open window and peered inside and saw someone on the floor. He climbed through the window, and there she was. Blood was everywhere. On her, the floor, the walls.

He was afraid, knowing no one would believe how he had come to be with her inside that house. He ran to the bathroom and threw up and then decided he had to get out. He was running toward the window when he saw something moving in the dark. He thought someone was lunging toward him. Then he realized he was running past a mirror, and the only person moving was him. It was his own reflection that had startled him. It was George.

Part Three

Tonja

Sixteen

In the beginning, the members of Karen's family had thought that after the arrest everything else would be simple. They'd had this idea that once a man was found and charged, the law would see to the rest. The case would be heard, and there would be something they thought of as justice. It might take a few months. Six at most. But the worst, they thought, would be over.

They did not know the criminal courts. They did not know they were entering a place where another language is spoken and where conventional notions of logic do not always apply. They did not expect that there would be a parade of judges and hundreds of motions and one bewildering delay after another and that there would be moments when they would want to stand up in the courtroom and cry out in pain. They thought the truth was what mattered. They did not understand that in court, the truth is cut up into little pieces and then rearranged and argued over, one piece at a time. The truth, they would learn, was subject to rules and procedures and maneuvers.

Once they'd seen what the courtroom was like, some of Karen's family decided they did not want to talk about her there. They did not want her memory brought up in a place that had become so hateful to them. Mark, Karen's brother, shuddered inside every time he heard a defense attorney speak of her.

Outside the courthouse, though, they talked about her constantly. They'd drive home, and they'd sit around the table and trade stories about her. Some of the stories were funny and had been told so many times they were almost legend; all of them were sad, because they brought Karen back for only a moment. Still, they went on talking about her each night. They kept her alive, as best they could, and they protected her from the courtroom, as best they could. It was a way of holding on.

Anita Kilpatrick wanted to see his face. If she saw him, she told herself, maybe she finally would understand. So on that day in March 1986 when Lewis was arrested, she asked when he would first appear in court. Tomorrow morning, she was told. At a hearing inside the jail.

The next day was Sunday, March 16. It was raining that morning when Anita showed up at the jail. David Mackey showed up as well. The two of them went to the front desk and said they were there for the hearing. A man at the counter asked for their names and the name of the prisoner they had come to see.

"George Lewis," said David.

The man wrote the names on a log. Then, in a space by David's name, he wrote that David was a friend of Lewis's. David did not see this, but Anita did, and she stopped the man before he made the same mistake with her. Later, when she knew more about the system, Anita would understand why the man had assumed they had come on behalf of the accused instead of the victim.

They walked through a metal detector and were directed to a small room next to the courtroom. The small room was for spectators. It had a window that looked out into the courtroom and a loudspeaker that piped in the sound. Six or seven other people were sitting in the room. One woman, it turned out, was a sister of Lewis's. She was by herself. She appeared to have been crying. David and Anita sat down and waited for the hearing to begin.

Lewis and other prisoners who had been arrested within the last twenty-four hours were brought into the courtroom. It wasn't much of a courtroom. There were benches and a few tables, surrounded by walls of concrete block. Sitting at the front of the room was Circuit Judge Harry W. Fogle, a white-haired man with glasses. When the prisoners were seated, Fogle explained that this was an advisory hearing. Its purpose was to make sure that newly arrested prisoners were aware of the charges against them, understood their rights, had access to legal counsel, and were not left to languish behind bars without appearing before a judge. Similar proceedings were held at the jail every day of the year, including Christmas, so that people would always see a judge within a day of their arrest.

Fogle called out the names of this day's prisoners and reviewed their cases, one by one. Anita and David barely heard what the judge said to the other prisoners. They were watching Lewis, who was sitting quietly in his dark-blue jail uniform. Two lawyers were there to represent him, and when it was his turn before the judge, they stood up and asked that bond be set for their client. They pointed out that Lewis had no criminal record and had strong ties to the community.

A prosecutor was supposed to have been at the hearing. He had even been told in advance that he should push for Lewis to be held without bond. But there had been an accident. The night before the hearing, an electrical storm had knocked out the power at the prosecutor's home. His alarm clock had not worked, and he had overslept.

Fogle, who did not yet know this, was not pleased. He said he was not sure what the law required him to do. He said he wished a prosecutor were there to argue the other side of this question. "If the state doesn't care enough to be here," he said, "then why should I?"

David and Anita wanted to stand up and pound on the window. Now that someone finally had been brought to answer for Karen's murder, no one was in the courtroom to speak for her. Anita and David, trapped on the other side of the glass, were powerless.

After listening to the arguments, Fogle set bond at $150,000. David was stunned. He didn't know if Lewis would be able to raise that kind of money, but he was sure it was an unusually low amount for a murder charge. He knew of drug cases in which the bond was five times higher. As soon as the advisory hearing was over, he went looking for a bailiff. He identified himself, said he had been a friend of Karen Gregory's, and asked to speak with the judge about the bond. The bailiff disappeared for a few minutes, then came back. The answer was no.

"The judge doesn't want to get into that for the time being," he said.

The next day, David called the state attorney's office to ask why no prosecutor had shown up at the hearing. An assistant explained and told him that the bond question was not settled. The state would have a chance at another hearing to ask that it be raised. These assurances did not make David feel much better. Already he was wondering whether Karen would be lost in the court battle ahead. He couldn't get over the fact that the case was known as the *State of Florida vs. George Lewis*. He thought it should be the *State of Florida on Behalf of Karen Gregory*. Wasn't it her murder that had brought them all into court?

Karen's family thought it was important to be part of the case as well. They did not know what to expect. So not long after the arrest, they arranged a meeting with Beverly Andrews and William Loughery, the two assistant state attorneys who were handling the case. Karen's family wanted to know what the chances were of winning a conviction.

Andrews and Loughery said the state had a strong case against Lewis but that he had hired two experienced lawyers—Joseph M. Ciarciaglino, Jr., and Robert L. Paver—who probably would try to stall and use smoke screens to obscure the facts against their client. Almost certainly they would try to put Karen on trial, perhaps by trying to make something out of the fact that she had been living with a man.

"It's going to be dirty," said Andrews. "There'll be a lot of ugly things."

Neverne Covington was at home one morning when a stranger knocked at her front door. He had gray hair and a moustache. He was smiling. Neverne studied him through the screen.

"Hello," she said.

"Hello," he said. "I'm an investigator with the Karen Gregory homicide."

"Who are you with?" she asked him, still keeping the screen closed between them.

"I'm here to find out the truth of what happened."

"Who sent you here?"

"I'm just trying to find out the truth."

The man showed her an ID card that confirmed he was a private investigator. Neverne opened the door and let him have a seat in her porch. She asked him again who had sent him.

"We're both on the same side," he said. "We're on the side of justice."

Neverne wasn't so sure. "Who signs your paycheck?" she said.

"Joe Ciarciaglino."

"That's what I thought."

"I just want to ask you a few questions," said the man.* "How did you know Karen?"

"I was her best friend."

"Where was she that night?"

"Right here. Where you're sitting."

As he continued, Neverne was growing angry. She had been warned that the defense might be digging around for information on Karen. And she did not like people appearing unannounced at her home. Especially this man, who worked for Lewis's attorneys. If he knew where she lived, Lewis knew where she lived.

Neverne told the man she wasn't sure if she was supposed to talk to him. She called the Gulfport police and left a message at the detectives' office, telling them this investigator was at her home and she did not know if she was obligated to speak with him. A few minutes later, Detective Barnes called back. He told her that the defense attorneys would have a chance to ask her questions later under oath, in the depositions. But this was different, Barnes said. This was a man sitting on her front porch, and she had the right to not talk to him if she didn't want to.

That was fine with Neverne. She asked Barnes if he would talk to the investigator over the phone and tell him to leave. Barnes did just that. When they got off the phone, Neverne was furious. She told the investigator she could not believe he had asked her

*The description of this meeting is based on Neverne Covington's recollections. When the investigator was approached for an interview to confirm Neverne's recounting, he disputed her account but said he could not comment on which points he disagreed with.

to help in the defense of the man charged with raping and murdering her friend.

"Don't you want to give George Lewis a chance?" he said. "What if it's not him? What if it's somebody else?"

"Yes, I'd like to give him a chance," Neverne said, motioning him toward the door. "The same kind of chance he gave Karen Gregory."

Seventeen

T he calls would not stop.

Tosi would be at home or down at the station, and the phone would ring. He'd pick it up, and there'd be a click at the other end of the line.

Then one day someone called and did not hang up.

"You've got the wrong man," said the caller, "and we're going to expose you."

"Well why don't you come on in and do all the exposing you want," Tosi said. "I've got the right man, and I've got the facts."

The harassment had started the day after the arrest, when the news first hit the papers. Early that morning, a friend of Lewis's had shown up at Tosi's house, banging on the front door. Debbie Tosi had answered. The friend was talking loudly. He wanted to know what the hell it was he was reading about Tosi charging George with murder. It was a mistake, he said. Larry had made a mistake.

In the weeks since then, the pressures had grown. Debbie Tosi and Glenda Lewis no longer spoke, not even at work at the bank. Glenda, whose lawyers had advised her not to talk with Debbie, had been transferred to another section. Meanwhile, coworkers were asking Debbie what was going on. How could Larry have arrested George?

Tosi himself was still trying to understand how it could have come to this. He kept taking out the tape of their final interview and playing it over and over, listening to George's voice.

"I didn't kill her, Larry . . . I looked, and I saw her laying on the floor. That's it. I didn't do anything else."

Tosi had wanted so badly to believe it, even when George was sending them off on all of those wild goose chases, running after Kumble and Mackey and the others. Tosi had tried for so long to make excuses for his friend. But now, as he listened to the tape, it seemed clear to him that George was still lying.

"I was scared. I saw what that guy did to her. He saw me. He knows what I look like right now."

If George was so afraid of this man on the lawn, Tosi asked himself, why would he have returned to the house without calling the police? He said he hadn't known whether or not someone else might be in there. If that was true, why would he have climbed through the back window in darkness and exposed himself to attack? Wouldn't it have been easier to use the front door?

"I saw her laying there in blood. I panicked. I didn't know what to do."

It made no sense. George was a firefighter and an emergency medical technician. He rode a rescue truck. He had been to accidents. And now he wanted them to believe that he had seen Karen's body and not known what to do?

Tosi sat at his desk, rewinding the tape, replaying the scene in his mind, trying to understand. He thought back to the times he and George had spent together, grilling on the barbecue or tinkering around in the garage. He tried to recall whether George had ever said anything strange, whether he had ever let anything slip. Was there something Tosi had missed? Some hint that had surfaced for a second before his eyes without his recognizing it?

The problem was, they were working in a vacuum. Other than the strangling incident described by Denise Lewis, Tosi had never heard of George's exhibiting the kind of deep emotional disturbance displayed by Karen's murderer. Yes, Tosi had noticed George's temper. But lots of people have a temper; few of them walk across the street, rape their neighbor, beat and stab her into unconsciousness, methodically attack her neck, and then return to the scene after dark the following evening.

Over the years Tosi had taken some classes on the background and psychological makeup of people who commit murders such as Karen's. Their early histories, he knew, tend to be littered with a telltale series of warnings. Usually there is a progression to their behavior, often beginning in childhood or adolescence with smaller acts of destruction, such as setting nuisance fires or torturing animals. Voyeurism is also common. Before they actually kill a human being, they may spend years spying on people through windows, fantasizing about them.

None of this sounded remotely like the person Tosi had hung around with. It was true that George had always been fascinated with fires. It was also true that some firefighters have been known to take such fascinations too far. Police files around the country contain dozens of cases in which firemen have been caught committing arson. Yet Tosi had never heard George accused of setting fires. Nor was there any proof that he had ever engaged in animal cruelty. As for voyeurism, George had never been charged with anything like that, either.

Still, as he went through it all in his mind, Tosi could not help but remember the history of prowling and peeping incidents around the neighborhood. He thought back especially to the incidents at the house of the black woman on Forty-eighth Street, the woman George had told another neighbor he was keeping an eye on for the police. Obviously George had kept an eye on a lot of people. He had seen David practicing his t'ai chi on the lawn; he had come running when Lawrence Sanders suffered his seizure; he had observed Peter Kumble in great detail. And on the night of the murder he had seen Karen coming and going and washing dishes at the kitchen sink. In fact, he'd told them he'd actually heard the clatter of the dishes. How far would that sound have carried? He'd told them he'd heard it all the way across the street in his garage. How could that be?

The more he thought about it, the more Tosi began to believe that George might have taken the watchful neighbor role to a perverse extreme. Perhaps he had been doing it for some time, using the garage as his base and then sneaking through yards at night to watch women. Perhaps, Tosi thought, he had been watching Karen.

"I would never do anything like that to a human being, ever."

Mentally shuffling through the evidence, Tosi found himself considering other possibilities that were equally disturbing. There remained, for instance, the question about the positioning of the clothing on the body. Had George really forced Karen to put on the black teddy before raping and killing her? Tosi knew George liked lingerie—Glenda had told Debbie. Then there was the white teddy, the one that Karen had bought not long before the murder and that David could no longer find. Was its disappearance related to George's enthusiasm for nighties? Could that be the reason that George—if George in fact was the killer—had apparently gone back to the house?

Tosi could not prove this theory; even now he could only guess at the motive for returning to the scene. He thought it more likely that George had gone back to clean up. That might explain why the house had been so neat when the police arrived. It also might account for their not finding any of his fingerprints, even though he had admitted being there. Perhaps, Tosi thought, George realized that he had left behind something incriminating, watched and waited until the following night, then slipped back across the street after dark to straighten up, wipe away his prints, and remove other traces of his presence. After all, he was friends with Tosi and other police officers, so he would have known what they would look for and how to make sure they didn't find it.

There was another possibility. It had occurred to Brinkworth, who had listened to Tosi running through all of his scenarios. It was conceivable, Brinkworth pointed out, that George had gone back to make sure that Karen was dead. Maybe he had sat there in his garage on Wednesday, wondering if she had survived somehow and was still alive in the hall, waiting to be found and to identify her attacker. Maybe, Brinkworth said, George had gone back to finish what he'd started the night before.

On April 9, 1986, almost four weeks after the arrest, the grand jury indicted Lewis on one count of sexual battery and one count of first-degree murder. He pleaded not guilty, and his attorneys filed a flurry of motions to have the indictment dismissed. They argued, among other things, that it was vague and indefinite; that it violated Lewis's rights to due process and equal protection under the law; and that it subjected him to the possible sentence of death by electrocution, which the lawyers said was cruel and unusual punishment, unnecessary mutilation of the body, and wanton infliction of psychological torture.

The person called on to rule on these motions was Circuit Judge Mark R. McGarry, Jr.

McGarry was not the first judge to have been assigned to the Lewis case. Though it had been filed only a month before, case number CRC86-03400CFANO already had bounced among four men in black robes. The first was Harry Fogle, who had presided at the hearing inside the jail. After that the case was assigned to Circuit Judge Owen S. Allbritton. It went to him because he presided over Division D of Pinellas County's criminal courts, where a court computer had randomly assigned the case. This was not unusual. The computer assigned all cases randomly so that lawyers could not shop around for judges, picking the ones most likely to rule in their favor.

Two weeks after the case was assigned to Judge Allbritton's division, however, he was transferred to another division in another courthouse. His replacement in Division D was Circuit Judge John S. Andrews. But Andrews could not take the case because his son had once been married to one of the prosecutors, Beverly Andrews. They were now divorced, but to avoid any appearance of bias, it had been decided that Judge Andrews should not preside over any cases prosecuted by his former daughter-in-law. So the case was reassigned to Division B, McGarry's division.

A circuit judge for nineteen years, McGarry was a thin, sandy-haired man who had never forgotten that there was a world outside the courtroom. He liked to play badminton during his lunch hours, and in years past, when he had a break during a trial, he had been known to retreat to his chambers and strum on a guitar. He also loved to draw cartoons that poked fun at attorneys and judges and their sense of self-importance. This quiet sense of humor served him well in court. Even when the lawyers before him were tearing into each other, he presided with an air of bemused tranquility. He was the calm not at the center of the storm, but above it. Seated high on the bench, he watched the lawyers fight their cases and gave them wide latitude to fight as they saw fit. There was no point in his getting upset about the fighting. That was what lawyers did.

When the Lewis case reached his division, McGarry wasted no time. He reviewed the defense attorneys' motions to have the indictment dismissed and denied them all. The prosecutors, meanwhile, had filed a motion of their own. Lewis was still being held in jail on the original $150,000 bond. To make sure he stayed there, they asked the judge either to increase that amount or to revoke bond altogether.

A great deal was at stake for both sides. The state knew that if Lewis were released, there was always a chance he might flee. If that happened, some of the witnesses would undoubtedly be intimidated. Neverne Covington, for one, already was afraid of Lewis, still remembering the day when he had driven behind her from one end of Gulfport to the other. Now that he was behind bars, the last thing Neverne wanted was to have him out again. She was tired, she said, of being afraid.

The defense was determined to keep the bond as low as possible. Lewis and his family were going to have enough trouble making a $150,000 bond, but they were willing to try. The case had been hard on all of them. Tiffany Lewis, who had just turned one, did not understand why her father suddenly had left them. One night at a restaurant Tiffany thought she saw her father and began crying. If Lewis were released, he could be with his wife and daughter and get a job to help pay his bills.

There were strategic advantages as well. If Lewis were allowed out on the street, the jurors might wonder whether the evidence against him was weak. It was one thing to see a man sitting in court in a jailhouse uniform, shackled and flanked by bailiffs. It was another to see him walking freely through the halls in a suit and tie, hugging his wife and kissing his little girl.

The question was not simply whether he would buy some time with his family before the trial. It was whether he would have a chance to buy a convincing impression of innocence.

David Roberts, a lieutenant with the St. Petersburg Fire Department, went to visit Lewis one day at the jail. He wanted to know if George was guilty. George said no.

"Why have they got you here?" Roberts asked.

"I don't know. You will hear a lot of stories."

"Okay. I believe you. Because I don't think you could have done it."

That was how many of the men and women at the fire department looked at it. They knew George, they said. Before the arrest, they had worked with him at the fire stations. They had joked with him and eaten with him and been willing to risk their lives with him in the flames. How could they have done that if they didn't trust him? George's family and other friends, meanwhile, insisted that he had been framed and that the police had made a terrible mistake. If anyone asked, they did not hesitate to offer the opinion that the world had seen better detectives than Larry Tosi.

"I've heard," said one person, "that he wasn't too much of a police officer."

Every night, Glenda visited George at the jail, taking different people with her to say hello and wish him good luck. So many people wanted to see him that the family had to keep a schedule of appointments. At the fire department, dozens of firefighters and paramedics were donating their vacation and holiday time so George could continue to draw a paycheck and help support his wife and daughter even as he sat behind bars. Technically, he was on vacation.

George also had the support of a Catholic bishop named J. Keith Symons. George's mother had been the bishop's secretary for fifteen years, working for him first at the diocese in St. Petersburg and then following him to the Florida Panhandle when he was transferred to Pensacola. Now Symons wrote a letter to Judge McGarry on George's behalf, proclaiming his belief that George was innocent and that if bond were granted he would not flee. Some of Lewis's friends and relatives, meanwhile, believed in him deeply enough to risk losing their homes for him. To help him get out of jail while awaiting trial, several people offered to secure his bond with their residences rather than cash. If Lewis fled under such circumstances, the county would have the right to take the homes and sell them. This was what is known as a property bond, and before it could be accepted, it needed Judge McGarry's approval. The defense attorneys had asked for that approval. At the same time, the prosecution was still pushing to have the bond increased.

The place where this question was to be decided—where all of the *State of Florida vs. George Lewis* was set to be decided—was the Pinellas County Criminal Courts Building. Filled with courtrooms as well as the offices of the state attorney and the public defender, the four-story complex was the heart of the county's overburdened criminal justice system. From a distance the huge white building appeared clean and efficient, shining in the sunlight like some monument to purity. Inside, however, it was cheap and dingy and bleak. The building was fairly new, having been erected only a few years before. But it had been falling apart literally from the day it opened. There were handprints on the walls and stains on the carpets and water leaks in one room after the other, and the elevators continually creaked and groaned, as if they were ready at any moment to pass final sentence on their occupants and plummet to the ground. The courtrooms were sterile boxes of beige with no more character than an insurance office; the judges' chambers were tiny rooms so lacking in privacy that whenever a judge interrupted a hearing to use the bathroom, the lawyers often could not help but overhear the unmistakable sound of his or her honor emptying a bladder.

Ciarciaglino and Paver, Lewis's lawyers, had hated the place from day one. They called it the Slum of Justice.

Still, when it came time for the first bond hearing, there they were, standing in a fourth-floor courtroom at the end of the dingiest corridor in the building. Nor were they alone. Dozens of people, many of them St. Petersburg firefighters and paramedics, had shown up to support Lewis. Several were standing outside the courtroom, waiting for the hearing to begin, when Beverly Andrews walked up. They knew she was one of the prosecutors, and as she moved through them, heading into the courtroom, they stared at her. One of them said something. Andrews didn't see the man who said it, but he spoke loudly, obviously wanting her to hear.

"She better hope she's never in an accident in St. Petersburg."

Andrews went inside the courtroom and complained to Ciarciaglino. The case was going to be tough enough as it was. She didn't need to be fielding vague threats from George's friends in the fire department. There was another problem as well. Andrews looked around the room and saw that there were some fifty people on hand to speak against her motion. Many of them were wearing their uniforms. Yet she had no witnesses of her own. Karen's family and friends would have been there if they had known, but no one in the state attorney's office had told them.

The hearing began a few moments later, and ended almost immediately. Andrews announced she was dropping the motion to increase the bond. She did not say she was doing so because she was outnumbered by Lewis supporters. (In fact, she would later deny that her retreat had anything to do with that.) Instead she simply stated that there had been a misunderstanding.

"I was under the mistaken impression," she said, "that the

bond was at $50,000. The file reflects it's at $150,000. Therefore, I'm withdrawing my motion at this time."

Within a few weeks, however, Andrews filed the motion again. When it came up for a hearing this time she had witnesses: Karen's brother Roy and sister Kim; David; Neverne; and Tosi. The defense, however, did not have its dozens of Lewis supporters. Paver said they had not been given enough advance notice for them to gather their witnesses again. He wanted the hearing stopped.

"There is just no reason to go forward on this," he said.

Andrews fired right back. "Judge, I take issue with everything Mr. Paver said."

The law, she pointed out, required only three hours of advance notice. She had given them several days. If the defense wanted more time to assemble its witnesses and bring them back at a later hearing, she said, that was fine. But she had witnesses of her own in court that day and she said they should be allowed to speak.

Judge McGarry agreed. He said he did not want to put the state's witnesses through the trouble of coming to the courthouse another time. He said he would hear them now, allow the defense to bring its witnesses in later, and then rule on the motion. He would not rule on the motion, he said, until he had heard from both sides.

Paver kept arguing. He said it wasn't fair.

"I'm letting you get your witnesses together," said McGarry. "What better deal can you have than that?"

A few moments later the bailiffs brought in Lewis from the jail next door. He took a seat beside Paver, directly in front of Karen's friends. Kim, who had never seen him before, felt her heart pounding. She couldn't look at him. Neverne, on the other hand, couldn't stop staring. It would have been easier if Lewis had looked like a monster. But he was clearly a human being. He appeared to have just gotten out of bed. He was wearing his blue jail uniform, and he was yawning and scratching his chin. His red hair was uncombed, his skin was pale. Neverne thought he looked vulnerable. She wondered if they fed him well at the jail.

Each of the witnesses explained why they did not want Lewis to go free before his trial. Tosi said that due to the brutality of the murder and to the fact that the grand jury had issued an indictment, he felt that Lewis might flee if he bonded out. Neverne talked about how frightened she'd been since she thought Lewis had been following her.

"My life," she told McGarry, "certainly has not been the same since this happened. I have not slept well for the past two years. Now this individual has been arrested and put in jail. I feel a little more comfortable, a little safer."

As she spoke in front of the judge, Neverne was aware that Lewis was sitting only a few feet behind her, watching. If he had wanted, he could have reached out his hand and touched her.

A month later, at the third bond hearing, McGarry heard from Lewis's friends and family. The first to speak was Ralph Hawkins, a captain with the fire department.

"How long have you known George?" Ciarciaglino asked him.

"Since he came on, about three years," said Hawkins. "He's worked for me for about two years."

"Do you believe, in light of the seriousness of the charges, that George would appear for his trial if he were released on bond?"

"Yes."

"Does he have the support of all of his coworkers?"

"Yes. Yes, he does."

The president of the local firefighters union stepped forward and voiced his assurance that George would not flee. George's sister Anita and his brother James and a couple of friends who had offered to put up their homes all said the same.

"I've known George for approximately 10 or 12 years," said Beatrice Madison. "His brother Jim is married to my daughter. He's practically a member of my family."

"You think he will appear at the hearings?" said Ciarciaglino.

"I know he will."

"And you recognize that the property would be forfeited should he fail to appear?"

"Yes, and it's all I have."

Evelyn Lewis, George's mother, spoke as well. She was a short, dark-haired woman who walked in small, careful steps. Her husband, she explained, had died a few months before. But the two of them, she said, had raised George to be a good boy.

"We taught our children to respect the law," she said, "to respect everybody, that whatever kind of job they do, do it with their whole heart and soul, and to have a good reputation, because that means a lot in this world, to be able to go somewhere and people look up to you, to always walk straight and proud . . ."

She went on for a few moments, talking about how George had always loved the outdoors, loved swimming and fishing and waterskiing, and how much it hurt him to be behind bars. She was thankful, she said, that her husband was not alive to see such a thing.

"I feel my son is innocent," she said, "and I know, I know and I promise on my husband's grave, he will appear for any charges against him if he is let out."

Ciarciaglino asked the judge to keep the bond at $150,000 and to allow the bond to be secured with the property that had been offered. Not many men, he said, have friends who would risk their homes for them. That trust, he said, would not be betrayed. On the day the case went to trial, George would be there.

The prosecutor at the hearing that day was Bill Loughery, who asked the judge to deny Lewis any bond at all, especially a property bond. Although such a gesture sounded impressive, he said, in reality it meant little. The county, he said, was not about to take these people's homes even if Lewis did flee. Besides, he said, Lewis's friends and family did not know the evidence linking him to the attack. All they knew was that he had been arrested almost two years after the murder.

After listening carefully, McGarry said that he was raising the bond to $300,000 and that he would not accept property bonds.

"It will have to be posted in cash?" said Ciarciaglino.

"Unless he comes up with something other than that," said McGarry. "I'm not going to have his friends and neighbors putting up their homes and residences and all their personal property based upon this case. Because it does sound like it's a serious case and does sound like the state's case is pretty—is stronger than I thought. So there it is: $300,000."

It was around then, just as the court case was beginning to move forward, that Tosi heard about something called Luminol. He was taking a course on homicide investigation, and he learned that Luminol is a chemical solution that reacts with an enzyme in blood, causing it to glow. It's used to find faint bloodstains or stains not visible to the naked eye.

Hearing this, Tosi remembered the section of the hallway carpet on which Karen's body had been found. Since David gave it to them that summer, the carpet had been stored in the evidence room at the station. By now the bloodstains that had been so obvious that first day were dried and faded, and against the brown color of the carpet it was impossible to see their distinct shapes. Perhaps Luminol could be used to find other usable footprints or handprints.

To test his theory, Tosi turned to some technicians with the Pinellas County Sheriff's Department who were familiar with Luminol. First, they scanned the carpet with a laser, searching for the general areas of bloodstains and any other evidence. Under the yellowish green beam of the laser, the stains appeared as black, velvetlike blotches. Then, inside a dark room, they sprayed Luminol over the areas with the stains. Immediately the stains on the carpet began to glow. One by one, bare footprints appeared. They could see the imprints of toes and arches and heels. There appeared to be at least a dozen footprints, all across the carpet, pointing in different directions, with some of them moving in a path that would have led toward the bathroom. Tosi, watching nearby, thought it looked as if the person who'd made the prints had been dancing.

Before the glowing footprints faded, the technicians photographed and videotaped them. One technician used a phosphorescent ruler to measure one of the prints. It was difficult to be absolutely precise, considering that he was measuring a stain that might have spread across the surface of the carpet. But the technician did his best. The footprint, he said, was approximately nine and one-half to ten inches long.

About the same length as Lewis's feet.

Tosi was still attending mass every Sunday, still praying for justice and for Karen's soul and for her family. But now he included others in his prayers as well. Now he was asking God to give strength and solace to Glenda and Tiffany and the rest of the Lewis family during the difficult times ahead. They are innocent, Tosi told himself. No matter what George may have done, they are innocent.

Eighteen

The sessions took place in small rooms at the courthouse. In these rooms were lawyers from both the prosecution and the defense, waiting to ask questions, and a court reporter, waiting to take down every word of every answer.

One at a time, the neighbors of Karen Gregory were summoned inside.

"Okay," one of the defense lawyers said to a retiree who had lived several houses away from Karen. "You have been listed as a state witness in this case. We are here today to ask you what it is you know about the case, what your first involvement was, and just exactly what happened."

"I, I heard a scream. Now, my first thought was—am I going too fast?"

"No."

"My first thought was that it was a brawl, a family brawl, and that the woman just screamed. And now this scream I should say lasted—I don't know—maybe half a minute. I really don't know, but at the end of it there was agony. At the end of the scream, agony. And I thought to myself, 'Somebody is in trouble.' "

A woman from across the street recalled the same moment: "Well, I was in bed when I heard the scream."

"How would you characterize the scream?"

"I would just say clear, very clear, and short."

"Did it appear to say anything?"

"No."

"Could you tell whether it was male or female?"

"It was definitely female."

Then there was the man who lived a couple of houses away. He too had been in bed. "To tell you the truth, the best way I can describe it—and I don't mean to be cruel—"

"Sure."

"—but I imagine if I put my hand over your mouth and then took a knife and cut your throat, what I heard was the air coming out of your throat. It was very short. It was very conclusive . . . I have no doubt in my mind that what I heard was her last breath."

First a question, then an answer. Another question, another answer. On and on until the lawyers were finished probing. Then another witness was brought in, and the questions began again. This was the process known as discovery, an established part of the Florida Rules of Criminal Procedure, designed to eliminate trial by ambush. In the early stages of a case, the prosecution and defense reveal their evidence to each other and share the names of their witnesses. That way, the logic goes, the lawyers will know as much as possible about the opposition's case before trial. Trials will be decided on the facts, not on surprises. At least that is the way it is supposed to work.

In this case, discovery began in April 1986, several weeks after Lewis was arrested. The prosecutors had given the defense a list of their potential witnesses, and now Ciarciaglino and Paver were calling those witnesses to the courthouse and questioning them under oath in depositions.

"Did you ever do anything to determine if this behavior was consistent with George Lewis and the person you knew as George Lewis?"

Tosi heard Ciarciaglino's question. But he wasn't sure he understood it. Which behavior were they talking about? The murder, said Ciarciaglino. Had Tosi found anything that explained how Lewis could be capable of committing murder?

"You knew this man rather well, didn't you?"

"Well," Tosi said. "How well do you know someone? I mean, I knew him. I mean, he's not a brother."

"You officiated at his marriage, didn't you?"

"Yes. I performed the ceremony. At the time, . . ."

Of all the witnesses, none was questioned as thoroughly as Tosi was. In the months that followed the arrest, Ciarciaglino and Paver summoned him to the courthouse repeatedly, quizzing him on every aspect of the case. During one of the depositions, Paver brought up the fact that Glenda Lewis had not reported seeing any blood on George's body when he returned to their house on the night of the murder. Had Tosi drawn any conclusions from that?

Tosi said he had. He told them the theory about George washing off with the hose outside the kitchen.

"Did you ever ask Glenda Lewis if George was wet when he came in the house?" Paver said.

"I didn't talk to her about that."

"Do you know if she was ever asked if there was blood on his clothing?"

"I don't know that either."

"Did you also conclude that the blood would wash off his clothing if it was present? Did you have any opinion as to that?"

"No. That's not what I felt. I don't feel that he washed blood off his clothing. I felt he changed clothes."

Paver asked Tosi if he had found any evidence of Lewis owning a knife that could have been the murder weapon. Tosi said a friend of Lewis's had mentioned that George once kept a knife in the garage.

"What did they indicate about the knife?"

"Just that he had a knife in his toolbox."

"Did you ever ask George about that knife?"

"No. I didn't get a chance to ask him much at all."

They asked Tosi to tell them all of his theories. So he did. He told them about George's feelings toward blacks and about his temper and about the arguments between him and Glenda and his sister Mary and about how his friends had noticed his acting wild around the time of the murder. He pointed out that it would have been easy for George to try to make a pass at Karen that night. Karen had been moving her belongings into the house. Maybe George had seen her carrying them and had used that as an excuse—either earlier in the evening or after midnight, when she returned from having dinner at Neverne Covington's house—to go over there and start a conversation.

"It's your hypothesis that he just knocked on the door and was allowed to enter?"

"My hypothesis is probably that," said Tosi. "And I base this on the fact that other neighbors had said that George Lewis was very helpful to them. If they got a flat tire, he would help them. He would help people make repairs on their homes, watch their homes for them while they were gone. It was my feeling that perhaps as she came home with some of these items, that he may have, in fact, walked over to her and offered to help her move some of these things and gained access in that manner."

There was one more thing Tosi had to tell them. He had learned that before the murder George had been a frequent customer at the Garden restaurant. Lots of off-duty firefighters and police officers hung out at the Garden. After the arrest, a bartender had seen Lewis's picture in the paper and thought he recognized it. He'd showed the picture to several others at the Garden, including the owner, and they remembered him too.

Hearing this from Tosi, the defense pressed for details.

"Do you know," Paver asked, "if these individuals indicated that Lewis came in alone, with a wife, with a girlfriend, with other firefighters—anything like that?"

"No."

"Any indication of how many times he came in?"

"No. I had asked them that, and they weren't sure."

"Any information you have at all that he ever even spoke to Karen Gregory while he was there?"

"Not at this time."

"Any indication that she was even working while he was there?"

"I'm not sure."

The defense asked other witnesses about Tosi's theories. Among them was Richard McCann, one of Gulfport's volunteer firefighters who already had been questioned by the detective. McCann confirmed that George and Glenda had argued vehemently in the days before the murder.

"Anything unusual about those arguments?" Paver asked.

"No. Just a lot of yelling."

"Both of them yelling?"

"Yeah."

"Do you recall what it was about?"

"No."

"Were you aware of an indication that George did not want to marry Glenda?"

"Yeah . . . He told me he didn't want to marry her."

"When was this?"

"I don't remember the dates, but it was after she got pregnant."

"Did he say he preferred to remain single?"

"Yeah, because when he told us he was getting married, I asked him why."

"What did he say?"

"He said he didn't want his daughter to grow up without a father."

Paver moved on. "Did you ever tell Tosi that you found it hard to believe or highly unlikely that Lewis would not render aid to someone in need? Do you recall telling Tosi that?"

"Yeah. He was the type of person that would help anybody."

"Did you ever tell Tosi that George had a very obvious temper and displayed it?"

"He had a temper, but it wasn't—"

"Was there anything unusual about his temper?"

"No. He was a normal person."

"Did he ever indicate to you one way or the other that he had met Karen Gregory?"

"No."

"Did he make any statements to you in regard to David Mackey?"

"No."

The lawyers also spoke with Richard Pashkow, another Gulfport firefighter who'd talked to Tosi. Pashkow was reluctant to talk to the lawyers. Aside from his volunteer firefighting, he was also a civilian fire inspector with the city of St. Petersburg, and he was worried that if he revealed anything negative about George—anything that might help him get convicted—he might incur the wrath of others in the department. He knew what firefighters were like, he said. He knew how deeply loyal they are to one another, and if he violated that loyalty, he was sure his job would be in jeopardy.

He said he hoped he wouldn't be asked to testify at the trial.

If that happened, he said, he might plead the Fifth and say nothing.

"I am caught between two things, between doing my civic duty as an individual in the community and between, you know, love between firefighters and the bond that they have. Okay? And you know, it's got me tore up."

Still, Pashkow did his best to tell the lawyers what he knew. He said that George had spoken to him about his dislike of blacks and about his belief that black firefighters were receiving special treatment. Not long after the murder, he'd told Pashkow he was so frustrated with the situation that he was thinking of quitting the department and moving to California to live with one of his sisters. Pashkow said he'd been surprised to hear this, that it seemed strange for George—who had worked so long to get into the department—to talk of leaving.

"Was there anything to indicate that George was serious about it," Paver said, "or was he just complaining about the treatment?"

"Well, he sounded like he was serious. Either he had contacted his sister or had gone out to California or had made plans to go out there to check into it, and I thought he was definitely serious."

Paver asked about any problems George might have been having around the time of the murder.

"Him and Glenda had just split up and were trying to get back together," Pashkow said. "And he was undecided on whether she was pregnant or whether she wasn't pregnant. Like, she was trying to hang this thing on him or whatever the case may be, for whatever reason, and he wasn't really happy about that."

Paver wanted to know if Pashkow had ever been with George at the scene of a serious accident, an accident where George would have had to see and deal with someone seriously injured. Sure, Pashkow said. And how, Paver asked, did George react? Like any emergency medical technician or firefighter, Pashkow said. Like a professional.

"In your experience, have you ever seen an EMT, paramedic not be able to treat someone because of the nature of the injuries?"

"No, I have not seen that."

Pashkow had something else to tell them. George, he said, had briefly been suspected of arson. This had been back when he was still a teenager, following the fire trucks around. The suspicions began, Pashkow said, when the firefighters noticed that George was showing up at some fires before they did.

"Everybody is a suspect in a thing when you get there and the same guy is showing up time after time," he said.

"Was there any more to that?"

"No," said Pashkow, explaining that the firefighters had told George to either join the department as a volunteer or quit following the trucks.

"And did he join?"

"Sure."

"Did he continue to be a suspect in any arsons?"

"No."

"Was there any evidence to indicate that he was involved in any of the arsons?"

"Just suspicion."

As the depositions continued, Lewis's lawyers were quietly pursuing an unusual and rather daring strategy. In April 1986, when the case was just starting, Ciarciaglino and Paver had filed a two-page document demanding that the state comply with the state's rules of discovery. The first page appeared to be written in the usual legal jargon and appeared to make the usual demands to see the state's evidence. But tucked away at the top of the second page was a startling sentence. It said:

No demand is made as to 3.220(a)(1)(i) and no reciprocal discovery shall be furnished pursuant to 3.220(b)(3).

Translated into plain English:

We're not asking you to tell us the names of your witnesses, because we're not going to tell you the names of ours.

Translated further:

We're willing to risk the chance that you might surprise us when this case goes to trial. We're willing to do that because we might just want to surprise you.

That one statement alone would have set the Lewis case apart. But when Ciarciaglino and Paver sent the document to the prosecutors in the state attorney's office, something else happened.

The prosecutors didn't read it. At least, they didn't read it closely enough to realize exactly what it said. Because the document looked like the standard demand for discovery, they answered it as such. They made a list of all of their witnesses and sent it to the defense. Then they sat by and watched as Lewis's lawyers deposed those witnesses, asking them to tell everything they knew.

It was an error of potentially devastating proportions. The prosecutors had revealed the foundation of their case to the other side while the defense had vowed to keep its case a secret until the trial.

Worse, they did not realize they had made a mistake. They were stumbling in the dark and didn't even know it.

Ciarciaglino and Paver knew how to fight against their opponents in the state attorney's office. They knew because before becoming criminal defense attorneys, they had worked for years as prosecutors. They'd learned firsthand how prosecutors think and how they act and how they go about building a case. Having learned that, they knew how to tear a case apart.

At thirty, Bob Paver was the younger member of the team. Though he'd been a lawyer for five years, he'd never tried a first-degree murder case before. The pressure was intense, because in Florida there are only two possible sentences for someone convicted of first-degree murder: death in the electric chair, or life in prison with no chance of parole for twenty-five years. But Paver was accustomed to pressure. Over the years he'd handled more than one hundred trials. In fact, later, in 1988, he would be elected president of the Pinellas County Criminal Defense Lawyers Association.

Ciarciaglino, forty, was the kind of man who could—and would, with the slightest encouragement—tell stories for hours. His background gave him plenty of material. When he was still a kid growing up in New York state, Joe helped his father truck chickens to slaughterhouses. When he was a teenager he sold used cars at auctions. After graduating from college he went to Vietnam, served as an Army lieutenant in field artillery, and won three Bronze Stars. Now, after thirteen years of practicing law, Ciarciaglino cut an intimidating figure. Even his last name was daunting. Almost no one could pronounce it right. He'd listen to people losing their way through all of those syllables and he'd sound the whole thing out for them. C-R-SA-LEE-NO, he'd say. Often they would get it wrong again. Remembering was too hard. Maybe that was why some people called him Joe Cigar.

Joe stood out, not just because of his name but also because he was loud and tall and undeniably large. Sometimes he told jurors he was chubby, but that was an understatement. The truth was he looked like a well-fed bear in a three-piece suit. He acted like one, too. In court he seemed soft and tame at first, like a teddy bear. Then, when the time came to attack, he would transform into a grizzly and start clawing away at the opposition. As it happened, Joe had a thing about bears. He thought they were beautiful, and he could talk on and on about what it was like to glimpse one through a forest. He liked to hunt them. He knew some people might find that strange—killing an animal he so admired—but he did not care.

Around the courthouse Ciarciaglino was known as the lawyer who looked out for people in uniform. He represented the local chapter of the Police Benevolent Association, and he taught criminal law at Pinellas County's police academy. The cadets there loved him. He'd tell them about search warrants and probable cause and how not to blow a case by trampling over a defendant's constitutional rights. Sometimes he even shared his theories on how judges interpreted the law.

"They make it up as they go along," he'd say.

When cops and firefighters got in trouble, it was only natural for them to seek him out. He respected them because they put their lives on the line every day. They respected him because he was tough and was not afraid of drawing blood while fighting for a client.

Ciarciaglino had a gentle side. He taught Sunday school classes at his church and he loved to brag about his nine-year-old daughter Ann-Marie. But in the courtroom he was a different man. There, he was not paid to be gentle. He was paid to win, and he was willing to do almost anything to throw his opposition off balance. While the other side was talking he would pull out an old pocket watch and wind it with a key, just to distract the jury. He would goad witnesses into losing their composure. He would shower them with sarcasm. If no one else was looking, he once told a reporter, he would even waggle his tongue and make faces at them.

"I'll do anything for a client, as long as it's not illegal, immoral, or unethical," he'd said. "Short of those three things, there ain't no line I won't cross. There ain't no fighting dirty other than those three."

Ciarciaglino and Paver went on questioning the state's witnesses. They did not restrict their probing, however, to the issue of whether their client was guilty. In fact, they were spending a considerable portion of their time asking witnesses to supply an intimate portrait of Karen Gregory's life. They asked about her relationship with David Mackey, and how she felt about their sex life, and what kind of contraceptive she used, and what sort of attire she wore to bed, and whether she used illegal drugs, and whether she might have dated other men while she was dating David.

Some of these questions were directed at Bill Brinkworth.

"Did you find anyone that indicated Miss Gregory was a sexually promiscuous woman?" Ciarciaglino asked the detective.

"No, sir," Brinkworth said.

"By that I mean had sex with anybody other than Mr. Mackey while she was dating Mr. Mackey?"

"No, sir."

"Went to bars to pick up young guys, anything like that?"

"No, sir."

Ciarciaglino also asked this:

"What type of person, from talking to the other people, did you feel she would be attracted to?"

"Someone that was very athletic."

"Macho, so to speak?"

"Yes. Very athletic, very well-built."

"Like a firefighter?"

"Some firefighters are well-built," Brinkworth said, "and some aren't."

The defense asked similar things of other witnesses, including David.

"With what regularity and what amounts," asked Ciarciaglino, "did Miss Gregory partake of alcohol?"

"Regularity and amount?" said David.

"Yes."

"I would say not very frequently."

"Once a week, once a month, only when she went out?"

"I'd say no more than once or twice a week, and generally

having wine with dinner or having a drink when we would go out."

"Did you ever see Miss Gregory drink sufficient alcohol to where you have thought she, for example, could not drive a car?"

"No."

Peter Kumble, meanwhile, was questioned at length about his intentions toward Karen.

"Did you ever have an occasion," Paver asked him, "to develop what could be described as a friendship with Ms. Gregory?"

"A distant friendship," said Kumble.

"Did you have any desire to make that relationship less distant and more intimate at any time?"

"No, sir."

"Would it be your testimony that you did not want to have sex with Ms. Gregory specifically? When I refer to intimate, that's what I mean."

"That's not a nice question," Kumble said. "I did not desire to have sex with Ms. Gregory."

"Did you desire in any way to have any kind of romantic relationship with her?"

"No."

"Did you find Ms. Gregory attractive physically?"

"Ms. Gregory was an attractive woman. But not to me."

Not realizing what they had done, the prosecutors waited for Ciarciaglino and Paver to send their witness list. Under the rules, they normally had seven days to hand it over. But when the seven days went by, the defense had not sent the list.

A month went by. Still no list.

Two months. Three. Four.

Nothing.

Nineteen

Anita Kilpatrick wanted the truth. Even though she had gone into the house that day in May and seen the aftermath of the attack—gone in with her spray cleaner and paper towels and seen the bloodstains reaching upward along the walls of the hallway—she still did not know what had happened to Karen. Now she wanted the facts. No matter how upsetting it might be, she wanted to understand. So she drove to the courthouse one morning, walked into the clerk's office, approached the front desk, and asked someone to bring her the file.

Like most court files in Florida, this one was public record. By now it had grown into several bulging volumes, each bound in a bright red folder. Anita carried the volumes to a seat across from the front counter. She sat there all day. She read through the arrest affidavit and the indictment and the growing stack of motions and orders and other papers. Near the bottom of the pile was the deposition of Dr. Wood. Anita knew that Wood was the medical examiner and understood that her deposition would undoubtedly include lengthy descriptions of Karen's wounds. Still, as terrified as she was of seeing such details, Anita was tired of wondering what Karen had suffered. She needed to know. She began reading.

> Q. Now let's return to the wounds. Did any of the knife wounds hit any vital organs, arteries, veins, bone?
> A. The stab wounds to the left neck incised the left jugular vein.
> Q. What does incised mean?
> A. That means it was totally cut in two under a stab wound of the left neck. The carotid arteries were intact. One stab wound created a wound on the front of the mid-cervical vertebral column, the spine.

As Anita's eyes moved across the pages, horrible images from inside the house, from when she'd stood in the darkness of the hall, trying to clean up the blood, flashed through her mind.

> Q. Did you form an opinion how long this activity would have taken?
> A. Well, taking into account the placement of the blood within the house, number of injuries to her, blood on the bed, the presumed sexual assault, it certainly took a few minutes, out to ten, fifteen, twenty.
> Q. Ten, fifteen, twenty minutes?
> A. It could have been.

Anita sat there, the file open in her lap, and wept. She'd had no idea the attack could have lasted so long.

> Q. How long after the assault—are you able to form an opinion as to how long after the assault ceased she would have been alive?
> A. My opinion, she didn't live any significant amount of time. We might be talking about a few, few minutes. She is bleeding massively from multiple wounds.
> Q. Are we talking probably five minutes?
> A. Probably.

Five minutes. Plenty of time for the police to have reached the house if any of the neighbors had reported the scream.

Q. Is the fact her eyes were open when she's dead in-
   dicative of anything?
A. She died with her eyes open.

Anita's body was shaking. She felt as if a wave of white light
were running through her brain. She stood up. She returned the
file to the front counter and somehow made it outside to her car.
She was driving home, trying to focus on the road through her
tears, when a police officer pulled behind her and turned on his
flashing lights.

When he walked up to her car at the side of the road, Anita
was still shaking, still sobbing. The officer paid no attention to
her crying. He told her she had been speeding, gave her a ticket,
and drove away.

Anita was not the only person reading through the depositions. A reporter for the *St. Petersburg Times* had been spending
days in the clerk's office, poring over the file.* The reporter had
never met Karen Gregory or George Lewis. But he had some
questions that earlier articles had not answered. Why had it taken
so long for the police to arrest someone who lived less than a
stone's throw away from Karen? How had Lewis, a man whose
job was saving lives, come to be charged with rape and murder?
And why had so many neighbors heard the scream and not called
the police?

This last element was particularly disturbing. That spring,
two years after Karen had cried out in vain, something similar
had happened in another house only a few blocks away. Two
children, fourteen-year-old Michelle Morris and her twelve-year-
old brother Eddie, had been stabbed to death. Neighbors had heard
Michelle crying and screaming for several minutes, begging someone not to hurt her, but none of them had called the police. When
the children's mother returned from her night job, she'd found
their bodies. A short time later, a neighbor who lived behind them
had been arrested.

Afterward, the reporter had written an article about the Morris case, Karen Gregory's case, and several others in which people
had decided not to pick up the phone to help their neighbors.
Through interviews with local police officers and with a social

*That reporter is the author of this book.

psychologist in New York who had made a study of such cases, he had learned that this was a common problem all across the country, in both big cities and tiny villages. In Pinellas County it happened all the time. People, mostly women, were being beaten, raped, and murdered, and their neighbors were routinely ignoring their cries for help. Now he wanted to write about one of these cases—Karen's murder—in detail. After reading through the court file, he had begun working on a series of articles chronicling the murder and the investigation that followed.

The editor on the series was Neville Green, who was shortly to become deputy managing editor of the *St. Petersburg Times*. Both Green and the reporter knew the project would be controversial; for one thing, Anita, David, and Neverne were urging that publication be postponed. The trial, they pointed out, was fast approaching. Though originally scheduled to begin in August, it was now set for November 12—not even three months away. Karen's friends did not want the newspaper to do anything that might affect the outcome of the case. Things were complicated enough already.

"These are our lives you're dealing with," David said.

Though sympathetic to their concerns, Green and the reporter believed the articles should be published as soon as possible. They argued that people needed to understand what was at stake when they heard a scream and chose not to call the police. As for the possibility that the series might cripple the case, Green and the reporter felt confident that would not happen. If the lawyers could not find enough impartial people to sit on a jury in Pinellas County, the venue would be changed to another part of the state. Such a drastic move seemed unlikely, however. In a county with close to a million residents, many of whom do not read the paper closely, if at all, lawyers rarely had trouble finding twelve unbiased jurors.

David and the others did not know what to do. To them the bottom line was that nobody else truly could understand what they had gone through since the murder. What gave the *Times* the right, they asked, to intrude into such private territory? What gave the paper the right to gamble with the future of the case? If the series affected the trial's outcome, Green and the reporter could just walk away and move on to their next project. But David and the others, not to mention Lewis's family, would have to live with whatever debris the series left in its wake.

"They don't care about us," David said. "They're just trying to sell more papers."

Still, as far as he and Neverne and Anita could tell, the paper had left them with only two choices. Either cooperate and grant interviews, or keep their mouths shut and let the series be published without the details they could provide about Karen and her life. Her friends did not want that to happen either, so they reluctantly consented to talk to the reporter.

The series began on a Sunday in late September. David awoke early that morning and went to one of the *Times* boxes. Before he'd even pulled out a copy of the paper, he saw a color photo of Karen's face on the front page. David was stunned. He'd known the picture was coming—he was the one who had lent it to the paper—but he wished someone had warned him it would be displayed so prominently. He wished he could have prepared himself. Now, as he held the paper in his hands, Karen was gazing up at him with those piercing eyes. Her face was serene, with a hint of a smile playing at the corners of her mouth. It was her Mona Lisa look.

Until that moment, the *Times* had covered the case in only the barest of details. Now, as the complicated and disturbing chain of events leading to the arrest was made public, readers began calling and writing by the dozens. Some wanted to say that after reading Karen's story they would never ignore another scream in their neighborhood. Some were outraged that the paper had published such a lengthy account before the trial. Many simply wanted to know why so much attention had been paid to the case in the first place.

"What was the big deal about her murder?" one irate woman said over the phone. "If she had been a senator's daughter or something, I'd understand. But she was nobody."

In the state attorney's office, Beverly Andrews saw the series and wondered how long it would take Ciarciaglino and Paver to ask for a change of venue.

Not very long. A few weeks after publication, the defense filed the motion, saying Lewis could no longer get a fair jury in Pinellas County.

The motion was heard by Judge McGarry. Paver pointed out that the *Times* series had been widely read. Many readers, he said, had followed the series as if it were a cheap murder mystery. Beverly Andrews argued that an impartial jury could be found in

Pinellas County. Not everyone, she pointed out, could have read the series. And not all of the potential jurors would be *Times* subscribers.

McGarry agreed, refusing to grant the change of venue. "I don't think you'll have any trouble picking a jury," the judge said afterward.

The day of trial was almost upon them. Ciarciaglino and Paver had asked for a continuance, arguing that they needed more time to prepare in such a complicated case. But McGarry had denied their motion. Meanwhile, the defense and the state attorney's office were still battling over discovery. Six months had gone by since the prosecutors had given the defense their list of witnesses. Ciarciaglino and Paver, however, had stuck by their original position and were refusing to hand over their witness list. They already had used the state's list to take depositions from more than twenty witnesses. But without a list from the defense, the prosecutors had not taken a single deposition. They were gathering statements from several people on the other side who obviously would be part of the case—Glenda Lewis, for instance—but they could only guess about the defense's other witnesses. So Beverly Andrews had filed a motion with Judge McGarry. The motion contained some jargon of its own:

> WHEREFORE, the State of Florida moves this Honorable Court to enter its Order granting the State's Motion to Compel.

Translated:

Dear judge,
Make them tell us who their witnesses are. Please.

The hearing was a week later, October 17, inside Judge McGarry's chambers. McGarry wanted to know what the problem was. Wasn't it only fair that the defense should hand over its list, too?

Paver said no. He pulled out a copy of the two-page demand for discovery that had been sent to the state in April. He pointed to the sentence at the top of page two. The defense, he said, had not asked for the state's witness list and therefore had no obligation to release its own witness list.

"I don't know how it could be any clearer," he said.

Andrews said she had not read the document that way at all. Her understanding, she said, was that the defense had demanded to see the state's list. If the sentence on page two said differently, she said, she had not noticed it.

McGarry studied the document himself. Paver seemed to be right, he said. The defense did not have to hand over its witness list.

"We'll deny state's motion," the judge said, "and press on."

Five days later, Andrews and Paver were in front of McGarry again. Andrews wanted the judge to reconsider.

This time, Andrews was the one reading aloud from the defense's demand for discovery. If the judge looked closely, she said, it would be clear that Ciarciaglino and Paver had in fact asked to see the state's witness list. There was another paragraph on page one, she said, in which the defense had demanded that the state hand over any statements made by the accused, any police reports that included such statements, plus—Andrews was reading aloud now—"the name and address of each witness."

"Let me see," said McGarry, looking at the document again.

The defense attorneys, Andrews argued, had tinkered with their demand just enough to be confusing. They had asked for the state's witness list on page one, then had slipped a one-sentence disclaimer at the top of page two saying they did not want the list after all. It wasn't right, Andrews said. The rules, she said, were not designed to obstruct justice.

Paver said the defense had not obstructed anything. He and Ciarciaglino had merely followed the rules, he said.

"I'm afraid I can't agree with you, Mr. Paver," said McGarry. If the defense attorneys didn't want the state's witness list, he said, they should have made that clear right up front. Instead, as he put it, they had practiced some "artwork." In the interest of justice, the judge said, the defense would have to hand over its list.

Ciarciaglino and Paver were not ready to hand it over. Not yet. Determined to keep on fighting, they decided to take the issue to Florida's Second District Court of Appeal. In the meantime, while they prepared the appeal, another piece of business had arisen. Although they still were keeping their witnesses a secret, the defense attorneys had sent written notice to the state informing the prosecutors that they did have a piece of evidence that might be used at trial.

Specifically: "One (1) knife."

The notice gave no description of this knife—not its size, not its weight, not even its type. And Ciarciaglino and Paver certainly were not about to reveal its significance or how it might be used in Lewis's defense, if it were to be used at all.

A viewing was arranged on October 30. The prosecutors, along with Tosi and two technicians from the sheriff's department, were ushered inside the hushed elegance of Ciarciaglino and Paver's offices, which occupied a renovated house overlooking a tiny placid lake in downtown St. Petersburg. When they were ready, Ciarciaglino and Paver ceremoniously placed the knife on a conference room table. It was a small pocketknife. The technicians studied it and photographed it, while the prosecutors tried to find out where it had come from and why the defense had listed it as evidence. Ciarciaglino and Paver were not saying. All they would say was that it had come from the custody of Glenda Lewis.

The next day was Halloween. That afternoon, Andrews and Loughery summoned Glenda to the state attorney's office to ask her about the mysterious knife. Glenda, accompanied by Paver, showed up in a flapper costume—a short red satin dress with frills, several strands of pearls, and a headband adorned with a plumed feather—she'd been wearing at the bank. She was embarrassed to be seen at the courthouse in such an outfit. She said she didn't know she was going to be called in that day. She did not want to talk. She said she needed to get back to work. But Judge McGarry had ordered her to cooperate. He'd decided she had to answer the prosecutors' questions; if she wasn't sure how to answer something, she could consult with Paver, who would not be allowed into the room during the interview but who could sit outside.

Even so, Glenda fought every step of the way. She sat with Andrews and Loughery and a court reporter in a small windowless room and gave them as little information as possible. They would ask her a question, and she would say she didn't know or didn't remember or couldn't be specific. Every few seconds she would step outside and ask Paver for advice.

"This is unreal," she told the prosecutors.

They showed her photos of the knife. Did she recognize it? Yes, she said. Where did she recognize it from? A toolbox. Whose toolbox? Her husband's. Did she know who had given the knife to the defense? Yes. Well, who? Her sister-in-law, Mary Lewis.

"When was it you saw this in your husband's toolbox?" Loughery asked.

"I have no idea."

"Did you see it before he was arrested?"

"I don't remember."

"Do you remember seeing it after he was arrested? I mean, did you go out or did Mary go out and visibly go through his toolbox and find this knife? Is that how you saw it?"

"I'll be back." Glenda stepped out, consulted with Paver, then returned. The court reporter read back the last question. Did she recall exactly when or how she came to see the knife? Yes, she said, she and Mary had found it in the toolbox.

And when, Loughery asked, did this happen?

"I don't remember."

"You don't remember at all?"

"No."

"You have absolutely no idea if it was a week ago or if it was six months ago?"

"No."

"I want you to remember, Glenda, you are under oath."

"I know. I don't lie."

"Did you find it within the last week?"

"No."

"Did you find it within the last month?"

"I don't remember, really."

"Where was the toolbox found that this knife was in?"

"Oh, boy," she said.

Again she stepped out to talk to Paver, then stepped back inside. The toolbox, she said, was in the garage.

They asked her why she and Mary had found the knife and given it to the defense attorneys. What was the knife's significance?

"I don't know."

"So you don't have any knowledge about what this knife is supposed to show, whether it's supposed to be a murder weapon or whatever?"

Again she stepped out. Again, when she stepped back in, they repeated the question. What was the reason for giving the knife to the defense?

"It was requested," she said.

"Mr. Paver requested this knife be brought to him?"

"Well, anything that we found."

"Anything that you found in regards to what?"

"I don't know."

"Glenda, again, all I want to know is, what's the story behind the knife?"

"It was just one that we had."

So the only significance of the knife was that Ciarciaglino and Paver had asked them to find it and bring it to them? Yes, Glenda said.

"Was there any blood on it?"

"No."

"Do you know if this knife was tested for blood or for fingerprints or anything along that line?"

"You would have to ask my attorney."

Finally the prosecutors had had enough. They told Glenda she had better call her office and let them know she wasn't going to be back for hours. If she was going to keep on making this difficult, forcing them to pull every single detail from her one at a time, then she was going to be stuck here for a long time. Because now that they had a court reporter, taking down her every word, they wanted her to go over again what she'd seen and heard the night of the murder.

Glenda was sick of it too. She was scared. She was crying. When she stepped out into the hall, people were staring at her in her costume. She said she wanted Paver to be allowed inside the room with her.

"I'm not going to keep running back and forth," she said. "He's my attorney, and I think he should be in here with me."

"Well, he doesn't have a right to be," Loughery told her.

They asked her how long she'd waited in the kitchen for George that night. From the moment she heard the scream until he walked back inside the house, how much time elapsed? She said she wasn't sure. Maybe seven minutes or so. Between ten and fifteen minutes at the most. And when George returned, they asked, what was he wearing? She said she didn't remember.

"I can't speculate."

"So you don't remember a single thing about what he wore?"

"No."

"And do you expect your memory to get better about what he was wearing?"

"Who knows."

"You're the only one that does, Glenda. I'm just trying to find out."

"Well, your mind can only remember what it can remember when it can remember. It's just been too long ago . . . And I don't want to speculate, and I'm not gonna."

She did not want to sit in the chair anymore. She was standing up. She was getting more and more upset. Finally Paver insisted they go see a judge. McGarry wasn't available, so they saw Circuit Judge James R. Case. Paver told him that the questioning had gone far enough. He wanted it stopped. Glenda, he said, needed time to compose herself.

When Case said no, Paver asked what would happen if Glenda refused to answer their questions at this time. She wasn't necessarily saying she was about to refuse. But she wanted to know, he said, what would happen if she did. What would the judge do?

"Well," said Case, "you can tell her that she's subject to the contempt powers of this court, and if she refuses to testify that the contempt powers include incarceration in the county jail."

Glenda said she didn't understand. "I don't know what you're saying," she told the judge. "I don't know."

"I'll make it very clear to you. You are to go back downstairs, and you are to answer the questions of the prosecutor. Can I make it any more clearer?"

So they did. Back in the investigation room, with Paver waiting outside, they continued with the questions. Glenda looked at Loughery, who had been in court all morning and in this room with her all afternoon and was now eating a sandwich.

"Is this your lunch?" she said.

"What can I do, Glenda?" he said, raising both hands in exasperation.

"Well, this is not a joke to me."

"This is not a joke to us, either," Andrews said. "We've got a ton of other things to do."

"We thought this would take a half hour, Glenda," said Loughery. "We are not trying to harass you or intimidate you. We just want some answers."

They took her through it, step by step. She told them George was innocent. He wasn't gone long enough that night, she said, to have committed the murder. And when he came in the house, she said, there was no blood on him. He wasn't out of breath.

"This whole thing is confusing me," she said. "I just know he didn't do it."

The Second District Court of Appeal was not sympathetic to the defense's position on the witness list. The court did not even want to hear their position. Judge McGarry's decision would stand; they would have to give the prosecution their list.

Still, the appeal was not a total defeat for Ciarciaglino and Paver. They had been pushing for a trial delay, and now they had it. By the time the appeal court dismissed their petition, it was already December. With the original trial date long past, the case was postponed until March. The defense, in other words, had lost the appeal but won more time.

Meanwhile, Andrews and Loughery had concluded that the knife from Lewis's toolbox was a red herring. They doubted the defense really intended to use the knife at the trial. As far as the prosecutors could tell, the defense attorneys' only reason for putting it on their evidence list was to waste the state's time. In fact, someone from Ciarciaglino and Paver's office—a reliable source, Loughery says—ran into Loughery at a party a few days after the viewing and told him that the defense had never taken the knife seriously. Not long before it was shown to the prosecutors, this person said in passing, Ciarciaglino and Paver had been joking around with the knife in the office. They'd made sandwiches with it, the source said. They'd used it to slice cheese.

Later, when asked about these allegations, Ciarciaglino and Paver would deny that they had been playing evidence games with the knife or that they had used it to make sandwiches.

"It didn't happen," Paver would say. "It just didn't happen."

Either way, the knife would never even be mentioned at trial.

On the night of December 31, Anita Kilpatrick and Neverne Covington ran into each other at a party. They talked about how glad they were that the man charged with killing Karen was still behind bars. They had been terrified for so long—not just of Lewis but of the world and so many of the people who walk through it. But now, as they stood there at the party, surrounded by friends toasting the end of 1986 and the dawn of 1987, Anita and Neverne felt relieved. They hugged. They danced. They walked outside under the stars and remembered what it was like to breathe the night air in Gulfport and not be afraid.

That evening, George Lewis walked out of jail.

For weeks his family had been talking to a private bonding company, trying to arrange the payment of the $300,000 bail that would free George. Finally the family had scraped together what the bonding company needed. Early that evening, agents for the company had gone to the jail and paid the bond.

It was dark when George was released. He was driven to a nearby office, where Glenda was waiting for him. It was time to celebrate. It was New Year's Eve.

Twenty

It was the first weekend in January. Detective Brinkworth was off-duty, hanging around the Gulfport marina. He had stopped in the marina supply shop to buy some ice—he planned to go sailing that day—when a red-haired man in blue jeans walked by the shop's front window with his head lowered, as if he were trying not to make eye contact.

Brinkworth could not believe what he was seeing.

"Lewis," he said. "That looked like George Lewis."

"Didn't you know he was out?" said the harbormaster, who was standing a few feet away.

Brinkworth did not know. Hardly anyone did. Not the police, not the state attorney's office, not Karen's friends. None of them had been informed that Lewis had bonded out. Now Brinkworth stood quietly watching as his old acquaintance—the subject of the longest and most gutwrenching manhunt in Gulfport history—moved freely a few feet away along the sidewalk.

Lewis stopped at a shrimp tank. He bought some bait. He walked away.

*　　*　　*

In Florida, where murder is so much a part of life it has become almost commonplace, it is still a rare and unsettling sight to see an accused killer strolling the streets before his trial. Almost all defendants charged with first-degree murder are held without bond or with a bond so hopelessly high that it might as well not exist.

Such had appeared to be the case with Lewis. The prosecutors had assumed that he never would be able to make his $300,000 bail. He wasn't wealthy or even well off. He was a young man with a high school education who had been living in a small house owned by his parents and who had been laying carpet in his spare time to pay the bills. The other members of his family, meanwhile, gave no indication that they were rolling in green either. Still, after Judge McGarry refused to allow them to free George with the property bond, his mother and the others had gone looking for help outside the court system. In early November, one of his sisters approached Al Estes, the owner of a local bonding company, and asked him what it would take for him to get George out of jail. Estes, a big burly man with a bushy white beard and an aura of controlled power, told her he would need the standard 10 percent fee—in this case, $30,000 in cash, which would be nonrefundable—plus enough property to serve as collateral for the entire $300,000 while George was out and awaiting trial.

Evelyn Lewis, George's mother, took out a second mortgage on her house to get Estes the $30,000. She also put up about $40,000 worth of rare coins and other valuables, and at least a dozen other people—family, friends, and several members of the St. Pete fire department—offered money, jewelry, a boat, and other property, including several houses. It was an act of collective faith in George. If he fled, his friends and family would lose it all.

Estes was impressed that the people around George believed in his innocence deeply enough to risk so much. Not everyone, however, was pleased. One day after the news of George's release made the papers, the phone rang at Estes's midcounty office. An assistant answered.

"You freed Lewis," said a man on the other end. "I'm going to kill you, motherfucker."

Click.

"I've been threatened for putting them back in jail," Estes told a *Tampa Tribune* reporter. "But never for getting them out."

Unanswered Cries

*   *   *

David Mackey wanted to know where all of the money was coming from. There was more involved than the $30,000 bonding fee. There was the question of the defense attorneys. Ciarciaglino and Paver were experienced and, presumably, expensive, and they had been working on the case for almost a year now. They had hired a private investigator. They had questioned dozens of witnesses. Paver had even flown to Arizona to take a deposition. Now David couldn't help wondering. Who was paying for it all?

Others close to Karen were afraid because Lewis was out of jail. Neverne lived only a few blocks from the marina where Brinkworth had seen him. Now she felt vulnerable. She knew that rationally, Lewis ought to realize it would be best to avoid any contact with her. But if Lewis was the murderer, he was not necessarily a rational person. How could she assume he would stay away?

Sometimes Neverne wondered what it would be like to make Lewis afraid. She imagined calling him on the phone. She knew just what she would say.

Hi. I'm Karen. I lived across the street from you. Remember me? Why did you hurt me? Did you know how much this has hurt so many people? I fought hard, didn't I? You didn't think I had that in me. Do you still think about me? When you make love with your wife, do you think about how you raped me?

When he left jail, Lewis did not return to the house on Upton. In the aftermath of the arrest, it had been sold to some friends of the family. So now he and Glenda and Tiffany found an apartment in northeast St. Petersburg. By this point he had been placed on judicial leave from the fire department. To pay some of his bills he worked in a machine shop in Gulfport.

One of George's friends had some advice for him. The friend said he knew what he'd do if he were facing a murder charge. He'd run, he said. But George did not run. Twice each day he checked in with Al Estes. Quietly, he tried to go on with his life. Sometimes it was not easy. The articles in the *Times* had given him a measure of notoriety. One day he was standing in an express line at a local supermarket when he realized the fresh-faced high school kid behind the register was staring at him with a look of fright in her eyes. She'd been ringing up his purchase and hadn't seen him until she'd rung the total and looked up. Now she was shaking.

"Yeah," Lewis said gently. "It's me."

He picked up his bag and left.

"Pardon?" said Milton Lewis, one of George's brothers.

"Do you know why he was arrested for the murder of that girl?"

"I don't know why."

"Did he ever tell you what the police had on him?"

"I have no idea what the exact evidence was. I realize—I understood there was a footprint involved, but that's all I am aware of."

It was March 3, exactly one week before the trial was to begin. Over the past several weeks, the defense attorneys finally had begun to give the names of their potential witnesses to the state. Now Andrews and Loughery were deposing some of those witnesses, questioning members of the Lewis family as well as George's friends and coworkers. Hardly any of these people, it turned out, knew much about the case. But they did know George and his background, so the prosecutors asked about that.

They asked Richard Campbell, one of the friends who had put up his house for the bond, whether George was the kind of person who looked out for his neighbors. Campbell said yes.

"Well, would you think he would be defined as a good neighbor?"

"Yes, yes. Probably better than a good neighbor."

They asked Roy Ozmore, another friend, if he thought George was a truthful person.

"Very truthful."

"Do you have an opinion as to whether George is a violent person?"

"No, he is not."

They asked Carl Lewis, Jr., another one of George's brothers, to share his theory on why George went inside Karen's house that night. Carl said George might have been trying to help Karen.

"All my life I have known him," said Carl. "I don't know if you would understand this, but our family lives to help people. That's what he lives for. Okay? Regardless of what he has done all his life, he has always made sure he helped people and cared about people. That's my brother. That's why he wanted to be a fireman."

They asked Anita Fridy, one of George's sisters, if she had spoken to George about the facts of the case. She said no. All she knew about the case, she said, was what she'd read in the paper.

"Do you think George could have done this?"

"No."

"Why is that?"

"Because he would not do such a thing."

By now yet another judge had been assigned to the case. Mark McGarry had been moved in a routine transfer to another of the county's courthouses, and his replacement was Circuit Judge William L. Walker, a quiet man whose white hair and white beard stood out above his black robe. Walker had served on the bench in Pinellas County for more than a decade. He was an affable, unassuming judge who had a slightly disconcerting habit of mumbling. The lawyers in his courtroom waged an ongoing struggle to hear him. They would stand there, leaning forward, cocking their ears in his direction, staring up at him with bewilderment clouding their faces. "I'm sorry, your honor," they'd tell him. "I didn't catch what you just said."

Luckily, Judge Walker had a sense of humor about this—he joked about it in court—and did not mind repeating himself. He often made jokes from the bench. The jokes usually weren't that funny, but they were well-intended—and they came from the mouth of a judge, so the lawyers usually smiled. It was usually a good idea to smile when a judge made a joke.

The past year had not always been easy for Walker. Three times the Florida Supreme Court had ruled that errors had been made during first-degree murder cases over which Walker had presided. The Supreme Court had overturned all three cases. The Lewis trial did not promise to make the judge's life any easier. It was a complex, drawn-out case in which the question of guilt or innocence was not clear, as it is in so many cases. In addition, the series in the *St. Petersburg Times* was bound to complicate the task of finding an unbiased jury. Finally, there was an underlying tension that came from the tangled personal histories of the people involved—people who now would soon find themselves on opposite sides of the courtroom.

Obviously there was the friendship between Tosi and Lewis and their wives. But there were other ties, too. Back when she was a law student, Beverly Andrews had served briefly as a clerk for Ciarciaglino. Later, when she was getting a divorce, she had hired him to represent her. Ciarciaglino, meanwhile, had also represented Tosi, along with other police officers, in a dispute with the city of Gulfport over back wages.

None of this had stopped the two sides from battling hard. They had argued with each other and picked at each other and accused each other of playing games. Word games. Witness games. Lawyer games. Now, as the final days before the trial ticked by, both sides were still arguing. They were arguing about evidence and witnesses and whether or not the pretrial publicity necessitated that the case be moved to another county. They had fought over this issue once already, but Ciarciaglino and Paver were not ready to let it rest.

The games had only begun.

Twenty-one

The trial began on a Tuesday morning in mid-March. The prosecutors arrived early, as prosecutors almost unfailingly do, lugging their files up to Courtroom B on the fourth floor of the courthouse. On her way in, Beverly Andrews stopped for a moment in the long carpet-stained hallway to gaze out a window. Camped down in the parking lot below, like some huge metal creature that had escaped from a national park, was a motor home that Ciarciaglino and Paver had brought to the courthouse as a mobile office. Equipped with typewriters, law books, and telephones, it was planted where no one could miss it, taking up at least three parking spaces directly in front of the building's entrance. Parked nearby were two silver Mercedeses, one belonging to Ciarciaglino, one belonging to Paver.

At the moment Ciarciaglino was standing outside the motor home, emanating exuberance. His suit jacket was off. He was smiling and laughing and talking with his assistants.

"He's holding court out there," said Andrews, shaking her head. "Unbelievable."

*   *   *

A few minutes later, after Ciarciaglino and Paver had made their way upstairs with Lewis and taken their seats, the proceedings got under way with some preliminary motions. The first thing that happened was that Ciarciaglino asked that David Mackey and Anita Kilpatrick, who were sitting in the courtroom, be ordered to leave.

"I would ask the court," he said, "to invoke the rule."

Ciarciaglino did not need to explain which rule he meant. The witness rule, as it is commonly called, says that anyone who might testify in a case cannot sit in court while other witnesses are on the stand. It's designed to prevent people from being influenced by the testimony of others and to prevent them from changing their own testimony. But lawyers, prosecutors and defense attorneys alike, routinely abuse it, using it as a tool to keep family members and friends of either the victim or the accused out of the courtoom. Lawyers do not want jurors to see a mother's tears or a brother's angry stare. They don't want jurors to be swayed by sympathy—at least not by sympathy for the other side—so sometimes they list friends and family as potential witnesses, even when they have no intention of calling those people to the stand.

That was not the case here. Both David and Anita were listed as witnesses, and there was little doubt that eventually both would be called to testify. Andrews, however, argued against having them removed from the courtroom so soon. She pointed out that the trial had not reached the stage where testimony would be heard. Why, she asked, should David and Anita have to leave now?

Ciarciaglino, who had already asked Glenda Lewis and other defense witnesses to step outside, said there was a good reason for David and Anita to do the same. The preliminary motions, he said, concerned the facts of the case.

All right, said Judge Walker.

"Out of an abundance of caution," he said, "we will just remove them."

David and Anita did not want to step outside. They had understood that they would not be allowed to stay during testimony. But they had been told it probably would be all right to listen to motions and jury selection. They had taken off from work just to be there. Once the judge ordered them out, though, they had no choice but to leave. A bailiff escorted them to the hallway, where Glenda and other people supporting her husband had gathered. It was a narrow hall with only a few benches, and the two groups were uncomfortably close to each other. David and Anita found seats and tried not to stare.

Inside the courtroom, the lawyers argued for two hours. They argued about the relevance of Sgt. Tosi's reputation among certain witnesses and about the relevance of what one of the psychics had said about the case and about all sorts of details over how the potential jurors should be questioned. When they were finished they moved next door to Courtroom A, the largest in the building. On that Tuesday morning the room was filled with spectators and a collection of lawyers and clerks who had sneaked away from their desks to watch the beginning of the trial. Seated in the center section of the room's benches was a group of fifty prospective jurors, quietly waiting.

A door opened at the back of the courtroom. The voice of a bailiff boomed out.

"All rise."

Judge Walker stepped into the room, his black robe flowing behind him. Almost immediately, the lawyers scurried to the bench for a whispered huddle with him. There would be dozens of such bench conferences in the days to come. The lawyers would use them to ask for a mistrial, to complain, to argue, to accuse each other of improper behavior, and to request to use the bathroom.

In this conference Ciarciaglino pointed out that David and Anita were now at the back of this courtroom after they had been told to leave the one down the hall. Again, Ciarciaglino asked the judge to have them removed. Again, Andrews argued that the witnesses should be allowed to stay for the time being. Andrews, in fact, had told David and Anita they could sit in the courtroom now. This was only jury selection, Andrews reminded the judge. There was nothing Karen's friends could hear that would prejudice their testimony. Andrews said it was important to them to be here and would be unfair to kick them out. Ciarciaglino, she said, was just harassing them.

Judge Walker agreed that rulings in the law might well have said it was permissible for David and Anita to stay. But he said he had to think about the possible appeal. What if he allowed them to stay and the status of the law changed? What if a higher court reversed him?

"I'm going to grant the motion," said Walker. "Get them out of here."

So Anita and David were removed again. They stood outside the courtroom and stared through the windows.

"Case set for trial today is *State of Florida vs. George Lewis*," Walker announced. "State ready to proceed?"

"Yes sir," said Andrews.

"Defense ready?"

"May we approach the bench?" said Ciarciaglino.

Back they went. This time Ciarciaglino wanted to ask that the trial be delayed.

"We are not ready," he told the judge.

"We will proceed as if you are ready," said Walker.

The arguments went on. Andrews bickered with Ciarciaglino. Ciarciaglino bickered back. When they were done, Ciarciaglino turned from the bench to return to his seat, thanking the judge as he went. Andrews immediately called him back.

"Judge," she said, turning to Walker, "before we go back— Mr. Ciarciaglino, can I have your attention, please? Years ago, I clerked for Mr. Ciarciaglino, and he told me that one of his tricks of the trade was to turn away from every bench conference and say, 'Thank you, your honor,' real loud."

It was an old ruse. Thank the judge loud enough, and the jurors might think you've won whatever dispute brought you to the bench in the first place.

"He just did it, judge," said Andrews. "I don't want to be up here out-shouting him, and I would ask that we just not play that game to begin with."

"Well, I apologize for being courteous," said Ciarciaglino.

"I'm not going to worry about it," said Walker. It was already close to noon. They had been haggling all morning and had not even begun picking a jury. The judge pressed on. "Would Mr. Lewis please stand, face the jurors?" he said.

Across the room, seated at the defense table, Lewis stood up in his jacket and tie and nodded toward the prospective jurors. He looked bored, as if he was not sure why he had to sit through all of this rigamarole.

Walker reached into a wooden box in front of him, inside

which were fifty slips of paper, each bearing the name of one of the prospective jurors. Walker pulled out twelve slips at random and read aloud the names. One by one, twelve people took seats in the jury box.

"Go ahead, Ms. Andrews," said the judge.

The prosecutor stood up and walked briskly to a lectern in front of the jury box. She was just introducing herself when Ciarciaglino interrupted her.

"Excuse me, Ms. Andrews," he said. He was standing again, looking toward the judge. It was the lectern. He said it blocked his view of the jury.

Walker asked him what he proposed to do. Ciarciaglino said they could move the lectern. Maybe, the judge replied, Ciarciaglino should move instead.

Ciarciaglino glanced down at all of the papers on the table in front of him. "I really have everything here," he said. "If you want, I will move. If that's the only resolution, I will be happy to."

Walker stared down from the bench. He looked as if he were trying to remain calm.

"Well," he said, as an edge began to creep into his voice, "there may be some other resolution that is fair . . . I'm willing to listen."

"No," Ciarciaglino said, "I'll do that, judge. Thank you, sir."

"You're welcome."

The defense attorney walked across the room, searching for a better vantage point. There were plenty of chairs to choose from. He chose the empty one at the state's table—Andrews's chair.

"Do you mind?" he said.

Some of the prospective jurors were laughing softly. Not Andrews. She was glaring at Ciarciaglino. Her head was slightly cocked. Her eyes were narrowed. She held them on her opponent for a few seconds.

"Are you ready, sir?" she said coldly.

"Yes," he said.

Andrews turned back to address the jurors. A few feet away, Ciarciaglino listened. He was the picture of graciousness now. He sat in her chair, at her table, with her notes and files stretched out before him, and smiled. He smiled as if he could not have found a better chair in the entire universe. And the prosecution and the judge had let him have it.

*   *   *

There were nine courtrooms in the criminal complex. Positioned on walls inside two of them, including Courtroom A, were video cameras. The cameras were hooked up to video monitors in the public defender's office, the state attorney's office, the bailiffs' office, and the office of the administrative judge. That way, others around the courthouse could watch what was happening in different hearings and trials. If they wanted to switch from one courtroom to the other, they simply flipped the channel.

That week, as jury selection in the Lewis case dragged on, lapsing into a second day and a third and a fourth, the word in the halls was that every monitor in the complex was turned to Courtroom A.

Ciarciaglino was giving a show. After beginning with the seizing of Andrews's chair, he now appeared to be taking over the jury box. When it was his turn to question the prospective jurors, he'd address them each by name. He'd lean on the lectern and speak with a twang and talk about how smart and good looking the prosecutors were—he said Loughery looked like one of the Kennedys—and how he hoped the jurors wouldn't hold it against him and his client just because he was fat and old. (He was only forty-one.) He said he also hoped they wouldn't hold it against him if he felt the need to keep running up to the bench. "Going to the mountain," he called it. He told jokes. He grinned. He delivered little speeches about America and patriotism and the law.

He did everything in his power to make the jurors feel comfortable with him. At the same time, he made the prosecutors profoundly uncomfortable. He would let Andrews get deep into the middle of a sentence, then cut her off and ask to approach the bench. He'd stand in front of the judge and complain that Andrews was interrupting him. One day, as they gathered in front of the judge, he complained about how she wouldn't sit still.

"Can you ask her to stop jumping up and down like a marionette?" he said.

"I'm intimidating you?" said Andrews. "I'm sorry."

The thing was, Ciarciaglino stood at least a foot taller and was a good 150 pounds heavier than Andrews. When the two of them went up to the bench, she almost disappeared in his shadow. Ciarciaglino's complaint might have been funny if this were not a murder trial. But he played it straight, knowing his height and weight would not appear in the written record if he had to take the case up on appeal. He complained about how tired he was. He complained about how the prosecutors were telling reporters what happened during the bench conferences. And a few days into the proceedings, when he was told to move his motor home from the front of the court complex to the back, he complained about that too.

Andrews tried to fight back. She argued to the judge that Ciarciaglino's conduct regarding the motor home had been an insult. She said that he and others had held what amounted to a cocktail party out in the parking lot, drinking and laughing in front of the complex, where prospective jurors could see them.

"Judge, let me say something," said Bill Loughery, trying to get matters back on track. "Whether Mr. Ciarciaglino's camper is illegally parked has nothing to do with the merits of this case."

Which was absolutely correct. The longer Ciarciaglino had them arguing about his motor home or whether or not Andrews should stay in her seat, the longer he kept them from the real question of the trial, which was whether or not his client was a rapist and a murderer.

Of all of the side issues he raised, one of the most time-consuming was the campaign Ciarciaglino waged to have Karen's friends moved farther and farther from the courtroom. He wasn't satisfied just to have them out of the room. He also didn't want them standing outside the courtroom door, even though Glenda Lewis was standing there as well, peering in. Ciarciaglino wanted Anita and David out of sight. He said their presence could taint the jurors with emotionalism. So Anita and David were told to not stand by the door. That wasn't good enough, either. Ciarciaglino complained that Anita was sitting in a chair outside the door, staring at the prospective jurors.

"She is five feet outside the door," he said.

"She is not outside the door," said Loughery.

"I want to avoid any problems," said Judge Walker. "Let's move her away from the door."

The prosecutors asked if Anita and David could watch the jury selection on a video monitor in the state attorney's office, far away from the prospective jurors. Walker said no. He was talking about appeals again. His sentences were starting to jumble together. "Let me tell you something," he said. "I have been reversed in cases where the law has changed, and you are talking about a death-penalty murder case, and you are talking about five different appeals, and a whole bunch of change, and lawyers have a great imagination in coming up with stuff, if we ever get to that point, and I don't want that type of thing to interfere with the decision."

So Anita and David were asked to move inside one of the witness rooms along the hallway. Neverne Covington had joined them by now, and the three of them went inside and sat down, wondering how much more completely their presence could be erased. A few minutes later the door from the courtroom opened, and Ciarciaglino, Paver, and Lewis walked in.

"Excuse me," said Ciarciaglino as he and the others retreated.

Soon a bailiff came into the room and told David and Anita and Neverne they weren't supposed to be there. So they left and moved somewhere else. By the end of the afternoon they had been kicked off the floor.

Just as he had worked on the prosecutors and the jurors, Ciarciaglino worked on the judge. He and Paver were constantly approaching the bench, asking for a mistrial, arguing that the entire panel of prospective jurors should be thrown out, dropping not-so-subtle hints about how easy it would be for the judge to be reversed on appeal. Day after day they fed Walker's obvious concern that he not have another murder case overturned.

"I think you are picking on me, Mr. Ciarciaglino," said the judge.

"I apologize."

The issue Walker seemed most worried about was pretrial publicity. Throughout the jury selection, Ciarciaglino and Paver kept up their demand for a change of venue. Not that many prospective jurors, it turned out, had read the lengthy stories in the *St. Petersburg Times*. Many of those who had seen them said they'd only skimmed or looked at a headline or read a part of the series.

"Candidly," Walker told the lawyers, "I don't think anybody has read the whole series."

Even so, the judge wanted to take extra care in making sure Lewis received a fair trial. Early on he began excusing virtually every prospective juror who had read or seen any part of the series, including those who said they didn't remember what they had read. He also bumped one juror who had not read the series at all

George Lewis's house, across the street from David Mackey's house, with the neighborhood crime watch sign in the yard at left. (*St. Petersburg Times*/Joe Walles)

Sgt. Larry Tosi, shown here testifying at the trial. He is holding an aerial photograph of the neighborhood where the murder took place. (*St. Petersburg Times*/Fraser Hale)

Neverne Covington, Karen Gregory's close friend.
(*St. Petersburg Times*/Ricardo Ferro)

Herman "Hap" Golliner, Gulfport's police chief at the time of the murder, shown in his office with his beloved baseball figurines.
(*St. Petersburg Times*/Charles Ledford)

The path of the struggle

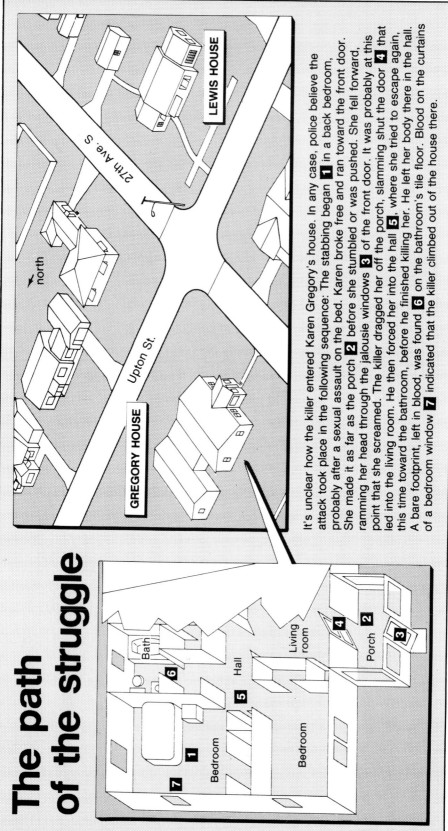

It's unclear how the killer entered Karen Gregory's house. In any case, police believe the attack took place in the following sequence: The stabbing began **1** in a back bedroom, probably after a sexual assault on the bed. Karen broke free and ran toward the front door. She made it as far as the porch **2** before she stumbled or was pushed. She fell forward, ramming her head through the jalousie windows **3** of the front door. It was probably at this point that she screamed. The killer dragged her off the porch, slamming shut the door **4** that led into the living room. He then forced her into the hall **5**, where she tried to escape again, this time toward the bathroom, before he finished killing her. He left her body there in the hall. A bare footprint, left in blood, was found **6** on the bathroom's tile floor. Blood on the curtains of a bedroom window **7** indicated that the killer climbed out of the house there.

(*St. Petersburg Times*/Art by Frank Peters)

David Mackey, Karen's boyfriend, shown standing in front of the Polk
County Courthouse.
(*St. Petersburg Times*/Ricardo Ferro)

George Lewis during the attempted jury selection in Pinellas County.
(*St. Petersburg Times*/Tony Lopez)

Assistant State Attorney Beverly Andrews, looking toward
Lewis and his attorneys at the defense table during the at-
tempted jury selection in Pinellas County.
(*St. Petersburg Times*/Tony Lopez)

Circuit Judge Crockett Farnell, who presided at the trial in Bartow, shown in his office.
(*St. Petersburg Times*/Ricardo Ferro)

Joseph M. Ciarciaglino, Jr., left, and Robert L. Paver, right, Lewis's attorneys, shown in their office. On the floor is the skin of a bear that Ciarciaglino shot and killed himself.
(*St. Petersburg Times*/Ricardo Ferro)

Prosecutor Richard Mensh talking to jurors at the trial in Polk County, June 1987.
(*St. Petersburg Times*/Fraser Hale)

Glenda Lewis, testifying at the trial.
(*St. Petersburg Times*/Tony Lopez)

Beverly Andrews and William Loughery, the two other prosecutors at the trial, shown in the courtroom.
(*St. Petersburg Times*/Fraser Hale)

Lewis, covering his face during the trial, seated between his attorneys, Ciarciaglino on the left and Paver on the right.
(*St. Petersburg Times*/Evan R. Steinhauser)

Tonja Dishong.
(*St. Petersburg Times*/Cherie Diez)

George and Glenda Lewis play with their daughter Tiffany in the rotunda out-side the courtroom on the first day of jury deliberations.
(*St. Petersburg Times*/Evan R. Steinhauser)

George Lewis, testify-
ing at the trial.
(*St. Petersburg Times*/
Tony Lopez)

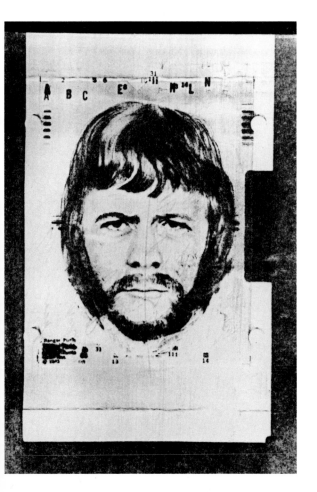

The composite drawing
that Lewis helped Tosi
put together of the man
Lewis said he'd seen on
Karen's lawn.
(*St. Petersburg Times*/
Photo of composite by
Fraser Hale)

Juror Tim Green, shown in front of the Mc-Donald's where he was working late nights during the trial.
(*St. Petersburg Times*/Ricardo Ferro)

Juror Dorene Cobb, who originally voted not guilty.
(*St. Petersburg Times*/Ricardo Ferro)

Juror Maytha Schafer, one of the last holdouts for acquittal, who remembered meeting John Wayne Gacy.
(*St. Petersburg Times*/Ricardo Ferro)

Juror Ruth Wunder, who conducted an investigation of her own after the trial and eventually came to doubt the verdict. Here, she's shown in the courtroom where the trial took place.
(*St. Petersburg Times*/Ricardo Ferro)

Glenda Lewis, screaming and hysterical, is led from the courtroom right after the verdict is announced.
(*St. Petersburg Times/* Cherie Diez)

George Lewis watches Glenda being led from the courtroom.
(*St. Petersburg Times/* Cherie Diez)

Evelyn Lewis, George's mother, testifies during the penalty phase of the trial: "All I can say—I know he's a good boy." (*St. Petersburg Times/* Kathleen Cabble)

Karen's mother Sophia and brother Roy standing outside the courtroom during the trial. (*St. Petersburg Times/* Kathleen Cabble)

From left to right: David Mackey, Anita Kilpatrick, and Neverne Covington, awaiting the judge's sentence. (*St. Petersburg Times/* Joe Walles)

but had heard his wife talking about it. Still, Walker was visibly worried. Late on that Friday afternoon, as they neared the end of the fourth day and still had not found a jury, Ciarciaglino and Paver warned him again about the dangers of being overturned. The record of these proceedings, they said, was brimming with possible grounds for reversal.

"Judge," said Paver, "I think that record is pretty big by this time."

"Pretty solid," said Ciarciaglino.

"We have a lot of problems that haven't gone away," said Paver.

Suddenly, in the middle of a discussion about whether to bump one of the jurors, Walker started talking about confessions. None of the lawyers had told him, he said, what Florida law said about confessions. He had heard somewhere that when a confession is published in the community where a case is to be tried, the trial judge must grant a change of venue. No confession had been printed in the *Times* series—the series had repeatedly quoted Lewis saying he was innocent—but Walker was no longer sure what to think. The series, he pointed out, described several conflicting statements Lewis had made. To the judge it seemed that the articles inescapably led the reader to conclude Lewis was guilty. Did that mean that publishing the articles was close to publishing a confession? Did that mean if Walker did not grant a change of venue he'd be reversed?

The prosecution saw what was coming and tried to stop it. Andrews said she did not know they were going to talk about this now. She had left her file on this subject in her office, she said. She reminded the judge that he had been careful to make sure they were finding impartial jurors. And the *Times,* she emphasized, had not printed a confession. There had been no confession to print.

No matter. Walker had made up his mind. "I'm going to grant the motion for change of venue," he said.

It was all over. The judge had decided that everyone would have to start over again with a new trial. Now Karen's friends were allowed into Courtroom A. Anita and Neverne looked dazed. David just stared at Ciarciaglino, Paver, and Lewis, who were quietly celebrating at the defense table. Both sides were checking their calendars to see when they could set the new trial date. They were debating where the trial should go.

Ciarciaglino was smiling again. "If we go to Miami," he joked, "do they issue Uzis?"

Walker chuckled. "Not to you."

Neville Green was sitting in his small, glass-enclosed office at the *St. Petersburg Times* that Friday afternoon when the phone rang. It was a reporter who had been covering the trial, calling with the news.

"The judge did it."

Green didn't know what to say. He hung up the phone, stepped out of his office, and took the stairs two flights down to the ground floor. He went outside—it was a warm spring afternoon—and walked slowly around the block, feeling sick. He did not believe it had been a mistake for the *Times* to publish its series before the trial. But he felt badly for Karen's friends and family, who already had waited so long for the case to be resolved. The *Times* had predicted correctly that the lawyers would find many prospective jurors who had not read the series. But they had not counted on how successfully the defense attorneys would play on Judge Walker's fears of reversal. Now the case would have to be delayed until it could be moved to another courthouse in another county.

At that moment Karen's two brothers, Roy and Mark, were on their way to Pinellas County. They had taken off work in New York and were driving down for the trial, having timed the long trip so they would arrive as jury selection was ending. They pulled up to their sister Kim's house in Dunedin on Friday night, just a few hours after the change of venue was granted. The trip, they were told, had been a waste.

Roy and Mark were stunned. So were the others. Ever since the case had begun, they had felt as if they had lost control of their lives. Institutions such as the police and the court system seemed to constantly be making decisions that affected their privacy, their memories, their safety. Now the newspaper had published a series, against their urging, that had led to a change of venue. Karen's friends and family had had enough.

A few days after the judge's decision, several of them went to the *Times* to complain. One by one they told Neville Green and the reporter who had written the series how they felt. They said there was no way to describe how painful it was to endure yet another delay. The paper, Roy said, had exploited them and their grief. He had not read the series—he could not bring himself to do it, he said—but it was clear that the articles had gone too far. As far as he was concerned, the *Times* had sunk to the level of the *National Enquirer*.

Sgt. Tosi was frustrated too. For a long time now he had felt the system was drifting in the wrong direction. There were too many tricks, too many ways for lawyers to obscure the facts. He said he was tired of making solid arrests and then seeing the bad guys back on the street, smirking at him. He talked about quitting and opening a general store in the mountains of Tennessee.

"I wish I could leave tomorrow," he told the other detectives.

The pressure was getting to him. One day in December 1986, he had collapsed. He and Debbie were at a state park across the bay, trying to get their minds off the case by camping out for the weekend. Suddenly Larry couldn't breathe, and his heart was thumping wildly. He sat down beside the tent. He thought he was about to die.

"I think I'm having a heart attack," he told Debbie. "You better try to go get some help."

An ambulance took him to a nearby hospital. After repeated tests, the doctors decided Larry had suffered a stress attack. He was overweight, had high blood pressure, and had developed an ulcer. He went on a diet, tried to quit smoking, tried to take better care of himself. Debbie, who was suffering from stress of her own, began having attacks too, one time hyperventilating so badly that Larry took her to a hospital.

Through it all, Tosi could not get the murder off his mind. So many unanswered questions remained. How had it all started that night? Had George talked his way into the house by offering to help Karen move her plants? Or was it possible that she'd caught him gazing through one of the windows? Tosi wasn't sure. He still wondered whether Karen had been forced to put on the black teddy, and what had happened to the white teddy that David could no longer find, and what it was that apparently had driven George back to the house the following evening.

After all this time, it seemed doubtful that any more light would be shed on these issues. Then one day something happened.

It was the last week in April 1987. The trial was now scheduled to be heard in Bartow, the seat of Polk County, about thirty-five miles east of Tampa. It was to begin in early June, just five weeks away. Tosi was at the Gulfport Police Station when a woman came in to pick up a report. They started talking, and she mentioned that she knew him. When Tosi had trouble placing her, she reminded him that she and her son and daughter had once lived in Gulfport, on Fifty-third Street, across from the city's police and fire stations. Her daughter's name, she said, was Tonja. Tonja Dishong.

Suddenly Tosi remembered how, months before, he had searched in vain for the young woman named Tonja. Now, he asked the mother if her daughter had ever known George Lewis.

Yes, she said.

That was it. Tosi had not found Tonja. Tonja had found him.

She came to the station for an interview on May 6. She was an attractive nineteen-year-old woman with dark brown eyes and curly dark hair that fell past her shoulders and a wisp of a figure that was the envy of her friends. She weighed ninety-three pounds and had a twenty-one-inch waistline; sometimes people asked her if she was anorexic.

Tosi asked her about the summer of 1984, when she and Lewis were together. He wanted to know, for one thing, whether George had ever given her anything. Tonja said yes. As a present he had given her a nightie. It was a white teddy, she said, with lace in the front. But there had been a problem with it. Even though it was marked a size "small," it was too big on her. Not that Tonja had complained. She thought it was sweet that George had been thinking of her.

Tosi asked Tonja if she still had the teddy.

Yes.

He asked if she would bring it to him.

Yes.

Twenty-two

One night in May, not long before the trial was to begin, Tosi ran into Joe Cigar at the Hilton on St. Petersburg Beach. Tosi was attending a panel discussion on the criminal justice system, and Ciarciaglino happened to be on the panel. Tosi was sitting in the audience, surrounded by other law enforcement officers, when a woman stood up and asked Ciarciaglino a question. She wanted to know how he could defend accused criminals. How did he sleep at night?

Ciarciaglino grinned and gave the members of the audience the answer he knew they wanted. He lifted his arms, shook them a little so the sleeves of his suit jacket dropped, then stuck out his hands. Wrapped around his left wrist was a gold watch studded with tiny diamonds that marked the hours of the day. Wrapped around the right one was a gold bracelet studded with diamonds that formed the scales of justice. He went on to give a long and serious answer about how he was part of a two-hundred-year tradition of Anglo-Saxon law and how defense attorneys protected the state from unjustly accusing the little guy and how it was easy to think of defense attorneys as snakes—easy that is, until you're the one on trial and you need a good lawyer.

But it was the joke that got the big response. When Ciarciaglino flashed the gold and diamonds, the audience burst out laughing. Not Tosi.

Larry liked Joe and respected him. But soon the two of them would be together in court in Bartow. Soon Ciarciaglino would be trying to prove that Tosi and the Gulfport police had bungled the most intensive investigation in the department's history and had arrested an innocent man. Now, after discovering Tonja Dishong, Tosi was more convinced than ever that he had arrested the right man.

Tonja had told Tosi all about the white teddy. She had sat in his office and told him everything she could remember about George Lewis.

To Tonja, George had always seemed like a nice guy.

She doesn't remember exactly when they started dating. She thinks it was within a week or two of the murder. The day they met, Tonja was on her front lawn in a bathing suit, throwing a Frisbee to her dog, Critter. Lewis was driving by in his pickup truck when he saw her. He took a good look at her, she says, and waved. When she waved back, he hit the brakes and backed up the truck.

He told her his name was George.

"Really?" she said. She didn't think anybody had a name like that anymore.

"Yeah," he said. "George."

He told her he worked at the fire station across the street and asked her if she wanted to go dancing.

"I don't dance," Tonja said.

George said he would teach her.

"How old are you?" he asked.

"How old do you think I am?"

"Twenty-three or twenty-four."

"You're close." Tonja was fibbing. She was only sixteen. But she didn't want to scare him away. "Are you married?" she said.

George looked at her. "What makes you ask that?"

"You look like you may be married."

"I'm not."

He was telling the truth. He and Glenda were not married yet. In fact, it was right around then that Glenda moved out of the house. In their early days together, Tonja noticed that George

222

wouldn't give her his home phone number. He told her not to worry. He said he would stop by and see her sometime.

It was a promise he did not hesitate to fulfill. He came back the day after they met, and the two of them went out. After that they saw each other regularly. They went camping and swimming and hung out together. They had a good time. Tonja thought George was funny. He could bark just like a dog—he drove a neighbor's dog crazy with it—and he did a great imitation of Yogi Bear. He also liked to drive around in his truck. It had four-wheel drive, and sometimes he and Tonja would head out into the bush and careen around.

George had a tape deck in the truck and enjoyed listening to music as he drove. He loved Huey Lewis and the News and had a tape of *Sports,* their hit album. George's favorite was a song called "Walking on a Thin Line," the popular tune with the chorus that goes, "Don't you know me, I'm the boy next door, the one you find so easy to ignore." When the song came on, George would play it loud. If Tonja was talking, he'd raise a finger to his lips so she'd be quiet.

One night George and Tonja were talking in his driveway, sitting on the tailgate of the truck, when the subject of Karen Gregory's murder came up. Tonja was afraid, knowing the killer had not been caught. She asked George where the murder had happened. He pointed across the street to the white house. Karen's boyfriend, he told her, had been out of town that night.

"It was his fault for leaving her like that," George said. "Because he knew what kind of neighborhood it was."

Tonja didn't think the neighborhood was so bad. Except for the murder, there didn't seem to have been much crime. And if it were so dangerous, she wondered, why would George be living there? They talked about what kind of person the murderer must have been. Tonja said the man would have to be pretty sick. George said that if they ever caught the guy, they should tie a rope around his genitals and hang him from a tree.

The murder came up frequently in their conversations. George liked to kid her about it.

"Don't forget to lock your doors," he'd say when he took her home. "There's a killer on the loose."

George and Tonja were comfortable with each other—comfortable enough that they opened up and talked about all sorts of things. Tonja eventually confessed that she wasn't twenty-three, and George began dropping references to someone named Glenda. When Tonja asked who she was, George said she was just someone he went dancing with. He was more open, however, when it came to stories out of the past. Sometimes Tonja wasn't sure whether to believe him. George told her that he had once had an affair with a woman who was a teacher. He said he liked older women. They knew all the tricks, he said.

Not that their conversations were always so wild. George talked about how much he loved kids and how he hated to see the way some parents treated them. He talked about his father, who was fighting cancer at the time, and how much it hurt to see him suffer. Often George talked about being a firefighter. He said he'd wanted to become one so he could help people. But he'd had to wait a long time before being accepted into the St. Pete fire department. The department, he said, kept hiring "niggers" first, even though he was just as qualified. George made other racial comments as well. One day he made a joke about how if you ever wanted to hit a black man, you better aim for his shins, because hitting him in the head wouldn't do any good. Another time, out at St. Petersburg Beach, he and Tonja saw an interracial couple walking hand in hand. Tonja said she thought it was gross, and George agreed.

To Tonja it seemed that George did not like the color black, period. She found that out one time when he saw her in a black nightie.

"You shouldn't wear that," he said. "Nice girls don't wear black."

"Why not?" said Tonja. "I'm a nice girl, and I wear black."

"It's just . . ." He struggled for words. "You know."

George had no problem with the color white, though. That was the color of the teddy he gave Tonja when her seventeenth birthday rolled around in late July. The two of them were going camping, and George had put it inside a bag with some supplies for their trip. He pulled it out and held it up for her by the shoulder straps. "Happy birthday," he said.

Tonja kidded George about how foolish he must have felt going into a store to buy the teddy. George teased her right back, saying how cute the sales clerk had been and how he'd thought of asking her to model it. George loved it when Tonja wore the teddy. She didn't mind wearing it, because she knew it made him happy. The two of them got along well. Sometimes he was a little risqué for her tastes—she politely declined his offer to take part in a sexual threesome—but he was never violent with her, and he never forced himself on her. She thought he was sweet.

That September Tonja fell in love with someone else. She and George remained friends and kept in touch, even after Glenda moved back into the house and they got married and had Tiffany. When the baby was about eight months old, George brought her over one day. Tonja could tell that George was crazy about his daughter. It was obvious from the way he held her and kissed her.

Tonja looked at her former boyfriend, showing off his little girl. "I bet you're a very good daddy," she told him.

"I plan to be," he said. "The only thing that could take me away from her is the Man Upstairs."

While Tonja talked, Tosi took notes. He wrote on a single piece of paper, veering all over the page in a tiny, cursive scrawl. He'd scribble a few words at the top, then a few more at an angle in one of the corners, then a few more down the side.

> . . . gave white nightie . . . didn't like black . . . was boyfriend's fault cause he left her in what he knew was bad neighborhood . . . Don't you know me, I'm the boy next door . . .

Tosi wanted to know as much as possible about the white teddy. Tonja told him that when George gave it to her, it appeared to be new. He had taken it out of the bag with the supplies for their camping trip. There was a receipt in the bag; she wasn't sure what the receipt was for, but she'd noticed that it listed several items. She thought there had been a tag on the teddy itself.

Tonja asked why Tosi wanted to know so much about this. "I can't really explain that right now," he said.

She brought the teddy to the station five days later, on May 11. She and Tosi talked some more. This time Tonja said she wasn't certain there had been a tag on the teddy.

Tosi called David Mackey and said he had a piece of clothing he wanted David to see. David asked where it had come from. Tosi said he couldn't tell him that right now.

They met in Tampa. Tosi showed the teddy to David. It looked, David said, just like the one Karen had bought herself for her birthday.

"Larry," he said, "that is exactly the way I recall the teddy. The lace on it and everything is exactly as I remember."

Tosi then went to Karen's sister Kim, who still lived in Dunedin. Kim remembered Karen talking about how she'd bought a white teddy, but Kim had never seen it. Kim did know one thing, though. She knew what Karen had liked—they had often traded clothes—and she said that the teddy looked like something Karen would buy.

"This is her," Kim said.

Tosi asked what size Karen would have worn.

A small, Kim said.

It was the spring of 1987. Karen had been dead for three years. Since then the criminal justice system had lumbered forward on a path designed to reveal the truth of what had happened that night. Whether anyone was any closer to the truth, after all this time, was a matter of opinion. By now the case file had grown so large it was kept in a cart that was wheeled in and out of court. A growing line of judges had presided over at least twenty hearings. Close to one hundred witnesses had been questioned under oath in depositions. And now, after the aborted jury selection, the trial was about to begin again in Bartow.

This time William Walker would not be the presiding judge. There had been a choice to make. Walker could have gone with the Lewis case to Polk County, leaving it to someone else to manage the other cases on his docket. Or he could have stayed in Pinellas, handling his regular caseload while another judge—perhaps a retired one with time to spare—presided over the Lewis trial. So it had been decided that it would be easier for everyone if Walker handled the many cases and let his replacement handle the one. Someone else would have to be found to go to Bartow.

Now, after watching the criminal courts system closely for more than a year, Karen's family and friends were disillusioned. In court, it seemed to them, the facts did not matter much. What seemed to matter were cleverness and intimidation and the art of massaging the rules. They were tired of the delays and the diversions and the hearings, where the prosecution and the defense maneuvered for strategic advantage as if they were playing an elaborate chess game. They were sickened by how Karen and her death seemed secondary amid all of the squabbling and the performing. They were disgusted that the defense had tried to dig up private details of Karen's life, and it frustrated them that the system so often seemed to treat those who cared about Karen as an irrelevant nuisance.

It was obvious to David and the others that the system was geared almost exclusively toward the accused. As David put it, every door was held open for George Lewis but closed to those who cared about Karen. If her friends wanted in, if they wanted to be heard and be taken into account, David said they had to keep pounding on the doors.

At the same time, those close to Karen were still dealing with the emotional aftermath of the murder. David kept imagining he saw her. He would be out driving and he'd see a white Volkswagen Rabbit, and behind the wheel would be a woman with long brown hair. He would see the back of her head, and he'd speed up so he could pull alongside and see her face. On many mornings he would wake up and have to decide whether he wanted to continue living that day. He thought of killing himself in a car accident, taking an overdose, poisoning himself with carbon monoxide. It seemed easier than trying to go on.

Karen's brother Mark struggled against fear. If his wife made an angry gesture at a bad driver on the road, he would yell at her. How did she know the guy wouldn't get out of his car and come after her? How did she know the guy wasn't going to pull out a knife? Karen's murder had changed the way Mark looked at everything and everyone around him. He had never noticed before how much violence there was in the world. He had never really cared. Now it seemed he was constantly reading about some nut putting cyanide into food or some guy pulling out a gun in a bar and opening fire. It seemed that people were out there slaughtering one another every day.

He tried going to a counselor, but the counselor didn't seem to take him seriously. He seemed to believe that Mark was inventing this elaborate story about the murder of his sister.

"Relax," the man said.

Roy, Karen's other brother, would go to a movie at night and be terrified to leave and walk out into the dark. He'd open the newspaper, read through the obituaries, and be shocked at the number of people who were dying. One day he saw an article about a man who had killed his wife and two sons, and it overwhelmed him to realize that these were not just names in the paper but had once been real people.

Memories of Karen haunted Roy. One day he took her pictures down off his apartment's walls. It was too hard to look at her. But that wasn't enough. Roy kept moving from one apartment to another, selling his furniture every time so he could make a clean start. He was trying to hide. He didn't want to talk to his friends. He didn't even want to talk to his mother or his brother, both of whom did not live far away. He did not want to acknowledge that he was part of a family touched by murder. In the morning he'd wake up and tell himself that today he was going to try to be a human being again. At night he'd drink in front of the TV. If the phone rang he wouldn't answer it. He was sure it was someone calling with more bad news. Things became so painful for Roy that he, like David, considered suicide. He thought about driving off one of the bridges that stretched across Tampa Bay. He imagined driving onto it late at night, reaching the crest, turning the wheel of his car toward the rail, and plunging into the black water.

Sophia, Karen's mother, broke into tears at the mention of her daughter's name. Sophia, who now lived in Dunedin during the winter months, still wondered, after all this time, why Karen had not managed to escape her attacker. Karen was strong, Sophia told herself. She could have made it. All she had to do was fight back. Some days Sophia was so depressed she did not have the energy to put on her clothes. She would sit around in her bathrobe, hoping that it had all been a mistake and that any time now the phone was going to ring and Karen would be on the other end of the line.

Kim wanted to talk about what had happened to her sister. But when she brought it up, people would get quiet and look away. It was as if they thought it distasteful of her to mention such a thing.

"Get on with things," they would tell her. "Put it behind you."

Kim could not. She tried seeing a counselor, as Mark had, but it only made her feel worse. The counselor was a nice enough woman, but when she heard what Kim was going through, she had no idea what to say. Kim had not even told her the worst of it. She had not told her about the nightmares or how she was plagued with the memory of what Karen had said after they saw *Looking for Mr. Goodbar* together.

"*I never want to die like that.*"

Kim didn't think the counselor could handle it. The woman couldn't even handle the sanitized version. She sat there listening with tears in her eyes and her mouth wide open.

"Oh my God," she said. "Oh my God."

Eventually Kim did find help. She found it through Lula Redmond, a Pinellas County family therapist who specialized in grief therapy. In the fall of 1986 Redmond had begun conducting something unusual—therapy groups for homicide survivors, people who have lost a loved one in a murder.

Redmond, who had counseled many homicide survivors over the years, knew that what Kim and the others were going through was all too common. Year after year, in tens of thousands of murder cases, friends and family members are left to drift through what has been described as "a realm of unresolved grief." Though victim advocates have long pushed for better treatment of crime victims, the plight of homicide survivors has only recently been recognized. Too often they struggle alone, isolated from those around them, unable to find anyone who can relate to what they are feeling. Redmond wanted to end the isolation. She wanted to bring homicide survivors together so they could see that they were not alone and so they could find ways to deal with their loss.

In December 1986, not long after the four-day series of stories on Karen's case, the *St. Petersburg Times* published an article about homicide survivors and the therapy groups Redmond was organizing to help them. Sophia and Kim decided to call Redmond. Sophia resisted initially, but Kim pushed her to do it.

"Mother," she said, "you've got to do something."

Redmond also was talking to David and Anita. Sophia, who was nervous about opening up in front of the others, agreed to work with Redmond in private sessions. It was not going to be an easy experience for any of them. Anita, for one, did not think the group would work. She had felt lost for so long that she doubted she would ever feel better. She wondered, as she put it, if she would ever find a way back to herself. The idea of walking into a roomful of other homicide survivors overwhelmed her. She did not know if she could face the fact that there was so much real horror in the world.

It was clear that the group would not be any picnic. For twelve weeks they would be traveling through difficult terrain, forcing one another to confront painful memories and emotions. But if they did not confront this pain, Redmond said, they would never put it behind them.

"It's a wound, and you've got to clean it out before it can be healed," she told them.

Their group had begun in February 1987. The members met every Tuesday night in a midcounty office building. Redmond was there, along with two other therapists who were learning to work with people who had lost someone in a murder. The rest of the group was made up of eight homicide survivors—David, Kim, Anita, and five others. The first night, they introduced themselves. There was a man whose twenty-four-year-old son had been stabbed through the heart in a bar. The son had not been carrying any ID at the time, so his body had lain unidentified in the morgue for days. There was a woman whose nineteen-year-old son also had been stabbed to death. There was another woman whose seventeen-year-old son had been shot through the neck.

Oh my God, Kim thought. These people are just like me.

Together the members of the group described their nightmares, both real and imagined. They talked about the moments and days immediately after the murders, when they felt the ground disappear beneath them, when they shuffled numbly through police stations, funeral homes, and cemeteries. They talked about the long years that followed, when their friends grew tired of hearing about it, when they retreated into their homes and hid, when they woke screaming in their beds. They remembered all of the things they wished they'd had a chance to tell the person who had been murdered, all of the unfinished business between them that had been left hanging. They carried on imaginary conversations with the people who were gone, berating them for not realizing how dangerous the world was, telling them how much they wished they could hear their voices and their footsteps in the hall again. They traded stories of wandering through a court system where defendants seemed to have all the rights. And they talked about their anger. They made lists of all of the people and things that had made them angry. Anita wrote hers so violently that the pen almost ripped the page. Her list included:

- The neighbors who had not called the police.
- The police officers who had left it up to Anita and her friend Michaela to try to clean up Karen's blood inside the house.
- Judge Walker.
- The *St. Petersburg Times.*
- George Lewis.
- Lewis's lawyers.

One night the members of the group talked about their fantasies of revenge. They described what they would do if they had free rein over the person who'd killed their loved ones. David, Kim, and Anita listened to one group member talk about cutting up the person into little pieces. They heard another member talk about burying the person alive in an anthill. It was frightening for the people in the group to admit that they had even fantasized about such things. But almost all of what they talked about was frightening. One night Anita broke down outside the building where the group met. The building was beside a crematorium, and as Anita pulled up in her car she noticed black smoke pouring from the crematorium's chimney. She already was dreading that night's session, and when she saw the smoke, she was instantly reminded that Karen's body had been cremated. Anita began to sob.

Slowly, though, she and the others realized that the sessions were helping. They knew now that there were ways to accept the loss and move forward. There were ways to regain control. One of those ways was to not allow the court system to shut them out. David and Anita already understood this. From the day of the advisory hearing onward, they had insisted on attending as many of the court dates as they could, even when it meant standing in the hall outside. But Karen's sister and mother weren't sure they had the strength to sit in court and hear the testimony and look at Lewis. Redmond urged Kim and Sophia to go to the trial and find out. She said that if they did not go, they would always ask themselves if their presence could have made a difference. They needed to face their fear, she said. They needed to hear the facts—as Anita already had forced herself to do by reading the court file—rather than spend the rest of their lives wondering what had really happened that night in the dark. Painful as the process would be, Redmond said, it was better to know the truth.

As the weeks went by, Kim and Sophia decided Redmond was right. Kim said she wanted to be Karen's eyes and ears and voice. Every time Lewis stepped into the courtroom, she wanted him to see her face and remember what had happened to her sister. Months before she had been too terrified of the man to even look at him. Now she was determined not to be afraid any longer. She said she was going to court to take back her life.

By now it was late May. Only a couple of weeks remained before the trial. But someone new would be joining the prosecution team in Bartow. Along with Beverly Andrews and Bill Loughery, there would now be a third assistant state attorney handling this case. His name was Richard Mensh.

It would have been hard to find a more experienced prosecutor in Pinellas County than Dick Mensh. He'd been with the state attorney's office for twenty-five years, and for the last eighteen he'd been the office's chief assistant. Mensh liked to call himself an "old workhorse." It wasn't a bad description except he wasn't so old—only fifty-three. Still, he'd spent more time in court than some people spend on the planet, fighting his way through one trial after the other. He was not a man known for backing down. Once he had refused to drop out of a trial even though he was struggling with pneumonia. He'd waited for the jury to return with its verdict, then gone to a hospital.

As chief assistant, Mensh also had worked with his share of young prosecutors over the years, including Joe Ciarciaglino. Joe and Dick were old friends. In those early days in the state attorney's office, Ciarciaglino had learned a great deal from Mensh. Dick, he said, was his mentor. It showed, too. Echoes of the old workhorse's style surfaced all the time in Ciarciaglino's. Both knew how to claim territory in a courtroom; both were masters at talking to a jury. Mensh had a soft Florida accent—he was from Indian River County, over on the state's east coast—and he portrayed himself as an unassuming cracker in search of simple fairness from honest citizens. Ciarciaglino, on the other hand, had been born in New York and sounded like it, at least when he was sitting in his office telling stories. In front of a jury, though, his northern accent tended to disappear, only to be replaced by the country twang and an overwhelming tendency to refer to people as "folks."

There was one thing different about the two lawyers: Mensh did not handle that many criminal trials anymore. But here he was, about to return to court to battle with his former student in the Lewis case. Nobody proclaimed that Mensh was joining the prosecution's trial team expressly for that purpose. But Karen's friends and family assumed that one reason he was there was because he had taught Ciarciaglino and therefore understood how he worked—and how he could be beaten—better than almost anyone else. With Mensh around, it would be hard for Ciarciaglino to seize control of the courtroom, as he had during the first attempt at trial.

As Beverly Andrews would later put it: "You need a good ole boy to counteract a good ole boy."

There had been another personnel change as well. Now that Judge Walker had decided to step aside from the case, B. J. Driver, a retired judge who'd left the bench only two years before, had been appointed as the sixth judge on the case. Driver was a straight-talking barrel of a man, a former Marine who had fought starvation and the Japanese at Guadalcanal. At sixty-four, with sharp eyes and an air of quiet determination, he still carried himself like a soldier. During more than two decades on the bench in Pinellas County, he had gained a reputation as a tough, no-nonsense judge who ran his courtroom firmly, efficiently, and without a trace of tolerance for lawyers who stepped out of line. He handed out so many long prison sentences that Florida inmates used to call him a "time machine."

"He believes in a lot of time," explained one of them. "They call him the hanging judge."

It came as no great surprise, then, when the defense moved to get rid of him. Ciarciaglino filed a motion, stating that the judge was prejudiced against him and might treat his client unfairly. To support this argument, Ciarciaglino cited several instances in which the two of them allegedly had clashed. One time, Ciarciaglino said, Driver had become visibly upset and stormed off the bench after Ciarciaglino had accidentally shown up late for a court appearance. Now, given this personal history, Ciarciaglino said Driver should disqualify himself from this case.

The judge considered the issue at a hearing in Clearwater on May 20. Mensh urged that the defense's request be denied. It appeared, he said, that the defense's biggest complaint with Driver was how tightly he ran his court. If Driver said a case was to begin at 8:30 A.M., Mensh pointed out, that did not mean 8:31. There was no valid reason, he said, for the judge to disqualify himself.

Ciarciaglino sat quietly a few feet away and let Bob Paver argue the defense's side. Paver said Judge Driver had little choice but to grant the motion. As every lawyer in the room well knew, one of Florida's rules of criminal procedure virtually requires judges to disqualify themselves when the prosecution or the defense accuses them of such prejudice. It does not matter whether a judge believes the accusation is true, so long as the accusation complies with the rule. Furthermore, the courts have upheld this rule, especially in capital cases. If Driver denied the motion and stayed with the case, Paver said, any conviction might well be reversed on appeal.

Finally Driver spoke. The rule, he said, was a bad one. It was bad, he said, because it allowed lawyers to shop around for judges—something, he hastened to add, that may or may not have been happening in this case. Still, the rule was the rule, and he was bound to follow it.

"It's an anomaly that the touchstone of the law is to seek the truth," he said. "But in this case, the Supreme Court tells us that truth is immaterial and irrelevant, and we shall not even consider the truth."

With that Driver granted the motion. He was disqualifying himself so that another judge—one more to Ciarciaglino's liking, he said, with just a touch of derision—could take over the case. Then he turned to Ciarciaglino.

"Over the years I've observed you, I never dreamed you were so sensitive," said the judge, a hint of a smile playing at the corners of his mouth. "I always had the impression that what would embarrass you would cause blisters on a washbucket."

The search for a new judge—judge number seven, now—did not take long. On May 20, the same day Driver stepped down, Circuit Judge Crockett Farnell was appointed to replace him. Despite the short notice, Farnell said he could begin with the trial on June 2, only one day later than planned.

At forty-seven, Farnell was among the most respected members of Pinellas County's judiciary. He was known as a judge who did what he thought was right, even if it meant taking some heat. He understood what it was like to be a criminal lawyer, slugging it out in what some have called "the pit." Before becoming a judge five years earlier he had practiced law for fifteen years, first prosecuting people as an assistant state attorney, then representing them as a defense attorney.

Farnell came from a family that had lived in Florida since the 1800s. He was also a pilot, the owner of two cattle ranches, an avid jogger who logged six miles a day, and a colonel in the U.S. Marine Corps Reserve. Farnell was proud of being a Marine. He drove a pickup truck, and on the back was a bumper sticker that proclaimed *Semper Fi*—abbreviated Latin for the Marine motto ALWAYS FAITHFUL. Every year on November 10, the birthday of the corps, the same motto found its way onto a cake served at a party in the judge's office. He'd invite lawyers and clerks and other judges to celebrate, cutting the cake with his Marine sword and playing "The Marines' Hymn" on a portable cassette deck.

That was Farnell. He had a dry but persistent sense of humor—persistent enough that it survived even when the lawyers in front of him were trying to extract a pound of flesh from each other. "Are you going to live through this trial?" he'd say. "I'm worried."

He could get tough if he had to. But he did so quietly, calmly, and without a hint of desperation. He rarely raised his voice and he never pounded a gavel. He had a gavel—the Clearwater Bar Association had given it to him when he was sworn in—but he never brought it to court. Unneeded, it stayed in his office.

Having stepped into the Lewis case at the last moment, Farnell was not familiar with the complexities of the facts and their emotional undercurrents. He did not realize, for instance, that Lewis and Tosi had been friends. Nor was he aware of what was happening with the investigation even as he came onto the case. He did not know, in other words, about the sudden appearance of Tonja Dishong and the white teddy.

Lewis's lawyers were in the dark on that subject too. Ciarciaglino and Paver were making last-minute preparations to defend their client against a possible sentence of death in the electric chair. But no one had told them what Tosi had uncovered. No one had told them, because the prosecutors had not thought there was much to tell. Tosi had explained to them about finding Tonja and the teddy. He'd explained that this piece of clothing might be the one missing from Karen's belongings But he'd said he wasn't sure. He wanted to find the store where the teddy had come from.

Maybe there would be a receipt that could tell them whether it was Karen Gregory or George Lewis who had bought it. So far, though, Tosi had not found such proof.

Then, on Tuesday, May 26, David Mackey called the prosecutors, wanting to know if they were going to try to use the teddy at the trial. They said no. It was their understanding from Tosi, they said, that David could only testify that this teddy looked similar to the one Karen had bought. That wasn't solid enough, they said.

David couldn't believe it. Somehow there had been a breakdown in communication. He didn't think this teddy looked similar to Karen's, he told the prosecutors. It looked, he said, exactly like Karen's. He thought it was the same one.

The prosecutors were stunned. Now that they finally understood how sure David was, they moved quickly. They called the defense attorneys to notify them that the state had something new and intended to use it. To make it official they sent a messenger on that Wednesday to hand-deliver two pieces of paper to Ciarciaglino and Paver's office. One of the papers said that the state was hereby acknowledging the existence of an additional witness, namely, Tonja Dishong. The other said that the state was hereby acknowledging the existence of an additional piece of tangible evidence, namely, a woman's white undergarment, in care of Detective Tosi.

The trial was only six days away.

Part
Four

The Good Neighbor

Twenty-three

The second attempt at trial began on June 2. That Tuesday morning, the skies over Bartow were a canopy of blue, dotted with clouds. It was the kind of day when a murder trial seemed all the more unreal, when you stepped into court and were struck all the more vividly by the realization that you had entered a different realm.

Outside, people were getting on with the business of living—cleaning cereal off the kitchen counter, wiping the baby's nose, hurrying off to work in the car, hoping that the left rear tire would hold out another five thousand miles. But inside the Polk County Courthouse, men and women were gathering to dissect ugliness and death. They were there to examine the brutal murder of one human being and to consider whether another human being should now be ordered to die in the electric chair. It did not matter how civilized they tried to make the process appear, one of Karen Gregory's friends pointed out. What had brought them to this place was inherently uncivilized.

The courthouse sat in the middle of downtown Bartow on the busiest road in town. It was an old-fashioned courthouse with massive white pillars out front and a domed clock tower rising from the roof. Respectfully known as the Hall of Justice, it felt entirely different from the run-down criminal complex back in Pinellas. It had more character and personality; it seemed more intimate. It felt like a courthouse, not a factory.

When George Lewis arrived there early that morning, he did not look like a man on trial for his life; if anything he seemed exuberant. Dressed in a grayish brown suit, he sprang lightly up the courthouse steps with his wife and his lawyers behind him. The defense team had brought dozens of files stored in boxes, and Lewis took off his jacket, loaded the boxes onto a dolly, and carted them up to the second floor to the courtroom, smiling for a news photographer. He seemed supremely confident. Those who sat close to him in the days that followed, however, could see that his nails had been chewed to below the tips of his fingers, well past the point of bleeding.

Judge Farnell showed up shortly before 8:00 A.M., carrying his robe and a black nameplate. The prosecutors and defense attorneys were already waiting for him. "Morning, sports fans," he said.

They went down a corridor behind the courtroom to a dark vacant office that would serve as Farnell's chambers during the trial. They sat around a long table that occupied most of the room. Farnell found a cup of coffee and lit a Honduran cigar. He asked the attorneys if any problems had arisen.

"Other than what was just handed to us?" said Beverly Andrews, angrily waving a piece of paper. It was a motion from Ciarciaglino and Paver asking the judge to delay the trial. The motion said they needed the continuance because of their last-minute notification about Tonja Dishong and the white teddy.

Judge Farnell looked slightly bewildered. "What's a teddy?" he said.

Paver told him, explaining how Sgt. Tosi had found Tonja and the teddy in early May. The defense, Paver said, needed more time to investigate this potentially critical new evidence. Even the prosecutors could not say for sure where the teddy had come from, although it was clear they would suggest that Lewis had stolen it from the murder scene. Given all of these questions, Paver said, there was no way they could be expected to go ahead with the trial now. It wasn't fair, he said.

Andrews disagreed. The prosecution had notified the defense about the teddy, she said, as soon as its importance became clear. Dick Mensh also questioned whether this presented a genuine problem for the defense.

Farnell looked at the senior prosecutor. "I'm sure it's a genuine problem," the judge said. Still, he denied the motion to delay the trial. He said he would try to give the defense time to investigate the teddy as the trial progressed. The question of whether the item would be admitted into evidence—whether the jury would be allowed to hear of its existence—would be tackled later.

There was one more thing. The prosecutors had noticed a defense witness—Glenda Lewis—inside the courtroom. They wanted to know: Were Ciarciaglino and Paver planning to allow her to sit there during jury selection? In that case, some of Karen Gregory's friends who were on the witness list would want to watch the selection as well.

"We'd ask that the rule be invoked at this time, judge," said Ciarciaglino.

"Fair enough," said Farnell.

That was that. Just as before, anyone listed as a potential witness would no longer be allowed in the courtroom while the trial was in session.

"Okay," said Farnell. "Let's go then."

From his seat high at the bench, Farnell looked out over the courtroom.

The court reporter who would take down every word of the trial sat forward in her chair beside the jury box, her fingers poised over the keys of a stenograph machine. The prosecutors—Andrews, Mensh, and Loughery—were at their table, with stacks of files and law books at their feet. Lewis sat at the defense table with Ciarciaglino and Paver. In the audience, meanwhile, were some fifty prospective jurors, all looking expectantly toward the judge.

"Good morning, ladies and gentlemen," said Farnell. "How's everybody today? Happy to be here?"

Some murmurings rose from the audience.

"I'm glad to hear that. We're here this morning on the case of the *State of Florida vs. George A. Lewis*. Do any of you know Mr. Lewis?"

More murmurings. No.

"All right. We'll have him introduced further in a few moments. Do any of you know anything about the case? All right. Have any of you . . ."

The selection of twelve jurors did not take long. The lawyers began that morning, asking the same questions and twisting through the same maneuvers that had occupied them for four days when they'd tried to pick the jury in Pinellas County. Only this time Ciarciaglino did not have a chance to dominate the courtroom. Farnell presided with a calm and steady hand. And Mensh, Ciarciaglino's old mentor, was there to match his former student's every move. Out in the real world they were friends who shared small talk and bummed cigarettes off each other. One night during the trial they would even go out for a drink together. But here in court they remained adversaries. As Mensh later put it: "I don't mind kicking and gouging my best friend when it comes to representing the people of the state of Florida."

Now the two of them went to work. Ciarciaglino showed, as he had before, an uncanny ability to memorize the names of the prospective jurors. So did Mensh. As a stream of men and women moved in and out of the jury box, he chatted with them one by one, making it look as if it were the easiest thing in the world to mentally juggle the names of so many strangers. Ciarciaglino went to the bench and complained to the judge that the prosecutors were lecturing the jurors on the law instead of asking questions. Mensh went to the bench and complained that Ciarciaglino was sharing anecdotes with the jurors instead of asking questions. Ciarciaglino said he hoped the jurors wouldn't be prejudiced against him because he was "fat and ugly." Mensh stood up and reminded the people in the box that it was irrelevant whether Ciarciaglino was "a little overweight."

"Because we're not on trial," said Mensh. "We're lawyers only."

That was how it went. Ciarciaglino would take one step; Mensh would take another. It was a kind of dance. Not a particularly graceful dance, but one that required skill and instinct and a peculiar willingness—you only see it in court—to argue about anything. They went at it all day, broke for the night, then came back the next morning and began again. That day, Wednesday, they found a panel of twelve jurors. There were five women and seven men, ranging in age from twenty to sixty-nine, all Polk County residents. One was a cook at McDonald's, another was a bookkeeper, another a chemical engineer, another the athletic director for the local school system. None of them had heard of Karen Gregory or George Lewis; none had read the stories in the *Times*.

Up at the bench, the lawyers said these twelve would do fine.

"Do you want to excuse anybody?" Mensh said to Ciarciaglino. "I don't."

"He accepts the panel?" said Ciarciaglino. "We accept the panel."

"Quickly swear the panel," said Farnell.

"Before anybody changes their mind," said Mensh.

Out in the audience, Karen Gregory's mother listened quietly. Sophia had chosen a seat at the back of the room because she did not want to be conspicuous. She was wearing sunglasses because if she cried she did not want anyone to notice. The prosecutors had told the members of Karen's family that they would not be allowed to shed tears or become visibly angry, no matter how upsetting they found the testimony. Otherwise, the state could be accused of trying to use the family to sway the jury's sympathies.

Sophia had come to the courthouse with Kim. One of the first people they'd seen was Lewis. He was standing on the second floor, leaning against a railing, looking down in their direction. Sophia grabbed Kim's hand.

"It's him," she said.

She had never seen Lewis in person before. She knew that he had been released on bond, but she had expected that at the trial he would be handcuffed or accompanied by a bailiff. But there he was, wandering freely through the courthouse. Sophia looked up at him. She was afraid. But she did not turn around and walk away.

"I know I can do it now," she said to Kim.

The two of them walked up the stairs and sat down in the courtroom. They did not sit together for long, because Kim was soon informed that she would have to leave. Knowing that Tosi had questioned her about the white teddy, Ciarciaglino and Paver were listing Kim as a possible witness. So not long after the trial began, she was relegated to the halls with the others.

Kim was furious. There wasn't much she could testify about. After all, she had never seen the teddy and could not say whether it was the same as the one now in the prosecution's possession. She was sure that Ciarciaglino and Paver had no intention of calling her as a witness, that they just wanted to keep her out of the courtroom. Her mother would have to sit in court alone.

"Counsel for the defense?"

Ciarciaglino stood up, walked over to the jury box, draped an arm across a lectern, and gazed into the faces before him.

"Ladies and gentlemen," he said. "Always wait to the end. Things are not always what they appear to be."

By now it was Thursday, the third day of the trial. The prosecution and defense were delivering their opening statements, presenting to the jury two radically opposing views of what they expected the evidence to show. Bill Loughery already had described the state's case, telling how the police had ended up arresting Lewis. Now Ciarciaglino was giving the other side of the story—George's side.

The jurors would not believe, the lawyer said, what had happened once the police investigation began. Evidence, he said, had been destroyed. Two friends of Karen Gregory's—throughout his statement he took care not to use Karen's name, referring to her instead as "the decedent" or "the deceased"—had been allowed to clean the house only several hours after the body was discovered. Afterward detectives had been forced to go back to search for more clues. Meanwhile, he said, the jurors would hear nothing to prove that the deceased had been raped. The evidence merely showed that she had had sex. It did not show, he said, that she'd had sex against her will. At the same time, he said, it would become clear that the Gulfport police had been pressured to solve the case. Someone—he did not say who, but it was obvious he was speaking of David Mackey—had complained about the handling of the investigation.

"The evidence will show," said Ciarciaglino, "that they needed to arrest someone."

He acknowledged that Lewis, whom he called George, had given a number of statements to the police. But he did not say that these statements were conflicting. They were "progressive," he said. Later in the trial, he said, the jurors would need to hear from George himself about what had occurred.

"You are going to see that George Lewis . . . is not some heinous criminal lurking in the neighborhood, waiting to commit this crime," said Ciarciaglino. "He was a young man, caring about his to-be wife, his home place, his family, his friends, his neighbors."

The lawyer did not say who he thought the real killer was, but it was suggested by the end of the trial the jurors might have some ideas of their own.

After Ciarciaglino took his seat the judge looked back toward the prosecution table. "Call your first witness."

"The state," Loughery said, "calls Neverne Covington."

She had been waiting outside, in a side room off the hall. Just a few minutes before, she had looked at a photo of Karen. It had been taken on Halloween 1983, when Karen had transformed herself into the gum-smacking waitress with the towering, tilted beehive hairdo. When Neverne saw the photo now, she burst out laughing. She'd forgotten how funny Karen had looked that night. She'd forgotten that sensation of indestructible giddiness she had felt when the two of them were together.

Not that she hadn't tried to remember. She had fought to remember everything, had consciously worked to hold onto Karen's face inside her mind, to engrave every detail into memory—the piercing quality of her eyes, the thickness of her eyebrows, the way she hid her mouth behind her hand when she laughed. But all of that had been so long ago. Amid all of the battles in court, amid the relentless need she and the others felt to make their presence known at every step of the court case, bits of these memories of Karen had begun to slip away. In all of the muck and mire, Neverne said, they'd begun to lose her.

Neverne stared at the picture. Remember why we're here, she told herself. Remember that silly girl?

"Did you know Karen Gregory?"
"Yes."
"How did you know Karen Gregory?"
"She was my best friend."
Neverne sat in the witness box, listening carefully to Loughery's questions, hoping she wouldn't say anything wrong. She had worried about that for months. She wasn't a lawyer. She didn't know what was acceptable in court. She didn't want to cause a mistrial and force them to start all over again.

"Now, do you know the defendant, George Lewis?"

"I have not been formally introduced to him."

"Okay. How is it that you know him, if you do, or know of him?"

Neverne fixed her eyes on Lewis. "I know of him," she said, her voice rising with barely concealed anger, "because he is the person that's been indicted by the grand jury for Karen Gregory's murder."

Ciarciaglino and Paver rose to their feet.

"May we approach the bench?" said Paver.

"Come forward," said Farnell.

The lawyers hurried to the bench and congregated in front of the judge, speaking softly so the jurors and spectators could not hear them.

"At this time I move for a mistrial based on the witness's statement," said Ciarciaglino.

Farnell turned to Loughery. "You had better get your act together with the witness."

"I will try."

"I am not going to have that nonsense."

Sitting a few feet away, Neverne could not understand what she'd said wrong. Was someone suffering under the impression that Lewis had been charged with jaywalking?

"Judge," Paver said. "We press for the motion for mistrial."

The charge was no secret. Farnell already had informed the jurors that Lewis had been accused of murder. But the indictment was not evidence, and Neverne's remark, Paver said, had made it sound as if it were. His complaint, in other words, was that Neverne had made it sound as if the indictment could be considered proof that Lewis was guilty. Farnell said he understood. He denied the motion for mistrial but said he would try to fix the problem.

The lawyers left the bench.

"Ladies and gentlemen of the jury," said Farnell. "You are to disregard the witness's last answer. That is not evidence to be considered in the case. Take the jury out, please, Mr. Bailiff."

A bailiff took the jurors into the jury room at the back of the courtroom. Farnell told Neverne he understood that this was not the most preferable way to spend an afternoon. But they did not want to be forced to take the case to trial again, he said, asking her to pay close attention to the questions.

Neverne was still confused. She thought she had paid close attention to Loughery's question. Had he not asked her how she knew who Lewis was? "I don't understand. How else would I have answered that?" she said. "I thought I was stating a factual, objective statement, and I was trying to answer it as honestly and innocently as I possibly could."

"Fair enough," said Farnell. "But it involves a matter that the lawyers are concerned about, technically."

The jury was brought back into the room. Neverne began answering Loughery's questions again. She told how Karen had come to her house for dinner the night of the murder and how they'd talked and drunk wine and celebrated the fact that Karen had just moved into David's house. Loughery asked how much wine Karen had consumed. Neverne said she wasn't sure exactly, maybe three or four glasses.

"Did Karen tell you she was going anyplace else besides Mr. Mackey's house when she left?"

"No. She said she was going straight home and going to bed."

"Cross-examination?" said the judge.

Paver rose and walked toward the lectern. "Ms. Covington," he began. "You recall . . ."

Neverne had braced herself for this moment. She had thought that the defense attorneys might ask her questions designed to make it look as if Karen were somehow responsible for her own murder. If they did, Neverne had rehearsed an imaginary answer.

Excuse me. I'm confused. I thought George Lewis was on trial. Not Karen Gregory.

Now, sitting in the witness chair, Neverne tried to remain calm.

Paver wanted to talk about the wine Neverne and Karen had drunk that night. Did they drink some before dinner? Neverne said yes. Some more during dinner? Yes. After dinner too? Yes. Did Neverne think Karen had had enough to have been impaired?

"What specifically do you mean by impaired?" asked Neverne.

Paver did not want to play this game. "Did you feel," he said, "that she was affected by the alcohol, Ms. Covington?"

"In what way?"

"In any way."

"Perhaps she was relaxed. If you could be more specific, I could answer that more appropriately perhaps."

Paver moved on. "And can you tell us, did you have an occasion to engage in any activity, particularly in the front yard of Mr. Mackey's house?"

The question was vague, but Neverne understood what Paver meant. He was referring to the times she and David had practiced t'ai chi.

"Yes," said Neverne.

"And can you describe for the jury, please, what that activity was?"

"I took a couple of classes with another woman from David Mackey on t'ai chi ch'uan."

Loughery stood up to object. These questions were irrelevant, he said, asking to approach the bench. Once more the lawyers gathered briefly in front of the judge and argued in low voices. Once more the judge sent the jurors out of the room. It was a pattern that would be repeated many times in the next two weeks.

Farnell asked Paver to explain what t'ai chi ch'uan had to do with this case. Paver said he was trying to show that Neverne was practicing martial arts. He said such behavior from one of Karen Gregory's friends fit generally into Karen's lifestyle. Karen's lifestyle, Paver added, also included her listening to reggae music and smoking marijuana.

"Judge," said Loughery. "That is an absolute character assassination."

Paver stood his ground. Karen's taste for reggae music, he continued, was important because two local reggae musicians had once briefly been among the many suspects. Part of the defense's case, Paver reminded the judge, was that the police had arrested the wrong man. Perhaps, Paver suggested, the police should have further investigated these two musicians.

Farnell said he understood. He said that if Paver wanted to build a case along those lines, he'd have to do it later with his own witnesses. The judge, however, was willing to let the defense take a proffer from Neverne—to go ahead and ask her questions related to these matters now, while the jury was out of the courtroom. That way the judge could hear the testimony, then decide later if the jury should hear it too.

Once the jury was gone, Paver asked Neverne if she knew whether Karen had smoked marijuana.

"She told me she had used marijuana in the past. I was not

aware of her using marijuana throughout the course of my contact with her."

Paver asked Neverne if Karen had liked reggae music. Yes, said Neverne. And did Karen, he asked, frequent a bar that featured reggae music?

"How do you describe 'frequent'?"

"Ma'am, she went there, and they played reggae music, didn't they?"

"She went there on occasion."

David Mackey was the state's next witness.

"Mr. Mackey," said Loughery. "How old are you?"

"Thirty-two years old."

He looked older. His hair was graying at the sides and the muscles in his face were taut, as if he had forgotten how to relax.

David explained how he and Karen had started dating and how she had just been moving in with him that May when he left for the conference in Rhode Island.

"After that time did you ever see Karen again?"

"Not alive, no."

He could have told the jurors about the next time he did see her, at the wake. He could have described her in the casket, wearing the purple burial dress her family had picked out. But he was sure that if he mentioned such emotional details, the defense would move again for a mistrial. So he stuck to the barest of the facts. He explained that he was still in Providence when he learned that Karen had been killed in their home.

"Did you ever spend the night in that house again?"

"I never—no, I couldn't do that."

Ciarciaglino stood up. He wanted to approach the bench again. Standing in front of the judge, he quietly complained that this last comment from David was improper. It was designed, he said, to inflame the jury.

"Judge," said Paver. "We need a mistrial."

Farnell denied the motion. Before they left the bench, though, Loughery raised another issue. He was ready to ask David about the teddy Tonja Dishong had given the police. Did the judge think they should take a proffer of this testimony? Did he want to hear what David had to say, outside the jury's presence, before deciding whether it was admissible? Farnell said yes and asked the bailiff to take the jury out.

It still was unclear where the teddy had come from. But both sides were trying to find solid proof that answered the question. Sgt. Tosi had started the search himself before the trial. Since he would be busy in Bartow, he had asked Brinkworth to take over the investigation. Brinkworth was calling the teddy's manufacturer, the manufacturer's distributors, retail outlets. He was working overtime to find the store that had sold the item. If he could find the store, there might be a receipt. If he could find a receipt, it might say whether the teddy had been bought by a Ms. Gregory or a Mr. Lewis. Meanwhile, the defense's private investigator was calling the same places, trying to learn the same thing. So far neither side seemed to have made much progress. But they were still pushing forward.

"I want positive results," Tosi told Brinkworth. "I don't care if it takes you twenty-three hours a day. I want to find out where it came from."

With the jury out of the room, David talked about Karen's teddy, explaining how she had bought it in March 1984 and he had been unable to find it again after the murder when he searched through her belongings.

Loughery handed him a manila envelope.

"Let me show you what's been marked as state's exhibit number 24 for identification purposes. Could you open this, take it out and tell me if you recognize it?"

David pulled out the exhibit. It was the small white teddy from Tonja. Once more he said it looked like the teddy Karen had bought.

When Ciarciaglino went to the lectern, David's face tightened even further. Ciarciaglino asked David if he was saying that the teddy in front of him was the one he had seen Karen wear. Again, Ciarciaglino did not refer to Karen by name, instead calling her "your girlfriend."

David stared back coldly. "I am not telling the court that, Mr. Ciarciaglino. I am saying that this looked exactly like the one I recall seeing."

Was there anything about this teddy, Ciarciaglino said, that made it different from others of the same design? David said he'd never seen other such teddies. He said he wasn't sure he could answer the question.

"Well," said Ciarciaglino, sarcasm edging into his voice. "Let's see if we can't help you."

He told David to examine the teddy closely. Did David see any distinguishing tears or marks that allowed him to say this teddy was Karen's? David said no.

"That's all the questions I have," Ciarciaglino said.

Loughery stepped forward again. Was there anything particular about this teddy, he said, that David remembered as being unique to Karen's? David said yes. He said this one had thin shoulder straps, lacy material in the front, and a button in the front—all just like Karen's.

"Are you aware of what size Karen wore?"

"Yes. She would have worn a size small."

Ciarciaglino wasn't through yet. About that button on the teddy, he said. What made it different? David was confused. Different from what, he asked.

"Any other button in the world. I don't know, maybe your girlfriend made buttons, and those are her handmade buttons."

David looked at the button on the teddy in front of him. "It doesn't appear to be handmade by Karen, no."

"Anything about the lace that is unique from other lace?" said Ciarciaglino. "Perhaps your girlfriend was a maker of lace, or you were . . ."

Loughery tried to object. "Judge—"

Ciarciaglino cut him off. "I want to hear what he can tell us that says that's the one the lady was wearing."

"Go ahead with your questions," said Farnell.

Was there anything about this teddy, Ciarciaglino asked again, to prove that it was Karen's? Could David say this was the one?

"I imagine I can't."

"You *imagine?*" Ciarciaglino made it sound like a dirty word. "Can you tell us that's the undergarment you saw for certain? Yes or no."

"No, I can't, Mr. Ciarciaglino."

When the sparring was over, Ciarciaglino told the judge the teddy was clearly inadmissible. There was no positive proof that this piece of clothing before them had belonged to Karen Gregory. There wasn't even any proof, he said, that Karen's teddy had been stolen. David had seen her wear it only once, two months before the murder. She could have returned it, given it away, thrown it away.

Andrews said the prosecution did not need to prove beyond a doubt that the two teddies were one and the same. There was enough evidence to show they might well be the same, she said, and that was enough to make it admissible.

Farnell called a ten-minute recess to think it over. When everyone returned he announced his decision: the teddy was admissible.

The jurors were brought back in. For their benefit, David again went through his recollections of Karen's teddy. Again Loughery handed him the manila envelope. Again he said this teddy looked exactly like the one he'd noticed missing from Karen's belongings after the murder.

Loughery asked if he'd told anyone when he first realized Karen's teddy was missing.

"I told Detective Lawrence Tosi of the Gulfport Police Department."

"And when was it you would have told him?"

"It would have been sometime probably in June or early July of 1984."

Then it was Ciarciaglino's turn.

"Good afternoon, Mr. Mackey."

"Good afternoon, Mr. Ciarciaglino."

The defense attorney reminded David that they had met at a deposition the past August. Ciarciaglino had asked questions; David had answered. Did he remember? David said yes.

Ciarciaglino had a transcript of the deposition with him at the lectern. He told David he was turning to page ninety-two, line thirteen. A few feet away, Loughery pulled a copy of the same transcript out of the prosecution's files. He flipped through it, searching for the page. Ciarciaglino watched him.

"Let's wait for Mr. Loughery," he said.

Loughery found the page, and Ciarciaglino turned back to David and began reading aloud.

Q. So you found—at no time have you ever found anything missing from that house that you thought should be there?
A. No.
Q. And from that house, I include her possessions.
A. No.

Ciarciaglino asked David whether he remembered those questions. Yes. He asked whether David had been given a chance to read over the transcript and make corrections. Yes.

David shifted in the chair. "May I clarify one thing, Mr. Ciarciaglino?"

"Sure."

When those questions had come up during the deposition, David said, they'd been talking about items that could have been taken as valuables or weapons. When he'd said nothing was missing, he said, he'd meant no items of that nature. "Frankly," David said, "I didn't think about the teddy at that time. I had already told the police about it. I mean, that was not new information."

Now that the jurors were back in the room, Ciarciaglino was more gentle with his questions. The sarcastic edge was gone from his voice. Gone, too, were the caustic references to "your girlfriend." Now Ciarciaglino spoke politely of "Ms. Gregory."

Soon it was Loughery's turn again. Quickly, he tried to remove any impression that David might have invented his story. Loughery again asked David to explain that he had told the police—specifically, Sgt. Tosi—about the missing teddy.

"Is there anybody else you can recall you told about this missing garment?"

"I told several members of Karen's family, yes."

"Do you recall telling a lady named Doris Hajcak?"

"Yes, I do."

"Was this prior to the deposition?"

"Oh, absolutely. Yes, sir."

A few minutes later David was done. He stepped out of the witness box and walked from the courtroom to join Neverne and Kim and the others out in the hall. The jurors, meanwhile, had been given a new name to think about. Loughery had asked David about Doris Hajcak, one of the psychics whom David had consulted in the long months after the murder. The jurors did not know who she was, of course. No one had told them. Loughery didn't think it was necessary. The prosecution, he felt, had already made it clear David was telling the truth.

Ciarciaglino knew who Hajcak was, though. She was on his list of witnesses. In fact, she already had told the defense about her talks with David. She'd even handed over tape recordings of every session the two of them had had. On one tape, made on November 6, 1984—long before he would have had any reason to lie about such a thing—David can be heard talking about how he couldn't find a piece of Karen's clothing. He describes it as white and like a night garment. He says he doesn't know if Karen might have misplaced it or somehow lost it when she was moving into his house.

"But that's just about the only thing that turned up missing," he says.

The courtroom lights were off. The jurors sat in the dark, watching a videotape flicker on a TV screen. A few feet away stood Dr. Joan Wood, telling them what they were seeing.

"We are now entering the house . . . The wooden front door with the smears of blood . . . Entering the living room, we could not see any blood on the carpet . . . Now, turning left into the hall, it's the first view we have of the body . . ."

The jurors were seeing the video that had been shot the day the body was discovered. They were being led through the house, room by room, with Dr. Wood as their guide.

". . . Again, past her, into the bedroom, in which the blood was on the bed. On the floor there in front of the white tennis shoes is a curved footprint in blood . . . The bed itself, with blood in at least two areas . . ."

Sophia, still in the audience, stared down at her lap. She did not want to look at the TV screen and the image of her daughter's body. But she wanted to hear the testimony.

The videotape ended. Wood returned to the witness stand to answer questions from Beverly Andrews. As the doctor began to speak, an investigator who worked with the state walked over to Sophia.

"Would you just step outside with me?" he said quietly.

Sophia followed him out. She had been warned that she might be asked to leave when the testimony became graphic. But as she stepped into the hall she was angry.

"I really don't want you to do that again," she told the investigator. "I know what I can take."

"We're only doing this for your own good," he said.

Sophia wasn't convinced. "I've been a grown-up now for thirty-some years," she said. "I know what happened to Karen, and I don't think you people know what I'm capable of taking. I'm not going to walk out with you again."

Inside the courtroom, Dr. Wood went on talking. She explained how at first, when she saw Karen's body curled in the hall, she had not been able to tell the nature of the injuries. Her first impression was that Karen had been beaten to death. But when Wood placed the body flat on the floor and looked closely, she saw that Karen had been stabbed in the neck.

"Did you later observe other wounds other than the stab wounds on the neck?" Andrews asked.

"Yes, but not until the neck was cleaned at the autopsy."

"What wounds did you observe then?"

"Cutting wounds upon the neck."

"Did you observe the cutting wounds on the victim at all at the scene?"

"No, not at all. I couldn't see them."

"And why couldn't you see them?"

"Because of the dried blood that was present all over the neck. I looked at it, along with several other people, and none of us saw them."

On cross-examination, Ciarciaglino asked Dr. Wood about some theories she had discussed when she was questioned under oath in her deposition, almost a year before. In the deposition she had talked about how she had considered the possibility that this might be a ritualistic murder and how she'd wondered about the unusual concentration of stab wounds around the neck; she also had mentioned that throat cutting is a method of killing sometimes found in murders committed by homosexuals. Now that they were in front of a jury, Ciarciaglino led Wood through some of this territory again—especially the fact that throats are sometimes cut in homosexual murders.

"And in this case," Ciarciaglino said, "there was an attempted cutting of the throat?"

"Yes," said Wood.

Even though he never said it out loud, it was obvious what Ciarciaglino wanted the jurors to think:

George Lewis has a wife. He's not homosexual. How could he have killed Karen?

Wood had already told the jurors how Karen's body had been found in the white T-shirt and the black teddy. Now Ciarciaglino asked Wood if she had found anything strange about that combination of clothing.

"A teddy, as the women on the jury probably know, serves as a form of slip," Wood explained. "And therefore, the way it was found, it had to be on over this undershirt, because the undershirt straps were in place. They were not removed to take the teddy down. So the teddy was over the top of the undershirt, and that's unusual, I believe."

Ciarciaglino asked Wood to talk about how much Karen had been drinking before the murder. A test of fluid from Karen's eye, the doctor said, had shown an alcohol level of .010 grams per deciliter—a relatively small amount, equivalent to about half a drink. But another test had been run on Karen's blood.

"And the results of that, please?" said Ciarciaglino.

"The result of the blood test," Wood said, "was .090 grams percent, or 90 milligrams percent."

That was high—just short of a .10, the blood-alcohol level at which it's illegal to drive in Florida.

Again, the unspoken message from Ciarciaglino was clear.

Are you listening? Remember the wine at Neverne's house? Karen might have had too much to drink that night.

Once it was her turn to ask questions again, Beverly Andrews did her best to erase any doubts Ciarciaglino might have created. She asked Dr. Wood if throat cutting was also seen in cases that did not involve homosexuals. She answered yes. And were there other common characteristics of homosexual murders that were not found in this murder? Again, yes.

"So is it your opinion," Andrews said, "that a homosexual killing has anything to do with this case at all?"

"Not to me, it has nothing to do with it."

Andrews went on. Did Dr. Wood, she asked, know of cases in which an attacker forces a victim to put on a piece of clothing?

"Certainly."

The unspoken point:

Remember the black teddy over the T-shirt? Even Dr. Wood thought the combination was strange. Why do you think Karen would have done that? Why, unless . . .

"Are you aware that a teddy was discovered to be missing by the victim's boyfriend?"

"Yes."

Are you following this? One teddy—the black one—was found on Karen. Another teddy—the white one—was missing from her belongings. Has it occurred to you that the killer might have had some fixation with lingerie?

Ciarciaglino was standing up. "Judge," he said. "I object."

Farnell looked down from the bench. "The objection is denied."

Andrews wanted Wood to talk some more about alcohol levels. One test suggested Karen had been almost stone sober. The other suggested she'd been nearly drunk. Which was it?

Wood said the lower alcohol reading, taken from the eye fluid, was more accurate. Karen's body had been lying in the house for about thirty-one hours before the police arrived. When a body decomposes, Wood explained, bacteria and yeast can produce alcohol in the blood, raising the level found there. But the fluid in the eye is different. Compared to the bloodstream, which is subject to contamination, Wood said, the eye is a sealed chamber. So the eye test, she said, was the more reliable indicator of how much Karen had been drinking.

Andrews asked if they also had tested Karen's body for the presence of drugs.

"Yes."

"And what was the result of that?"

"It was negative."

Karen wasn't drunk that night. She wasn't high, either. Do not let Ciarciaglino confuse you.

Twenty-four

On Monday, June 8—the sixth day of the trial—one of the jurors asked to speak privately with the judge. Her name was Beverly Collier. She wanted off this case.

Collier, a thirty-two-year-old homemaker from Lakeland, was having back pain and felt distracted. Plus, the things she'd heard and seen in court—the descriptions of Karen Gregory's scream, the videotape from the murder scene, the photos of the body—were giving her nightmares.

"I'm not sleeping at night," she said back in chambers with Judge Farnell. "I've spent the last two nights hearing screams. I can't do this. I'm sorry."

"You know, this is an awfully important matter," said Farnell.

Collier was crying. "I know it is," she said. "I knew that it would bother me a little bit. I knew that I probably wouldn't sleep as well . . . I don't know what to say, Your Honor. The screams are very real."

Reluctantly, Farnell excused her. She was replaced by an alternate juror who had been chosen at the start of the trial in case something like this came up. The alternate had been sitting in a chair at the end of the jury box, listening to all of the witnesses. Now she moved into Collier's seat in the front row.

Nightmares had become part of the pattern of the case. Some of the neighbors who had heard Karen scream had thought it might have been someone calling out from a bad dream. David, meanwhile, had dreamed repeatedly that he was inside the house that night. In the dreams he was always too late. The attack would have just occurred, and he would be standing in the dark, trying to decide whether to stay with Karen or to run out and search for the killer. He never knew what to do. Then there was Cheryl Falkenstein, the young police officer who had found Karen's body in the hallway. She too had been bothered by nightmares; two months later, still disturbed by that memory, as well as by other problems with her job, she had left police work.

George Lewis was not immune, either. In his final statement to Tosi and Hanson, he'd told them that images of what he'd seen on the night of the murder kept entering his sleep.

To this day, I still get bad dreams about that.

The two sides of the case could not escape each other. As the trial moved forward, day after day, they were constantly thrown together. Inside the courtroom, Sophia sat only a few feet from Lewis. No longer did she stay in the back, hiding behind the sunglasses. She'd decided she'd had enough and had taken off her sunglasses and moved to the front. Neither she nor Lewis said a word to each other.

Outside the courtroom, Karen's friends and her sister wandered the same corridors as Lewis's wife, mother, and many of his friends. All of them were listed as possible witnesses, and since they had been relegated to the other side of the courtroom door, they had little choice but to wait, together but apart, within the confines of the halls and the second-floor lobby. They maintained a fragile, unspoken arrangement. Forced to spend days in the same space, they inevitably brushed shoulders, bumped into one another in the bathrooms, stood in line together at the water fountain. Still, they gave one another as much distance as possible, avoiding unnecessary contact, each side politely pretending that the other did not exist. The air almost shimmered with the effort.

Complicating matters was the fact that the design of the courthouse nearly forced them all to stare at one another. The lobby outside the courtroom—the place where they spent much of their time—was a rotunda, a circular room beneath the building's domed ceiling. The benches were arranged along the curving walls of the rotunda, so that they faced the center. Anywhere people sat, they naturally faced everyone else.

"This is the center ring," one person said. "This is the center circle."

At night some of them made the hour's drive back to Pinellas County. Others remained in Bartow, taking rooms at the Davis Brothers Motor Lodge, an inexpensive, no-frills motel that appeared to be the only motel of any size in the city. Judge Farnell stayed there, as did the prosecutors, the defense lawyers, and George and Glenda Lewis, who had a first-floor room only a few doors down from Sgt. Tosi. David, Neverne, and Anita had second-floor rooms overlooking the motel pool; in the evenings they'd look out and see George and Glenda swimming. It was an almost surreal sight. Lewis was on trial for his life, and yet there he was, laughing and splashing in the crystal blue water.

One night Karen's friends saw a strange man by the pool. It was hard to miss him. He was wearing typical poolside attire— shorts, a casual shirt, sunglasses—but next to his patio chair he had a briefcase. He sat there for hours, looking up at their rooms and the prosecutors' rooms, scribbling notes on a pad. At one point he held a newspaper as if he were reading it, even though it was long past dark and there was hardly any light by the pool. Was he supposed to be spying on them? Tosi, who saw him too, didn't think so. The sunglasses and the briefcase were too obvious. The man was down there, Tosi said, not to spy but to intimidate. Not to watch, but to let them know they were being watched.

At the beginning of the trial, when they were questioning prospective jurors, the lawyers had cautioned them to remember that this was real life, not "Perry Mason." Dick Mensh had asked the jurors to put aside whatever "garbage" they might have learned from TV.

"Can each of you tell me you'll do that?" he had asked.

The jurors had nodded.

It was a standard speech. Lawyers love to knock "Perry Mason." Don't expect real trials to be anything like that, they say. Don't expect surprise witnesses to pop up at the last minute; don't wait for a sudden confession from a tearful member of the audience. Those kinds of things, they say, don't happen in real trials, which, to hear them tell it, are conducted in an orderly manner according to strict rules.

This is only partly correct. Most real trials, it's true, are fairly dull. Even the most fascinating cases include long stretches of numbing boredom—hours of listening to highly technical testimony on ballistics and fibers, hours of waiting around in the halls, doing nothing. But almost all trials invariably have moments so outrageous or ridiculous or tragic that they surpass anything on television. Rules are routinely bent. Rules are routinely broken. And surprises are in fact sprung at the last moment. Witnesses make bald-faced lies. Judges occasionally snore at the bench. Lawyers, meanwhile, yell, deceive, badger, flirt, and mock at random. Time and again they attack the attorneys on the other side as if they're emissaries from the devil. Then, at the end of the day, they all go out together for beers.

A real trial, in other words, can be extraordinarily disorderly. It's not presented in a tidy package as it is on TV, where all of the loose ends are gathered before the final commercial. It's confusing and messy, just like real life. The facts of the case are almost never simple. Much of the time the "facts" that are presented aren't facts at all but theories, educated guesses, probabilities, likelihoods, insinuations, and points of dispute. That's what a trial is. Not just one dispute, but a thick fog made up of hundreds of tiny, interconnected disputes. The witnesses may be asked to tell the whole truth and nothing but the truth. But what's astonishing is how hard lawyers work at reshaping the truth to fit their needs. The whole truth is no good to them. It's too big and complex; it includes too many things that might hurt or complicate their case. What lawyers show the jury—or what they try to show the jury— is their own version of the truth, a carefully edited version containing only the "facts" they've chosen.

At the moment, the team from the state attorney's office was showing the jury its version of the case. For six days the prosecutors summoned their witnesses into court. They called in the neighbors who had heard Karen scream, and the FDLE blood pattern specialist who had been summoned to process the scene, and the detectives who had handled the initial stages of the investigation, and John Saunders, the FBI print expert who had sealed Lewis's arrest. One by one these people were brought in and asked to tell the jury what they knew.

The prosecutors tried to keep the story simple. They also

tried to keep it from straying into gray areas that might cause a mistrial. They did not ask their witnesses, for instance, to talk about how racism might have played a role in the attack. This possibility had been explored in the months before the trial, during the depositions. But no solid evidence had been offered to prove the connection—at least no evidence solid enough that it would be likely to stand up in court. So the prosecutors stuck to the basics of the case: Lewis's changing stories, his bloody bare footprint in the bathroom, the other bloody footprints on the hallway carpet, the white teddy.

Meanwhile, the murder investigation was continuing outside the courtroom. As witnesses appeared before the jury, both the prosecution and the defense were trying to track down the source of the teddy, trying to determine whether Lewis had stolen it from the house or bought it in a store, as he'd told Tonja.

Unfortunately, it was beginning to look as if the question would never be answered. Ciarciaglino and Paver weren't saying what their investigator had turned up, but it was a fair bet that they would hardly be keeping it a secret if their man had uncovered anything proving that Lewis was telling the truth. The prosecution's search appeared to have stalled as well. Brinkworth came to Bartow one morning and told the judge and the lawyers what he had learned. Testifying in chambers, away from the jury, Brinkworth said he had called the teddy's distributor and learned that in Tampa Bay this particular item of lingerie had been sold only at Robinson's outlets, including the one at Tyrone Square, a large shopping mall not far from Gulfport. Still, that didn't prove much. Either Lewis or Karen easily could have gone to the store and bought it. So Brinkworth had called Robinson's to find out whether the store still had receipts from the spring of 1984, when the teddy had been sold. Robinson's said no. The section inside the store that had stocked the teddy—Robinaire—had since been liquidated and all receipts had been destroyed.

The jurors were not aware that the search for the teddy's origins had hit a dead end. They were not even aware there had been a search in the first place. All they knew was that they were being told repeatedly to wait in the jury room, often for hours at a time, while some battle was waged out of their hearing.

Actually, the prosecution and defense were fighting dozens of battles outside the jury's presence. They were arguing about what the witnesses should say and not say once they took the stand. They were arguing about which pieces of evidence the judge should allow and which he should exclude.

At the same time, another explosive issue had entered the case. Late one afternoon during the first week of the trial, Ciarciaglino and Paver were reviewing some of the prosecution's items of evidence when they found an empty brown envelope. On the back was some writing that said the envelope had contained the diary of Karen Gregory.

The Gulfport police had come across the black-bound book, filled with Karen's neat handwriting, while searching through the house after the murder. The diary had been taken to the station for further study, and Tosi had read it, looking for leads, scanning for any mention of people who might have wanted to hurt Karen. He hadn't found anything, though. He had decided that the diary contained nothing pertinent to the investigation and had returned it to Karen's family. Now Ciarciaglino and Paver had stumbled onto the envelope in which the diary had been kept. Until that moment, they hadn't known a diary existed.

The two defense attorneys were furious. They told Farnell that this was yet another example of the police and prosecutors withholding evidence, just as Tonja and the teddy had been withheld. They said Farnell should declare a mistrial. They needed to read the diary, they said. What if it contained some clue crucial to their case?

The prosecutors said that argument was ridiculous. They said the diary contained nothing related to the case, only Karen's personal thoughts. The defense, they said, had no right to read it and invade her privacy.

"The diary," said Dick Mensh, "contains no evidence."

Ciarciaglino did not want to take the prosecution's word for that. He said that if Judge Farnell was going to be deciding whether it was important for the defense to read the diary, he needed to know more about the defense's case. But Ciarciaglino did not want to reveal any such strategy in front of the prosecution, so he asked the judge to let them talk to him privately, without the prosecutors. This request was made on Monday, June 8—the same day Beverly Collier asked to be excused from the jury.

The two sides had been arguing about the diary for days, first in chambers and now in the courtroom, while the jury was out. Karen's mother sat in the front row, listening in horror. Sitting beside her, just as shocked, were Karen's brothers, Roy and Mark, who had arrived at the trial that day from New York. All of them were incensed that the defense attorneys were trying to push their way inside the diary.

The fact was, though, that Ciarciaglino and Paver were defending a man on trial for his life—a man who was still presumed innocent until and unless the charges against him were proven. It was the duty of his lawyers to fight as zealously as the rules and the law allowed. And if they'd been free to discuss their case in open court, they probably could have reeled off a long list of explanations for why they wanted to delve into Karen's past. What if it led them to evidence that showed the killer was not George but someone else?

Yet, to those close to Karen it was hard to accept the notion that Ciarciaglino and Paver were merely defending a client. David and the others thought it was clear that from the start the defense had been manipulating the rules to attack Karen and the people who loved her. Now, with the move to open the diary, the family and friends decided they'd had enough. They wanted a chance to tell Farnell what they thought.

When this request was forwarded to Farnell, the defense protested. Ciarciaglino said they did not have the right. He said they should not be allowed to address the judge.

"May it please the court," said Mensh. "That's not my understanding of the law." A person didn't have to be charged with a crime, he argued, to win an audience with a judge.

Farnell agreed. Nevertheless, the diary put him in a difficult position. He didn't want to cause those close to Karen any more pain. But he also didn't want to take the chance that Karen's writings might hold something critical to the defense. He did not want to find out later that he had made a mistake and that the case would have to be tried again.

So on that same Monday, Farnell met in his chambers with Ciarciaglino and Paver, listening carefully as they shared their strategy and explained why they thought they should see the diary. Then, understanding what they had in mind, Farnell asked for the diary—Karen's family had brought it to court—and skimmed through it himself, trying to find out if it contained anything potentially relevant. He thought it did. Ciarciaglino and Paver, he decided, could see the book. They were not to tell anyone what it said and were not to talk about it in front of the jurors, but they

could read it and try to develop any leads they found. The two
lawyers began flipping through the pages.

Later that afternoon, after Farnell and the defense had returned
to the courtroom, Mensh reminded the judge that Karen's family
wanted to speak with him.

"Okay," said Farnell. "Just have them come forward."

Sophia was first. Talking quietly at the bench with the judge,
she said she felt they had suffered enough. There was no reason,
she said, for anyone to read her daughter's personal thoughts. It
was sacrilegious, she said.

"I feel that we have very few rights," she said.

"Ma'am?" said the judge.

"I feel that we have very, very few rights."

"I understand that. And I—"

"We're the only ones that can speak for her. It's very one-
sided, as far as I'm concerned. I have nothing else to say."

Karen's brother Mark stepped forward. "I just wanted to add,
my sister had a very—well, it would be easy to misconstrue the
way she lived her life."

"I understand that."

"Mr. Ciarciaglino is a very clever man, and if I was in his
position, I would—I can see where that journal, that diary could
be used to really paint a pretty inaccurate picture."

Finally it was David's turn. David said he knew what was in
the diary. Karen had not shown it to him when she was alive, but
once the investigation began, the police had asked him to read it.
So he knew, he said, that it contained nothing related to the case.
Ciarciaglino and Paver just wanted to read it, he said, so they
could search for dirt. David pointed out that he'd already lost
Karen, lost his home, lost any sense of privacy. How much more
was he supposed to take?

"This entire process feels like it is beyond any control," David
said. "I have been very, very restrained. I have been cooperative.
There has got to be a line drawn somewhere."

What David and the others did not know was that the line
had already been drawn. As they tried to stop the defense, they
did not realize that Ciarciaglino and Paver had already been allowed to read the diary. It was too late.

Twenty-five

C iarciaglino looked at the man on the witness stand as if he were an insect.

". . . you say that Ms. Gregory invited you to dinner?"

"Ms. Gregory invited me to dinner, she and David."

"She said, 'David and I want you to dinner?' "

"She used the word—"

Ciarciaglino cut him off. "Tell us what she said, as best you recall."

"She said she would like to have me over to dinner."

Peter Kumble sat trapped in the witness box, dodging repeated insinuations that he was lying.

"She said she wanted you to come over to dinner with the two of them?"

"Yes."

"And that was to be Wednesday?"

"Yes, sir."

From the start of the trial Ciarciaglino and Paver had been fighting to shift attention—and the blame—away from their client and onto a host of other people. They had tried to suggest that Karen was a woman who got drunk, smoked dope, listened to reggae music, and who might not have been raped at all, who instead might have been wild enough to have taken advantage of the fact that her boyfriend was out of town and gone to bed with someone else. They had also tried to paint Karen's friends as a bunch of latter-day hippies, and attacked David Mackey's credibility, and tried to make the entire Gulfport Police Department look like bumbling idiots who couldn't solve a murder if their own lives depended on it.

Still, even as they pounded away, the defense had a problem. No matter how far out of the mainstream Karen had lived her life and no matter how many mistakes the police had made, none of that changed the evidence against George Lewis. Even if David were lying and there had never been a missing teddy among Karen's belongings, that did not alter the fact that Lewis had been caught lying repeatedly to the police and that his footprint had been found inside that house in Karen's blood.

The defense attorneys already had told the jurors that George was not the murderer. But if it wasn't George, who was it? A few days before, up at the bench, they had hinted that maybe—just maybe—it was the two reggae musicians. Now they had apparently abandoned that theory and were ready to point the finger at someone else.

Ciarciaglino had waited his turn, listening patiently as the prosecution asked Kumble to explain to the jurors who he was and how he had come to visit Karen's house on the evening after the murder. The explanation, however, had not satisfied Ciarciaglino. In his best mocking voice, the voice he saved for those times when he wanted to humiliate someone, he gave the witness the grilling of a lifetime.

He walked over to the clerk's desk and picked up the photos of the outside of Karen's house that had been taken immediately after her body was discovered. With an air of almost imperial disdain, he dropped one onto the stand in front of Kumble. It showed the front porch into which Kumble had walked that evening—showed the jalousie door with the hole through which Karen's head had been rammed.

"You notice the cut in the screen?"

"Yes, I do, sir."

"You did not see it that day?"

"I didn't notice it, no."

Ciarciaglino dropped more photos before Kumble. Had the witness noticed the broken glass on the walkway? Not that he recalled, Kumble said. He said he had approached the house on the grass, not on the walk. Had he noticed the blood on the hand crank of the jalousie door? No. Had he seen the blood on the interior door of the porch, the door that led into the living room? No.

"Before you left, you wrote out a note and left it there. Correct?"

"Yes, sir."

Ciarciaglino was holding the note. He handed it to Kumble and asked him to read it aloud for the jury. He asked if the note said anything about a dinner invitation.

"No, it did not."

"No reference to dinner at all, is there?"

"No."

"You waited 10 minutes, and no one was there for dinner, so you left?"

"Yes, sir."

Ciarciaglino asked Kumble to think back to the night before his visit to Karen's house, to the night of the murder, Tuesday, May 22. What had Kumble been doing that evening? Kumble said he'd probably gone shopping.

"You're sure of that?"

"To the best of my memory."

Ciarciaglino asked if anyone else had been home when Kumble returned from shopping. Kumble said yes. His roommate, Kenneth Kuhar.

"Did you ever leave that evening?"

"No, I didn't."

"Did Mr. Kuhar ever leave?"

"No, he didn't."

"So your alibi as to where you were—"

Over at the prosecution table, Mensh was standing, a pained expression on his face.

Alibi?

"Excuse me," Mensh said. "I'm going to object. That is highly improper."

"Sustained," said Farnell. "The jury will disregard the attorney's last comment."

Ciarciaglino kept going.

"You were attracted to Ms. Gregory," he said. "Weren't you?"

"No, sir."

"It was your desire to have a romantic relationship with her, was it not?"

"No, sir."

"I can't hear you."

"No, sir."

Kumble swallowed hard, shifted in his chair. He looked helplessly toward the prosecutors, as if they could stop what was happening.

Ciarciaglino's voice was rising. "When you went over to that house on Wednesday—the Wednesday you did not see all of the things on that porch and you had the dinner invitation—you only waited 10 minutes?"

"Yes, sir."

"No mention in that note what happened to dinner, is there?"

"No, sir, there's not, sir."

Ciarciaglino was almost shouting now.

"Isn't it a fact, sir, that on Tuesday evening, you and Mr. Kuhar were out for the evening and you went by the Mackey residence?"

"No, that's not a fact."

"You stopped there to see Ms. Gregory. You made advances. She became angry with you, and you killed her."

Kumble's voice dropped to a near whisper. "No, sir."

Mensh was on his feet again, objecting. He was so angry he was stumbling over his words. He said that what Ciarciaglino had just done was improper. He said Ciarciaglino had absolutely no good-faith basis to accuse Kumble.

"Sustained," said Farnell. "Ladies and gentlemen, you should disregard the last statement by counsel."

It was too late. Ciarciaglino had called Kumble a murderer and had suggested that Kuhar was at least an accomplice. He would have a hard time proving it; no evidence, after all, had been found to show that either man had ever set foot inside Karen's house. Still, he had made the accusation and the jurors had heard it. What were they supposed to do? Erase the moment from their memories? Cut the words out of their heads?

Out in the courthouse halls, another kind of war was being declared. Now that Karen's friends had learned that the defense had read the diary, the delicate balance that had generally been maintained between the two sides slipped away. It appeared that the defense had not found anything inside the black-bound book that could be used in the case. After thumbing through it, Ciarciaglino and Paver had made no requests—at least in open court—to tell the jurors any of what the book contained.

Even so, Karen's friends were outraged. As far as they were concerned, the defense had stripped away the last vestige of decency. To them, it was as if Karen had been raped all over again.

David began standing at the courtroom door, staring at Lewis and his lawyers. Out in the rotunda, Neverne worked on Lewis's wife; she figured that the best way to get to George was to go through Glenda. So Neverne stared her down, trying to imagine what was going on inside her mind.

You must wonder. You must have some questions. Doesn't the evidence make you pause? Do you even know what the evidence is?

The prosecutors were wrapping it up.

They brought in Timothy Whitfield, the sheriff's technician who'd used the Luminol to find the footprints on the hallway carpet. He was not allowed to tell the jurors that the footprints were roughly the same size as Lewis's feet—and therefore too small to have been made by Kumble's—because the judge had ruled that the measurements were too imprecise and left too much room for inaccuracy. Whitfield was permitted, however, to show the videotape that had been shot of the footprints as they briefly glowed in the dark.

Next came Tonja Dishong, who quickly explained how Lewis had given her the white teddy. She said she believed the teddy had been new; she did not think it had ever been worn before.

Then, not long after she'd walked into the courtroom, she walked out.

Only one of their witnesses remained.

"The state," said Beverly Andrews, "would call Detective Sgt. Larry Tosi."

He stepped through the doorway, a rumpled figure in a gray pin-striped suit, carrying a briefcase filled with reports that even then he still had not completed. He looked stiff and uncomfortable. He looked as if he would have preferred to take off the jacket, light a cigarette, and just chat with the jurors. But that was not the way it worked. He took the oath, moved to the stand, and sat forward in the chair, his back erect.

"Detective Tosi," said Andrews. "I'm going to call your attention now to May 24th, 1984 . . ."

By now, after listening to the other witnesses, the jurors had heard most of the pieces of the state's case. Tosi's job was to put the pieces together. He talked about the months of working day and night on the case. He talked about going to the house, trying to visualize the murder. He talked about how David had given him the hallway carpet and other items from the house that he'd thought might be useful to develop leads. David, Tosi said, had been concerned about the investigation.

"Did you feel that your job was in jeopardy in any way because of his concern?"

"Not at all."

"Did you feel you might be demoted if you didn't make an arrest in this case?"

"No."

Andrews wanted to know about Peter Kumble. During the investigation, hadn't Tosi met with Kumble? Tosi said yes.

"And was Kumble cooperative with law enforcement?"

"Very cooperative."

"Did he voluntarily give hair samples, fingerprints?"

"Yes, he did."

"And voluntarily appear for interviews when requested?"

"That's right. Without hesitation."

Later Tosi would also point out that no evidence had been found to show that Kumble had been inside Karen's house, other than in the front porch. And as far as the police had determined, Tosi said, all of Kumble's statements had checked out. Furthermore, he noted that Kenneth Kuhar did not match the description Lewis had given of the man on Karen's lawn.

At last they came to the subject of Lewis. Tosi told the jurors he had known George long before the murder.

"George Lewis," he said, "was a friend of mine."

Being so close, Tosi said he knew that George was the type to call the authorities if he saw something suspicious in his neighborhood. At the same time, Tosi said, George was a certified EMT and was not the type to walk away from someone who needed help.

"Did you ever see anything to indicate that he was squeamish in any way?"

"Absolutely not."

Andrews wanted Tosi to discuss how dark it had been inside David and Karen's house. Tosi explained that at night, with the lights off, it was hard to see much of anything, especially with the big oak tree on the east side of the house blocking the light from the street lamp.

"What if you stood in the area where the body was found?" Andrews asked. "In that hallway, what could you see?"

"Nothing."

Tosi said that one night he'd turned off the lights and had an assistant lie down on the floor where Karen had been found. Tosi had waited a few minutes to allow his eyes to adjust. But he still couldn't see the assistant. It was too dark.

"Did you try the old putting-your-hand-in-front-of-your-face?"

"Yes."

"Could you see your hand?"

"No."

Andrews asked Tosi to talk about the different statements Lewis had given about the night of the murder. Then she asked if the sergeant had compared all of the versions.

"Yes, I did."

Ciarciaglino rose to his feet, asking to approach the bench. Once he and the other lawyers were gathered, he said he was trying to prevent a mistrial. He said he assumed that Tosi was about to say he'd compared the statements and found that they were conflicting. Ciarciaglino did not want Tosi to say the word "conflicting." He said it was up to the jury to decide that.

"Your honor," said Mensh, "with all due respect, Mr. Ciarciaglino is not concerned with avoiding a mistrial. What he's concerned with is avoiding testimony that's awfully damaging to his client."

"Fine speech," said Ciarciaglino. "Now, if we could stay with the law. The law is . . ."

When the lawyers finished arguing, Andrews went back to the lectern. She did not ask if Tosi had found the statements conflicting. Instead she asked if he thought the statements were "progressive"—the same term Ciarciaglino had used in his opening statement to describe his client's stories. But Ciarciaglino didn't like Andrews using that word, either. Approaching the bench again, he said Tosi should not be deciding whether the statements were "progressive."

"You guys are driving me crazy," Judge Farnell said.

"Ladies and gentlemen," he said, turning toward the jurors, "please disregard the use of the term 'progressive' in this matter, whether or not Mr. Tosi says it was or wasn't."

Tosi continued, explaining how he had tried in vain to identify the mysterious man that Lewis had reported seeing on David and Karen's lawn. He told how he'd collected the photos of various suspects and showed them to George, asking if any of them was the man.

"Was Peter Kumble's picture in that group?"

"Yes, it was. Absolutely."

"And did he identify the picture of Peter Kumble as being the person he saw?"

"No, he did not. He said it was not him."

A few moments later, Paver was standing up at the defense table. "Excuse me, judge," he said. "I wonder if we could approach for a minute?"

That was how it went. Andrews would ask a few questions and then the defense would head for the bench. A few questions more, and back to the bench. In the approximately three hours that Andrews devoted to direct examination of Tosi, Ciarciaglino and Paver requested seventeen bench conferences, making objections at virtually every one of them. They asked for a mistrial five times. Six times they stood up and voiced objections in front of the jury.

Eventually Andrews had had enough. "With the constant

objections," she complained in front of the jury, "it's rather hard to get to the end."

The moment she said this, Ciarciaglino and Paver were on their feet, plowing back toward the bench. They said the jury had been tainted by these personal attacks and that they wanted a mistrial. Farnell denied the request. Calmly, patiently, he reminded the jurors that the lawyers were obligated to make every objection they thought proper.

Finally Tosi told the jurors how he'd ended up arresting Lewis on March 15, 1986—how he and Lt. Hanson had questioned George that one final time, on tape, before taking him into custody.

"May I play the tape now, your honor?" Andrews asked the judge.

"You may."

The cassette was slipped into a tape player. At the defense table, Lewis listened quietly. Hanson's voice came first, reading George his rights and asking the first questions.

"Okay . . . were there any lights on in the house?"

"No."

"Could you see in there in any way?"

"No."

The jurors could hear him and George going through it all, step by step.

"Were you ever up on the lawn at the house?"

"No."

"Were you ever on the sidewalk in front of the house?"

"No."

"Were you ever in the house?"

"No."

Hanson's voice grew louder.

"You've never been in that house?"

"No."

"You're sure you've never been in there?"

"Uh-huh."

"Were you in there that night?"

"No."

Finally Tosi told him about the FBI and the footprint. Still Lewis would not admit to being inside the house. He said he wasn't even barefoot that night. He said he was innocent.

"I didn't do it to her, Larry."

"I've got no choice, George. All indications are that you did."

There was a pause.

"I saw the guy. I went in the house."

His voice began to break. He started to cry.

"I heard Karen scream. Okay? Oh God. I never seen anything like that before. I didn't see the guy do it, okay? I saw the guy outside. I went in after that, real quick. I still don't believe it."

He just kept going.

"I saw her laying there with her throat cut open. The guy had seen me. When he left, I ran back in the house, okay? . . . I looked, and I saw her laying on the floor. That's it. I didn't do anything else . . . I would never do anything like that to a human being, ever."

The tape ended.

"Your honor," said Andrews, "I have one question for Detective Tosi."

"Yes, ma'am."

Andrews turned back to the witness.

"Detective Tosi, at the time the interview took place and the defendant was arrested, did he know where the footprint was from that had been identified to him?"

"No. We hadn't told him where."

The bathroom. When they told him his footprint had been found in the house, they didn't tell him it had been found in the bathroom. And in all of that long rambling story, the story where supposedly he was finally telling them everything, he had not said a word about going in there. The one room he absolutely had to account for, and he hadn't even mentioned it.

The tape connected many pieces. The jurors had heard Dr. Wood describe how she'd stood in that hallway in the light of day and not been able to see all of Karen's injuries. In fact, Wood had explained how it wasn't until later, when the body was taken to her office and the dried blood was cleaned away, that she had realized that the murderer had not just stabbed Karen's throat but also had tried to cut it.

But on the tape, they could hear Lewis saying he had been able to see Karen that night in the dark. He said he had stood there without the lights on—stood where Tosi said you couldn't see anything without the lights—and had seen Karen lying on the floor with her throat cut open. How was that possible? How could he have seen Karen, much less her wounds? Why had he said that her throat was cut open? Was it just a coincidental choice of words, or had he slipped?

Across the courtroom, Lewis sat with his face in his hands.

Twenty-six

The tension was getting to all of them. It was mid-June now and getting hotter. Karen's friends, still forbidden from entering the courtroom, wandered the air-conditioned corridors of the Hall of Justice. Posted on a wall near the rotunda was a sign that seemed to have been sent from somewhere in the distant past.

NOT ALLOWED IN COURTROOM:
SMOKING
GUM CHEWING
DISRESPECT
TALKING
SHORTS
BARE FEET
BARE MIDRIFFS
FAR-OUT CLOTHES
WEAPONS

The trial was nearing the two-week mark. At the end of each day's testimony, David, Anita, and Neverne would retreat to their rooms at the motel. Soon they would see George and Glenda slipping into the pool for their evening swim. It was impossible to know what to make of this nightly ritual. Were they swimming merely because they enjoyed it? Or were they making a statement, trying to rattle the other side with their confidence?

Karen's friends said nothing. They would wait until George and Glenda had left before they went down to the pool. Even then they did not swim. It just didn't seem right.

Late at night, back in their rooms, they tried not to stare at the walls. They read. They turned on the TV. But they could not rid themselves of their uneasiness. One evening Neverne left her room for some ice and panicked briefly when she heard footsteps behind her. Meanwhile, some of the men connected to the case, including one of the prosecutors, were receiving obscene phone calls in their rooms. The person on the other end of the line was anonymous and spoke casually, as if they were all old friends.

In the morning the cycle began anew. They would get up, go to the courthouse, wander the halls again. Time was all they had. Waiting was all they could do. David paced. Anita looked through an album filled with photos of Karen. Neverne sketched and made notes in a journal. One day she wrote:

> . . . it is imperative to get through the maze, to get through the maze one has to know the rules and I don't know the rules.

"State your full name for the record, please."

"Glenda Grace Lewis."

"Glenda, are you married to George Lewis?"

"Yes, I am."

When she first settled into the witness chair, she'd looked down and smiled at the court reporter who was seated a few feet away, taking down every word. It wasn't much of a smile, just a quick, small, nervous one, as if she was grateful to have found at least one neutral face.

"And how long have you been married to George?" Paver asked from behind the lectern.

"Two and a half years."

"And can you tell us if you have any children?"

"We have a little girl, 2 years old. Her name is Tiffany. And we're expecting our second child in January."

There was a pause as the announcement registered with the

rest of the room. It was a startling piece of news. It was also irrelevant to the facts of the case. Soon, those close to Karen would begin the mental calculations, counting backward through the months.

. . . July, June, May, April. She probably would have conceived in April, just after the change of venue, when George was out on bond. Could she be offering her unborn child as a statement of faith in her husband's innocence?

Paver continued.

"Glenda, I'd like to direct your attention to approximately 1:15 A.M. on May 23rd, 1984 . . . Can you tell the jury, please, where you were at that time?"

"I was in bed."

"Were you asleep?"

"Yes."

"Did anything happen that awoke you at that time?"

"I was awakened by a scream."

Step by step Glenda gave her account of that night—how she climbed out of bed and looked for George, how frightened she was when she didn't find him. As she waited for him, she said, she noticed something out of the corner of her eye. The silhouette. It was in a window behind her, she said. She thought maybe it was a cat, but she wasn't sure. After that, George returned. He looked a little pale, she said, as if he'd been sick. They talked briefly about the scream, and they hugged and kissed, and Glenda asked if George was coming to bed. He said sure, as soon as he put away his tools and locked everything up. Then he came in, took a shower, and joined her in bed.

"Did you find anything unusual about the fact that George took a shower before he came to bed?"

"No. He always takes a shower before he goes to bed."

In the weeks that followed the murder, George took a number of safety precautions, Glenda said. He installed spotlights, bought a big dog, pulled out a .22-caliber rifle and showed her how to fire it. He told her that if she was going to sunbathe out in the yard in her bathing suit she should move toward the back. There was more. When he went to work, he sometimes drove her car and left his truck at the house. That way, she said, if someone were watching the house they wouldn't know when George was home and when he was not.

Paver stopped and looked down at his notes.

"Glenda, from the time that you heard the scream that woke you up—OK?—until the time that you actually saw George coming up the walk—can you tell us exactly how long that was?"

She said she wasn't sure. She wasn't wearing a watch that night, she said. But she had tried to figure it out later. She had sat down, this time with a watch, and attempted to mentally recreate how much time had elapsed before George walked in the door. Her estimate, she said, was that he was gone about ten minutes.

"Is that exact? Could it be longer or shorter?"

"It could have been longer."

"Longer?"

"Yeah."

"No further questions."

Any one of the three prosecutors could have cross-examined her. But the one chosen for the job was Bill Loughery, who at twenty-nine was the youngest member of the state's team. He was the one with the good looks and the fresh, clean face, the one who would be hardest for the jurors to dislike, even if he was about to fire some tough questions at the defendant's vulnerable wife.

"Good morning, Ms. Lewis," he said.

Glenda shifted in her chair. "Good morning."

They began where Paver left off, on the question of how long George had been out of the house that night. Politely, Loughery reminded Glenda that she had once said that George had been gone for a long time. In fact, hadn't she said twenty to thirty minutes?

"No," said Glenda. A chill entered her voice. "I don't recall saying that."

"Do you recall telling Debbie Tosi that?"

"Debbie Tosi? No . . . I might have said that it felt like that, because I was sitting there. But I don't recall saying that actual time."

Loughery wanted Glenda to talk about the tensions that were building in their house around the time of the murder. Wasn't it true that she had become pregnant with George's first child that May, the same month Karen Gregory was killed?

"Right," she said. "But I didn't know it until a couple of months later."

Before the murder, Loughery said, weren't there problems

with the living arrangements? Weren't she and George sharing the house with Mike Blank and Mary Lewis? Yes, Glenda said. Wasn't there friction between them all? Yes. And didn't Blank move out just before Karen's murder? Yes.

"And George wasn't too happy about Mary moving in, was he?"

"I don't think he had much of a choice."

"Right, because the house was owned by George's parents?"

"Right."

Afterward, didn't Glenda herself move out of the house for several months? No. She was only gone, she said, for about a month and a half. But she and George had been having problems, hadn't they? Yes.

"In fact, you were pregnant at the time, and he didn't want to get married, did he?"

"There was a lot involved. It wasn't only the pregnancy."

"There was definitely a strain in your relationship, was there not?"

"Right."

What about all of those safety measures designed to protect her? Didn't George take some of those precautions during the time she was no longer living in the house, when she did not need protecting? No, Glenda said. Even when she had been living there, wasn't she often totally alone at night? Didn't Mary Lewis work late? Didn't George's shifts at the fire station go for twenty-four hours? Yes. And yet, Loughery reminded her, George had not told her about this man on the lawn. Wasn't that true? George didn't warn her about that man, did he? No, she said. Not for months. Not until he told the police.

Loughery kept going. Wasn't George the type who kept an eye out on the neighborhood? Didn't he watch people's houses when they were gone? Didn't he know who was home and who was away? Who was old and who was young? Glenda said she didn't know. He might have kept track of the people who lived in their immediate area, she said. Wasn't George the type to stop and help if he saw an accident? Yes. Didn't he carry a first-aid kit in his truck? Yes. Didn't he also carry a knife with him, even when he wasn't at work? No. Didn't he have knives out in the garage with his tools? Glenda knew this was correct. After all, she had seen the knife out in the toolbox herself, the one that the defense had included in its evidence list. But now, with her husband's life on the line, she hedged. She said she did not pay much attention to his tools.

What about George's feet? Didn't he often go barefoot as he worked around the house and in the yard? Yes. And when he was done working, wasn't he in the habit of hosing himself off in the yard? Yes, Glenda said, when it was warm outside.

Loughery paused. "It was warm in May, wasn't it? Late May?"

"I don't remember the weather, really."

"You had your windows open, didn't you?"

"I'm not sure, really."

She looked nervous now. She looked as if she wanted to get up and run and was desperately trying not to show it.

"Isn't it a fact," Loughery continued, "that your memory of what George looked like that night is pretty vague?"

"It didn't seem important."

"You don't even know if he had a shirt on, do you?"

"I don't remember. I can't say at all."

"And you don't know if the reason he looked pale or not is because he just killed somebody. Right?"

Glenda stared at the prosecutor.

"I know he didn't kill anybody."

When Loughery finished, Paver went back to the lectern and asked Glenda to return to that crucial moment when George came back to the house.

"Did you notice whether or not George was wet?"

Glenda brightened. "No, he couldn't have been wet, because I would have been wet. I hugged him."

"So he was or was not wet?"

"No."

"When the hose was turned on outside your house, could you hear the hose on out there?"

"Yes."

"Did you hear the hose on that night before George came in?"

"No. I was sitting right there next to the window."

Paver was almost done. His voice was different now. It had become more careful, more deliberate. He asked if she'd ever seen photos of the murder scene.

"Yes."

"Where did you see them?"

"At Debbie Tosi's house."

"Having seen those photographs, Glenda, are you telling the truth here today?"

"Yes."

"Did you lie for George here today, having seen those?"

"No."

Loughery stood up. "Objection, judge. Self-serving."

"Sustained," said Farnell.

It didn't matter. The jurors had heard the answer. They had seen Glenda's face.

The judge looked toward the defense table.

"Call your next witness."

Ciarciaglino stood up.

"Call Mr. George Lewis."

Twenty-seven

I n the movies, the man on trial almost always takes the stand. It's dramatic, it's powerful, it satisfies the audience's desire to let the accused have his say. But in reality, it usually doesn't happen. Knowing they have the right to remain silent, many defendants do just that. There's too much to lose. If you testify, the state may be allowed to ask about convictions in your past—a question that's generally prohibited as long as you stay out of the witness box. And even if you have been unjustly accused, you run the risk that you won't be articulate or believable enough, that you'll squirm and sweat as the prosecution challenges you. Say nothing, and you're still presumed innocent. Testify, and you could end up talking your life away.

Yet there had never been much doubt that Lewis would take the stand. He had no past convictions to hide, and the prosecution had raised too many points that demanded explanation. So he and everyone else had waited for this moment.

For two weeks he had sat quietly beside his lawyers, taking notes. Outside the courtroom he'd sat with his mother, chatted with his friends from the fire department, stood still while Glenda straightened his tie. When he walked past the cameras that waited for him outside the courthouse, he smiled. When he swam in the pool at their motel, he floated happily in the water, not seeming to realize why anyone might have thought it strange to see him there. It was as if he did not understand the seriousness of his situation. But he did understand. One night during the trial, Glenda wanted to go out. It was her birthday, and someone had suggested that George take her somewhere nice for dinner. But George was reluctant. He didn't want to stray too far from the motel. He said he didn't want to disappear, even for a few hours, and have people think he had run away.

"George, you're going to have to speak up now."

He leaned closer to the microphone. He spoke softly, tentatively.

"George," said Ciarciaglino, "let's go to the early morning hours of May 23rd, 1984 . . . Did you hear a scream?"

"I heard what appeared to be a scream."

"Where were you?"

"I was inside my garage behind my house."

George explained that he often worked out there past midnight. His shift at the fire station made it easy. He'd work for twenty-four hours, then be off for forty-eight. That night, he knew he did not have to get up in the morning. He'd gotten off work earlier that day—Tuesday—and did not have to return until Thursday. So he was in the garage, welding and listening to the radio. He was wearing a T-shirt and shorts, he said. Over those clothes, he wore a long-sleeved flannel shirt and jeans so he wouldn't be burned during the welding. He'd also been wearing boots, he said, but his feet had hurt and so he'd taken them off.

Then he heard what he thought was a scream, he said. He wasn't sure where the sound had come from. He went out and walked up and down the street, looking. He was walking past the corner of David and Karen's yard when he noticed the man with the beard walking across the lawn. He asked the man if anything was wrong, and the man told him to get lost, to not say he'd seen him, to get the hell out of there. George went back to his own property. From there he watched the man walk north, along Upton Street and out of sight. By this point, George said, he was not particularly afraid. He wanted to find out why this stranger had tried to scare him away.

"Why didn't you just call the police then?"

"I wanted to investigate it more. I had done that before."

"Yeah. We heard you were called the crime watch guy or something of the neighborhood. Was that you?"

"More or less, yes, sir."

So he went back to Karen's house, he said. He went to the front jalousie door and saw glass on the walk. Now he was sure something was wrong. He knocked on the door. When no one answered, he walked around the house, found another door, and knocked again. No answer. He walked around to the other side of the house. He found a window, the only one with its shades open. The curtains were partially open. Through the window he could see some light.

"A faint light? A strong light?"

"It was a faint light."

He called out, asking if anyone needed help. No answer. He peered inside and saw a body lying on the floor.

"At that time, I felt that somebody needed help, and I crawled through the window."

"Why? Why did you go through the window?"

"At that time, that was the way in."

"Have you ever gone into houses and through windows before?"

"Yes, sir."

"When?"

"On several occasions with the fire department. We were trained to make entry in through windows."

"Tell us what happened when you got inside."

"When I got inside, I saw a person, which was a female, white female. And when I took a look, there was blood all over the place. There was enough light in there to where I could see it. And she was laying there half-nude . . . and I got scared."

"Could you tell what happened to her?"

"I couldn't tell what type of injuries she had, but I knew that something definitely terrible had happened."

"Did you touch her?"

"No, sir."

"Take her pulse?"

"No, sir."

"Why not?"

"At that time, I felt as though there was nothing I could do that would help."

"Why?"

"She appeared to me as though she was dead."

"How close to her did you get?"

"Within a few feet."

"Did you realize that at any time you had stepped in blood?"

"No, sir."

"What did you do then, after looking at her and seeing this blood?"

"I started to get sick, and I ran into what was the bathroom then, and I threw up."

"Where was this light coming from?"

"It was coming from the bathroom."

"What did you do then after you threw up?"

"I got out of there."

"Anything happen on the way out?"

"As I was running around the corner into the bedroom to go through the window, I—off the corner of my right—I saw movement, and I thought somebody was jumping after me. And after, I realized that it was the mirror and all I saw was my reflection in the mirror."

He crawled out the window and ran back toward his property, he said. He thought that the man he'd seen might have gone over there, looking for him. He went up to a window of his own house and peered inside. But he couldn't see through the window's blinds, so he went to the garage and shut its door and then went back to his house, entering through the utility room. There he took off the flannel shirt and jeans.

"How long did that take?"

"About 10 seconds."

"Why did you take off your flannel shirt and the jeans in the utility room?"

"That was something I always did whenever I came in from the garage or anything like that. That was where I always kept my work clothes."

Glenda was waiting for him, he said. She mentioned the silhouette she'd seen at the window. She asked if it had been him, standing outside their house. George said no.

"Why did you tell her no?"

"I don't know, sir. I was just shaken up. I was terrified of what I had seen."

"George, why didn't you just call the police now and tell them what you had seen?"

"I was scared and terrified. And besides, with being inside there after that, I didn't know how to explain being in there without them thinking that I did it."

Now that George had told the essence of his story, Ciarciaglino helped him fill in the blanks.

"Did you take a teddy out of the house, this white lady's undergarment that we saw?"

"No, sir."

"Okay. You saw Miss Tonja here tell us that you gave her a—this particular lady's undergarment or negligee, I guess they're called."

"Yes, sir."

"Do you know where you bought that?"

"No, sir. I don't recall exactly where I bought it at."

Carefully, Ciarciaglino guided George from one point to the next. Did he tell Glenda about what he'd seen that night? No. He didn't tell anyone. He wanted to, he said, but he was too afraid and did not know how to tell what had happened. Why did he repeatedly change his account with the police, gradually giving new details? Why didn't he just say nothing? Because even though he was afraid, he said, he wanted to help the police as best he could. What about the composite drawing of the man on the lawn? Did George help Sgt. Tosi put it together? Yes. They'd worked on it for more than an hour. George had done his best to make it look like the man on the lawn.

Ciarciaglino walked toward the stand and handed George several sheets of paper, each marked with a drawing of a bearded man.

"What are they, George?"

"This is the composite that I helped Sgt. Tosi do."

Ciarciaglino handed him another exhibit. It was a photograph of Kenneth Kuhar, Peter Kumble's roommate. The photo had been taken in the fall of 1986 by the private investigator working for the defense. It was blurry, but it showed Kuhar with a beard.

"Is that the person you saw that night, George?"

"It sure looks like him. I can't swear to it, but that's him."

"Okay. Does he look like the composite you drew?"

"Yes, he does."

Ciarciaglino handed the photo and the composite drawing to the jurors. One by one they compared them. When they were done, Ciarciaglino asked George if he'd ever seen the man on the lawn before that night.

"No, sir."

"Had you ever met Kenneth Kuhar before?"

"No, sir."

"George, did you rape Karen Gregory?"

"No, sir, I did not."

"Did you murder Karen Gregory?"

"No, sir."

The senior prosecutor did not bother to say good morning.

"Mr. Lewis?" said Dick Mensh, looking disgustedly across the room at the witness.

"Yes, sir."

"Today you're under oath. Correct?"

"Correct."

With that the questions began. Mensh reminded Lewis that when he stood in his own garage he could see across the street and into the house Karen had shared with David.

"Correct?"

"I would assume, yes."

Assuming wasn't good enough. So Mensh asked again: could he see inside the house?

"Yes."

"As a matter of fact, you can see all of the way back into the bedroom of the Mackey house from your garage when you're looking that way."

"I don't ever recall doing that."

"Can you, from your garage, look into the Mackey house and see all of the way back into their bedroom?"

"I don't know."

Lewis, Mensh noted, had just told the jury how he had taken off his boots before he heard the scream. Wasn't that correct?

"Yes, sir."

"But you didn't tell the folks what kind of boots."

"They are regular work boots."

"Laced boots?"

"Yes, sir."

"So you have to undo the laces to get your boots off, right?"

"No, sir, because I never laced them up that night. I didn't have them on that long."

"So . . . after you got through working, you just took your boots off. Is that right?"

"Yes, sir."

"OK . . . So you were barefoot then. Is that correct?"

"Yes, sir."

Mensh reminded Lewis that he'd told Lt. Hanson and Sgt. Tosi differently. In his final statement, the one the jurors already had heard, he'd said he was not barefoot that night. Hadn't he?

"Yes, sir."

"That wasn't true, was it?"

"No, it wasn't."

"So that was really just a lie to Lt. Hanson on the day of the tape, right?"

"Yes, sir."

Mensh paused a moment. What about after the murder, he said. What about after George saw this man on the lawn and then witnessed this terrible scene inside the house? Didn't he return to work at the fire station that Thursday, only a day and a half later? Yes, said Lewis.

"Performed your duties in your normal routine fashion, right?"

"No, sir. I was upset Thursday."

"But yet you weren't upset enough even on Thursday to tell any of your coworkers, right?"

"I was upset, but I was afraid to tell anybody."

But isn't it true, Mensh said, that firefighters depend on one another in a special way? Aren't they a close-knit society? Yes, said Lewis, to a point. Didn't he have close friends in the fire department? Yes. Didn't he have close friends in the police department, too? Tosi was a friend, wasn't he?

"He was a friend, yes. But he wasn't close, what I call close."

"He was close enough that you wanted him to have the privilege of . . . performing the wedding ceremony for you and your wife. Correct?"

"Yes, we had him do that."

"And you had been at his house many times before Karen Gregory was killed, hadn't you?"

"Yes, on several occasions."

"You had confidence in Sgt. Tosi. Otherwise, you wouldn't have had this relationship with him, right?"

"I had confidence to a point, yes."

"Now it's 'to a point'?"

"Well, I had confidence in him, but everybody has doubts about everybody."

"And even at that time, you never bothered to say anything to Sgt. Tosi, did you?"

"No, sir, I didn't."

Mensh wanted to go back to this man on the lawn. This man—"this alleged person," Mensh called him—told Lewis to go away? Yes. And yet Lewis was not afraid after the man said this? No. Lewis decided to investigate around David and Karen's house? Yes. And when he saw the broken glass on the sidewalk, that was when he realized something was wrong? Yes. But on the tape, with the detectives, didn't he say that he heard the glass breaking before he went over to the house? Yes, Lewis said. He heard it, he said, but he hadn't been sure what it was.

But Lewis had changed his stories so many times, Mensh said. He'd added so many facts. Was this yet another new fact?

"I'm telling the truth here today," Lewis said.

Mensh stared at him in disbelief. He didn't tell the truth before, did he? All those times he talked to the police, Mensh asked, did he tell the truth? No. But hadn't he just said that he'd wanted to help the police? Wasn't that what he'd just told the jury? Yes. Did he think he was helping the detectives by lying to them? Did he think he was helping by frustrating the investigation and prolonging it? No, Lewis said. He wasn't suggesting that, he said.

"I was afraid to tell them the truth," he said.

Mensh scoffed. There was no one else at the house that night, he said. "There was no one else in the house but you, Mr. Lewis, who had gone over there earlier in an attempt to have sex with Karen Gregory, who told you no, and that's when you became enraged, assaulted her and then cut her throat, slashed her about the body and left her for dead. Isn't that what happened?"

"No, it isn't."

"All right. Let's go on a bit further then with your testimony . . ."

Having tried the blunt approach, Mensh now returned to picking at details. He kept shifting around with his questions, moving back and forth through time, twisting and turning from one point to the next, dragging Lewis back through each section of his story.

So he was telling them that he saw Karen lying on the floor in her blood. Yet he did not even touch her? Correct. But Dr. Wood, Mensh pointed out, had testified that Karen could have lived for several minutes after the attack. Had Lewis heard that testimony? Yes. But wasn't he supposed to be the one-man neighborhood crime watch? Yes. Wasn't he also a firefighter, trained for medical emergencies? Yes.

"And you're suggesting to the jury that you didn't even bother to look to see whether that girl was alive or dead?"

"I was too upset."

"Too upset to even immediately pick up the telephone, if you didn't want to touch that girl, to call 911? Right?"

"Yes."

But as a firefighter, he'd worked around crime scenes before, hadn't he? Maybe, Lewis said. He couldn't recall any in particular, he said. But didn't he know how important it was for the police to reach a crime scene quickly, to get the investigation started as soon as possible? Lewis said he wasn't aware of that at the time. He hadn't logged many hours on the rescue truck, he said.

Mensh wanted to talk about Lewis's getting sick inside the house. Before today, had he ever told anybody else that he'd thrown up in that bathroom? Yes, Lewis said, he told his lawyers. Anybody other than them? No. So this was yet another addition to his story? Yes. And when he threw up, Mensh asked, was he calm and collected enough to flush the toilet? Yes. Did he clean up the bathroom afterward?

"No, sir. I didn't make a mess."

"You didn't make a mess. Yet you had told us that you saw all of this blood all over the place. You obviously walked through it, right?"

"Apparently, yes."

Mensh asked Lewis to think back to his arrest on March 15, 1986. That day, Tosi and Hanson did not tell him exactly where the footprint had been found, did they? No, Lewis said, they didn't. That was a long time ago, Mensh said. Plenty of time for Lewis to read through the depositions and review the evidence—and to learn that the footprint was in the bathroom. And now, having learned that, he was telling them this new detail about throwing up in that room. Wasn't that what he was telling them?

"I'm telling you the truth," Lewis said again.

"All right."

Mensh circled back. He wanted to go over the details of how Lewis approached Karen's house that night. He had testified that he walked up to the front door before he went to the window and climbed in. But wasn't the front door open?

"It might have been ajar. But it wasn't open."

Mensh stopped. So it was ajar, not open. But Lewis could have walked right inside the house, correct? Yes. Wouldn't that have been easier than climbing through a window? Did he even try the door? No. What about the screen on that window? When he climbed in, he pulled back the screen and left it hanging? Yes. But wasn't that the window the police had crawled through when they'd found the body? Hadn't one officer already testified that when she climbed in, she had to take the screen off? Yes.

"And there were paramedics there watching while she was doing this, right?"

"Yes, sir."

"These are the people you work with, right?"

"Yes, sir."

Then there were the neighbors who had heard the scream. Several had gone to their windows and stood there, watching and listening for any further sign of trouble. Two of them had a clear view of Karen's house and the corner of Twenty-seventh Avenue and Upton Street. One of them had looked out at the area just north of the house, the direction in which the man on the lawn supposedly had disappeared. Yet none of them had seen Lewis walking in the street, checking the neighborhood. None of them had seen or heard him talking to a man on the corner, or walking up to Karen's front door, or walking around to the bedroom window, or climbing inside.

Lewis, Mensh pointed out, had heard those neighbors testify to those things in court. Hadn't he?

"Yes, sir."

Did he know of any reason why they would tell anything but the truth?

"No."

What about all of those security measures, Mensh said. What about all of Lewis's concern for Glenda? Didn't he put up all the lights and buy the dog and take all of those other precautions in June? Yes. But didn't Glenda move out in June? No, said Lewis.

Mid-July. But wasn't it in June when he began dating Tonja? Wasn't that when he started having sex with his sixteen-year-old girlfriend? No. Lewis said he did not recall going out with Tonja in June.

Mensh wanted to return to the question of why Lewis had not called the police. He was telling them that he didn't call because he thought he would be accused of the murder? Yes. But what about an anonymous tip? Couldn't he have called the police without giving his name?

"You didn't even do that, did you?"

"I didn't even think about that."

Contempt rose in Mensh's voice. "You walked out of the house and left this girl, who you knew being dead, just to sit there a day, two days, literally rotting, without notifying any-body . . . Right?"

"That's correct."

Mensh didn't want to leave this point. Lewis was afraid of being accused—was that right? Yes. But not too afraid, Mensh noted, to send the police chasing after other suspects. Lewis said he didn't mean to send the police chasing after other suspects.

"That's what you did, though. Isn't it?"

"Yes, it is."

"You even wanted them to believe that Mr. Kumble did it, didn't you?"

"To this day, I don't know if he did it or not."

Yet he pointed the finger at Kumble, didn't he? And didn't Kumble leave a note at the house—a note with his name on it? Wasn't that right? Yes. But what did Lewis leave at that house? Wasn't he the one, Mensh said, who left a bloody footprint? Yes. And now he was trying to tell them that Kenneth Kuhar looked like the man on the lawn. Yes. Well, Lewis had read through all of the depositions in the case, right? Yes. So didn't he know full well that Mr. Kuhar did not have a beard on May 23, 1984?

"I do not recall that."

Sitting at the state's table, Beverly Andrews scribbled some-thing on a piece of paper and handed it to Mensh. He paused, read it, then looked back at Lewis.

What about the light, he said. Lewis was telling them a light was on inside the house that night. Right? Yes, Lewis said. In the bathroom, he said. But on the tape, the tape the jurors had heard, didn't he say there were no lights on inside the house?

"Yes, sir."

"And now you're suggesting that also was a lie to Lt. Hanson on tape?"

"Yes, sir."

"Lying is helping the police?"

"No, sir."

"And yet you had lied to Tosi, right?"

"Yes, I did."

"You lied to your wife, right?"

"Yes, I did."

"You lied to the people at work, right?"

"Yes, sir."

"Your family, right?"

"Yes, sir."

"And today, for the first time, we hear how the footprint got in the bathroom. Is that correct?"

"Yes, sir," Lewis said, looking straight at the prosecutor. "The truth is my best defense."

Everybody has doubts about everybody.

That was what Lewis had said. With one sentence, he had struck at the heart of it all. Can we assume the benevolence of our neighbors? Ask those who peered out their windows the night Karen's cry rang down their streets. How much confidence should we place in our friends? Ask Larry Tosi. And what do we really know about the person who climbs into bed beside us? Can we be sure where our lover has been? No matter what she believed, no matter which way the jury voted, Glenda Lewis would live in the shadows of these questions for the rest of her days.

Twenty-eight

C all your next witness," said the judge.
"The defense rests," said Ciarciaglino.

Yet the testimony was not quite over. Now that the defense had spoken, the prosecutors had the right to answer, and they called two people briefly to the stand.

The first was Kenneth Kuhar, a young man with brown hair and no beard. Under questioning from Loughery, he acknowledged that he had worn a beard in the past. But when Karen was killed in May 1984, he said, he was clean-shaven.

Loughery handed Kuhar the photo the defense had taken of him in the fall of 1986—the photo that showed him with a beard and that George had said looked like the man on the lawn. Usually, Kuhar said, he wore a beard during the winter and then shaved it off.

"Do you recall when it was you grew that beard, Mr. Kuhar?" said Loughery, indicating the one in the defense's photo.

"It was a long time after 1984."

There were other differences between him and the alleged intruder. Lewis had described the man as anywhere from about five eight to six four, weighing about 230 pounds, with collar-length hair that was light red or auburn, a light red or sandy beard, sideburns, a pitted complexion, broad shoulders, and muscular arms. He also had said the man wore a watch and may have worn a necklace.

"How tall are you, Mr. Kuhar?" said Loughery.

"Five-eleven."

"Back in May of 1984, did you weigh 230 pounds?"

"No, sir."

"How much did you weigh?"

"Approximately 140 to 150."

"How much do you weigh now, sir?"

"About 155, 160."

"Any reason why you know you weighed less than you do now?"

"I played soccer back then."

"Back in May of 1984 was your hair auburn or light red?"

"No, sir."

"Was it the same color it is now?"

"Yes, sir."

"Back in May of 1984 did you have sideburns?"

"No, sir."

"What was the length of your hair?"

"Pretty much the way it is now."

Kuhar's hair was wavy. But it fell several inches below his collar.

Loughery asked Kuhar to step down from the witness box and stand before the jury.

"Mr. Kuhar, could you roll up your sleeves and show the jury your biceps?"

Kuhar did, stretching out his arms, which were not particularly muscular.

"Have you ever been a weightlifter?"

"No, sir."

"Do you have a pitted complexion?"

The jurors could see for themselves that his face was smooth.

"Has your skin complexion changed at all from May of '84 to today?"

"No, it hasn't."

Loughery asked the witness to return to the stand.

"Mr. Kuhar," he said, "have you ever worn a watch?"

"I don't wear any jewelry."

"Have you ever worn a necklace?"

"No, sir."

"Is there a reason why you never have worn any jewelry?"

"I just find it uncomfortable."

On cross-examination, Ciarciaglino wanted to return to the beard.

"Evidently," he said, "you grow and shave off beards pretty regular. Is that right?"

"Not pretty regularly, no, sir."

"And when you shaved the beard off, it was just before the last time the case was set for trial, wasn't it?"

"No, sir."

When Kuhar was done, the prosecution recalled Tosi to the stand. Lewis had told the jury that he had run into the bathroom, thrown up, then run out—all without cleaning up. Now Tosi tried to show that this explanation was impossible. Lewis obviously had been carrying blood on the bottom of at least one of his feet and had set that foot down on the bathroom's tile floor. But the footprint, Tosi pointed out, had been found just beyond the doorway, about five feet from the toilet. There had been no other prints in the bathroom, Tosi said. There was a small blood spot on a green throw rug, he said, but the rug was close to the solitary footprint.

The question was obvious: how could Lewis have reached the toilet without leaving any other trace of his footsteps?

"Anything further?" said Farnell.

"No, sir," said Mensh.

Tosi stood up and left the courtroom. With that, the testimony ended. All that remained was for the lawyers to deliver their closing arguments and for Farnell to give his final instructions. Then the jurors would be sent out to deliberate.

That afternoon the lawyers met with Farnell in chambers to hammer out the precise wording of his instructions. They argued for hours, because they knew that the jurors would take typed copies of the instructions with them into the jury room. That text would be the jurors' only guidance on how to apply the law to this case and how to conduct their deliberations. It would be their Bible. A slight change in the phrasing here or the addition of a paragraph there might mean the difference between conviction and acquittal.

Ciarciaglino and Paver tried to include something in the instructions that might tilt the odds in their favor. They asked for the addition of an unusual sentence. A "zinger," the judge called it. It said:

> The fact that a person charged with a crime who was free on bond appeared for all required court appearances may be considered evidence of consciousness of innocence.

Translated into plain English:

When you sit down in that jury room, remember this: Lewis did not run. He showed up at the trial, every day, on his own. Would a guilty man do that?

It was certainly no secret to the jurors that Lewis was out on bond. Some of them would admit later that when they'd first seen him sitting at the defense table in his suit and tie, they had mistaken him for a lawyer. They'd assumed the defendant in a murder case would be in custody. The fact that Lewis was allowed to wander on his own had led at least one juror to wonder whether the state's case was weak. Now, with their zinger, the defense attorneys had asked Farnell to encourage such thinking. They had asked him to give the credence of the law to the notion that innocent men show up for trial.

Farnell would not do it.

"Good argument," he said. "But not good jury instruction."

Closing arguments were heard the next day—Saturday, June 13. That morning the courtroom was packed, with Karen's mother and two brothers seated in the first row.

First, Loughery spoke for the state. Then Joe Ciarciaglino spoke for the defense. Then came Mensh, bringing up the rear, speaking again for the state. They went at it for hours, their voices rising and falling and rising again like preachers delivering a marathon sermon. The attorneys wound through the days of testimony, making connections, drawing conclusions, urging the jurors to use their common sense, to remember their duty, to follow the law, to bring back a verdict that spoke the truth. But the two sides could not agree on what the truth was.

Mensh and Loughery said the evidence was overwhelming. George Lewis, they said, was a rapist, a murderer, and a liar—a poor liar at that. He went to Karen's house that night, knowing she was alone, and made sexual advances, they said. When Karen rejected him, he forced himself on her, then killed her so she wouldn't identify him. In the months that followed, they said, he trapped himself in one conflicting story after the other. He'd talked his way into this courtroom, and even then he'd kept talking, giving yet another account brimming with inconsistencies.

Now Lewis and his attorneys wanted the jury to believe that Peter Kumble was the real murderer and that Kenneth Kuhar was the stranger on the lawn that night. The prosecutors scoffed. This was the final insult to the jurors' intelligence, they said. From the start, they said, Lewis had pointed the finger at others, even at Lawrence Sanders, who clearly did not match George's description of the stranger he had supposedly seen. Why, the prosecution asked, would Lewis have done that? If he weren't the murderer, why would he have tried to drag an innocent man into the case?

When it came time for the defense to speak, Ciarciaglino didn't exactly answer that question. Instead he attacked the prosecutors' case.

"Look at two sides of everything," he told the jurors, "and you'll see they ain't got it, folks."

Ciarciaglino leaned against the lectern, his suit jacket unbuttoned, a straightened paper clip dangling from his mouth like a silver piece of straw. His twang, which had faded in and out over the past several days, now returned in full strength.

There were some hard questions that should be asked of Kumble and Kuhar, Ciarciaglino said. He acknowledged that he could not prove that these two men had anything to do with the murder. But the state, he said, had not proved that his client was the killer, either. There was no question, he said, that George had made a mistake. He'd played police officer. He heard Karen scream and saw the stranger on the lawn, and then he was foolish enough to climb through that window to help Karen. Once he did that, he realized no one would believe him. So he lied. Now the prosecutors were trying to say that George's lies showed he was guilty. What had they offered to prove it? Circumstantial evidence, Ciarciaglino said, uttering these last two words as if they were a crime unto themselves. Actually, there's nothing wrong with circumstantial evidence. It's perfectly legal and can be conclusive or inconclusive, just like other evidence. One study after another has shown, for instance, that eyewitness statements—which are popularly assumed to be reliable—are often wrong. Still, years of TV drama have left the public with the impression that anything circumstantial is suspect, and now Ciarciaglino took advantage of that belief.

The evidence was not even clear, Ciarciaglino said, that Karen Gregory had been raped in the first place. True, the medical examiner had found semen. But how could they be sure, Ciarciaglino asked, that Gregory didn't willingly have sex with someone in the hours before the murder? Wasn't it possible, he suggested, that she went drinking late that night? Couldn't a man, he suggested, have gone home with her?

Ciarciaglino made sure he talked, too, about the white teddy that had been submitted into evidence. There was no way, he said, that the prosecution could prove it was the same teddy that Karen had bought before the murder and that had later been reported missing. David Mackey, he pointed out, had seen Karen with the teddy only once, a couple of months before the murder. If she'd kept it, he said, wouldn't she have worn it for David again? Couldn't she have returned it before the murder?

Ciarciaglino was on a roll. He waved his arms. He yelled. He paced back and forth, complaining that the state was playing games.

"This boy's life," he said, extending a finger toward George, "is on the line."

When the lawyers were done talking, Judge Farnell read the jurors his final instructions. He reminded them that Lewis had pleaded not guilty and was therefore presumed innocent unless the state proved the charges beyond and to the exclusion of a reasonable doubt. He explained to them that circumstantial evidence was legal. He told them they were not to be swayed one way or the other because they felt sorry for anybody. Once they had been sent into the jury room, he said, the twelve of them would have to reach their verdict alone, and they would have to reach it unanimously.

Done reading, the judge looked up from his text.

"Mr. Bailiff," he said, "you may retire the jury."

The jurors walked single file down the aisle to the small room at the back of the courtroom. This was the jury room, where they would sit and talk and try to figure out the truth of what had happened that night in May 1984.

The door closed behind them.

Twenty-nine

That Saturday, as the jurors prepared to deliberate, Tiffany Lewis played outside the courtroom. She was two and a half years old. Though she did not know it yet, her entire life had been entangled in the case that was now rising toward a resolution around her. She had been conceived within days of the murder; she had been born just as her father became a suspect; and she had celebrated her first birthday when a family friend, whose wife sometimes babysat her, arrested her father and took him to jail.

Now, on this day, of all days, Tiffany had been brought to the Polk County Courthouse. She wore a patterned dress and sandals. Her dark curly hair had been pulled back into a little ponytail. She padded around the halls, gazing up at all of the strangers with dark eyes that were mirror images of her father's. For a moment she stood beside David Mackey, who looked down at her and lightly caressed the top of her head before she walked away to someone else.

During the breaks in the trial, George Lewis would go out to the rotunda to join Tiffany and Glenda. These were precious moments for George. If convicted, he might never again have a chance to see his family outside a prison. Now, as the three of them sat together on a bench, George kissed Tiffany and held her in his lap and smiled at her as she made silly faces at him.

One of the jurors, an older woman named Maytha Schafer, happened to glimpse them there. Not long before she and the others were to begin deliberations, Schafer went out into the hall, and there was Lewis, playing with his daughter. Schafer felt bad when she saw them. But she suspected she was supposed to feel that way. Lewis, Schafer told herself, wanted to be seen with his daughter. He was putting her on display so the jurors would notice her and think about her while they deliberated. He was using that child, she thought, to win their sympathy.

The jury room would have made a fine jail cell. It was a drab little box of a room, perhaps ten feet by twenty. There were no pictures on the walls, which were covered with peeling paint, and there was only one window and a pair of adjoining bathrooms, so that the jurors would not have to step into the halls and mingle with anyone while they were deciding the case. There was only one door out, and on the wall beside it was a buzzer the jurors were supposed to press when they had a question or had reached a verdict. Other than these few necessities, about the only things in the room were the evidence, including the rolled-up section of carpet on which Karen Gregory had died, plus a table and chairs, some typewritten copies of the judge's instructions, some verdict forms, and the jurors themselves, who were now sitting around the table looking at one another.

"Well," someone said. "Here we are."

Over the past two weeks, the jurors had been thrown together for hours at a stretch in this room. They'd learned a few things about one another. They had memorized names and nicknames, talked about their families and their jobs, told jokes, and gossiped about Jim and Tammy Faye Bakker, whose troubles had recently hit the headlines. One of the jurors had celebrated a wedding anniversary during the trial, another a birthday. Two of them, it turned out, had been neighbors as children and had not seen each other for the last fifteen years.

In alphabetical order, the jurors were:

- Gregory Blessing, thirty-five, a food and beverage director who recently had moved from New York.

Single. He had served for ten years, in the north, as a volunteer firefighter.

- Leif Bouffard, thirty-seven, a chemical engineer. Married, with two children.
- Elizabeth Carter, sixty-five, a school custodian. Widowed, with two daughters.
- Dorene Cobb, fifty-three, a homemaker who also cleaned houses and prepared meals for the elderly. Married, with four children.
- Timothy Green, twenty, a cook at McDonald's. Single.
- Gary Haeusler, forty, a production supervisor at a plant. Married, with two children.
- Robert Lancaster, forty-nine, a supervisor at a chemical company. Married, with two children.
- Terry Nicholson, forty, a railroad employee. Married, with one child. He and Lancaster were the long-separated neighbors.
- Theodore Saliba, sixty-one, director of athletics for the Polk County school system. Married, with three children.
- Maytha Schafer, sixty-nine, a retired accountant who enjoyed collecting shells. Married, with one child.
- Eulalia Whitcomb, sixty, a bookkeeper. Married. She was the one who originally had been picked as an alternate but had been moved onto the jury midway through the trial after Beverly Collier was excused due to her nightmares.
- Ruth Wunder, thirty-eight, a sales representative and seamstress. Married, with four children.

These were the seven men and five women who had been chosen to decide whether Lewis was guilty. Yet they knew less about the case than almost anyone else involved. They still did not know, for instance, about all of the legal battles that had been fought over the white teddy and Karen's diary. They were not even aware that Karen had kept a diary, because the judge had ordered that this detail not be mentioned in front of them. Day after day the twelve of them had sat in this room, waiting for the lawyers to settle whatever they were quarreling about. Boredom had set in quickly. Some of the jurors had taken naps. One had bought a *National Enquirer,* and they'd taken turns reading it.

It had not always been easy inside the courtroom, either. Tim Green, the McDonald's cook, sat at the far end of the back row and had encountered some difficulty hearing the witnesses. He'd had an especially hard time making out the testimony of the soft-spoken Glenda Lewis. Green was a polite, friendly young man who loved to watch old episodes of "Star Trek" in his spare time. Each day he'd gone to court to hear the lawyers and the witnesses; then, in the evenings, he'd gone to his regular job at McDonald's, flipping quarter pounders until midnight. The long hours had caught up with him. That Saturday, as the lawyers gave their final arguments, he'd struggled to stay awake. He'd even nodded off occasionally when the lawyers went to the bench.

Throughout the trial, Green and other jurors had been distracted—and sometimes irritated—by the continual objections from the attorneys, especially the defense attorneys, who never seemed to tire of jumping up and interrupting witnesses in mid-sentence. Several jurors, meanwhile, had been surprised that they could not ask their own questions of the witnesses. Unbeknownst to them, this was standard procedure at a trial. If jurors were given the chance to question witnesses, the lawyers and the judge would relinquish control over what the jurors heard. It simply was not allowed. Still, this made no sense to some of those on the Lewis jury. A man's life was in their hands, and yet they felt as if they'd been left with gaping holes in their understanding of the facts. One juror had wanted to ask if photos of the bloody handprints found on Karen's body had been enlarged and sent to the FBI. At least two wanted to know if Lewis had a temper—a critical point on which they'd heard nothing.

Hungry for insight into his personality, many of the jurors had studied Lewis during the trial, noting the moments in the testimony when his face grew red, checking to see if he was ever reluctant to look them in the eye. Tim Green had stared across the courtroom and tried to visualize Lewis inside the house that night, stabbing Karen over and over. It didn't seem possible. Lewis looked too nice. The thought had occurred to other jurors as well. But they tried to remember that even the nicest-looking people can commit horrible crimes.

Maytha Schafer, the retired accountant, had learned this the hard way. Before she and her husband retired to Florida, Schafer had worked as the office manager of a car dealership in Chicago. There was one customer who came in every year to buy the first new car of the season. He was a friendly man who sometimes dressed up as a clown for children. When he visited the dealership, he always brought a young boy with him. The man's name was John Wayne Gacy, and in the late 1970s the police made the gruesome discovery that he'd killed thirty-three boys and young men, then buried many of them in the crawlspace under his house. The news had shocked Schafer. One of the worst serial killers in history had stood in front of her, year after year, and she'd never guessed it. For all she knew, some of those boys he'd brought into the dealership had been among his victims.

Now, sitting in the jury room, Schafer thought back to Gacy. It was foolish, she told herself, to think you really know what anybody is capable of.

Schafer was the oldest juror. A graceful woman with striking white hair and a disarming smile, she and her husband lived in a small, comfortable home in Lakeland—a placid city just north of Bartow—that was decorated with her seashells and with photos of her grandchildren and greatgrandchildren. Her life was a peaceful one. But since the trial had begun, Schafer had been uneasy. She was having trouble sleeping; when she closed her eyes, she kept thinking about the case. She'd found it upsetting to see the photos and videotape of Karen's body, surrounded by blood. At the same time, Schafer found herself thinking a great deal about Lewis and how his future was in her hands.

Her husband said she shouldn't bother worrying. Maytha hadn't told him about the case—the judge had ordered the jurors not to discuss it—but he did know it was a first-degree murder trial. Mr. Schafer, a retired ironworker, was one of the many citizens who have grown cynical about the criminal courts system. He told his wife it didn't really matter what she and the other jurors did, it would only be overturned later on appeal. She was wasting her time, he said.

The first thing they did was pick someone to lead the deliberations. They settled quickly on Greg Blessing, the former firefighter.

Born and raised in New York, Blessing carried both the accent and the confidence found in so many from that city. Working at a country club restaurant near Sebring, he was an extremely busy man. He walked fast, talked fast, and generally seemed to be in a hurry. To the others, he seemed a natural choice for foreman, not because of his background in firefighting but because he sat at the end of the front row and was closest to the judge. Besides, someone said, a person in the front row is always the foreman on TV.

Once that decision had been made, the jurors dove into the larger one, looking through the photos, throwing out questions that had lingered in their minds. Many of them had been struck by the conflicts between Lewis's earlier accounts and the one he'd given on the stand, when he knew all of the evidence against him and knew what he had to account for. Suddenly now he was offering this new detail of how he'd run into the bathroom that night and thrown up. But if he had gone in there, why didn't the police find any sign of him walking to the toilet? The one footprint that had been found was at the edge of the room, approximately five feet from the toilet.

Greg Blessing picked up a photograph of that solitary footprint. To him, it looked as if the print did not even point toward the toilet. To him, it looked as if Lewis had made that print while standing in the doorway, with his right foot in the bathroom and his left on the hallway carpet. Already, Blessing was fairly sure which way he was going to decide. He thought the defense had made some valid points. He agreed, as did other jurors, that the police work in this case had been far from perfect. Blessing was still surprised that weeks had gone by before the hallway carpet, on which the technicians had later discovered so many bloody footprints, was removed from the house and taken as evidence.

But the mistakes of the police had not stopped Lewis from opening his mouth. To Blessing, it seemed that the man had lied so many times it had become impossible to know when to believe him. Even his latest story, delivered on the stand, did not seem to add up. Besides, as a former firefighter, Blessing brought a special perspective to this case. With that in mind, he tried to put himself in Lewis's place, tried to imagine what he would have done if he'd crawled through that bedroom window and seen Karen's body on the floor. If it had been him, Blessing thought, he would have called the police. No question. Years in uniform also made it hard for Blessing to believe that an innocent man wouldn't have shared his secret with some of his pals in the fire department. He hadn't even told Glenda. In fact, he'd left her alone that night while he went investigating at David and Karen's house. Why, Blessing asked, would Lewis have done that? Why would he have gone over there without first checking on Glenda?

After the jurors had talked over some of these points for a little while, Blessing suggested they take an early vote to see which way the group was leaning. He borrowed someone's pocketknife and cut a blank sheet of paper into twelve pieces. There weren't enough pens to go around, so they took turns. They marked their ballots quietly, covering their slips with their hands. Later, one of them would say they were like high school kids guarding their answers on a test. Most of them wrote "G" for guilty or "NG" for not guilty. They did not even discuss voting on the lesser charges that were listed in the judge's instructions, such as second-degree murder or manslaughter. Nor did they cast separate votes for the murder charge and the rape charge. In their eyes, Lewis was guilty of both or guilty of neither.

They folded their ballots and gave them to Blessing, who mixed them up so no one would know who'd voted how. Then he opened them, one by one, and read them aloud, placing the Gs in a pile to his left and the NGs in a pile to his right. When he was done there were eight ballots on the left and four on the right.

They had only started.

Outside the jury room, a bailiff sat in a chair, listening for the buzzer.

Others waited and listened as well. Knowing the buzzer could sound at any time, the lawyers and families on both sides of the case stayed close. They roamed the courthouse, sent out for a late lunch, retreated to quiet side rooms, tried not to stare at the clock. It was useless to guess how long it would take before they had a decision. Some juries finished in fifteen minutes; others went for days, only to announce they were deadlocked. The conventional wisdom held that quick verdicts were usually convictions. The longer the deliberations lasted, the better the chances were supposed to be for the accused. But even this rule was routinely disproven. Ciarciaglino said he didn't predict verdicts anymore. He'd been wrong so many times, he said, that he no longer even bothered trying.

His reluctance was well-founded. Once a jury disappears behind that closed door, its members do whatever they want. No one is allowed to sit and watch how the jurors arrive at their verdict. No one is there to speak up if they stray from the instructions or if their recollection of the evidence is faulty.

Trial lawyers have a saying they tell their clients. When you put your fate in the hands of your fellow citizens, they say, you always roll the dice.

Maytha Schafer thought Lewis probably had done it. But she wasn't sure. She needed more time to think, more time to go over the evidence—none of which, as far as she could tell, sealed the case beyond every reasonable doubt. When they'd counted the first ballots, she'd been surprised that eight of the jurors had been willing to vote for a conviction so quickly.

It was midafternoon now. By this point, each of the twelve knew where the others stood. There had been no formal announcements, but as they sat around the long table, battling questions back and forth, their comments made it obvious that the NGs had been cast by Schafer, Leif Bouffard, Dorene Cobb, and Ruth Wunder. One of these four—Wunder, the seamstress—almost hadn't made it to deliberations. She'd been ill during the first week of the trial but had pushed herself to stick it out, explaining to the judge how badly she wanted to be part of this case. She'd told Farnell that this was "a chance of a lifetime."

But as the deliberations began, Wunder was discovering how difficult this rare opportunity could be. But she was not about to change her vote just to agree with the majority. A short, soft-spoken woman who chose her words carefully, Wunder was no pushover. Like the others, she had questions about what Lewis had said on the stand. She did not understand how he could have thrown up in the bathroom and not made a mess. It also bothered her that he had lied so many times. But Wunder did not believe that just because a man lied that necessarily proved he was a rapist and a murderer. There was more. Wunder was having trouble accepting some of what she'd heard from the prosecution's expert witnesses. One of them—Joan Wood—had testified that scrapings had been taken from underneath Karen's fingernails. As she said this, Dr. Wood had smiled.

"Why are you smiling?" Ciarciaglino had asked her.

"Well, it's just an irony. Somebody back in Germany in about 1801 got a positive sample from fingernail scrapings, so ever since we've all done them. They never have showed anything."

Now those words nagged at Wunder, because they did not

agree with something she'd seen on TV. She and the other jurors had been asked repeatedly to put aside whatever notions "Perry Mason" had pounded into their heads. But it was not "Perry Mason" that Wunder was remembering. It was "Quincy," the long-running show in which Jack Klugman played a crime-solving coroner. In one episode, as Wunder recalled, Quincy had used fingernail scrapings to identify a murderer. Why, then, she asked, was Dr. Wood trying to tell them fingernail scrapings were no good? Was that true? What if Wood was wrong? And if she was wrong about that, was she wrong about anything else? What if all of the "expert witnesses," on whose shoulders the state had built much of its case, didn't know what they were talking about?

The other jurors listened as Wunder asked some of these questions aloud.

"Maybe we're looking at too much television," said Schafer.

Dorene Cobb, the homemaker who helped care for the elderly, had doubts of her own about Lewis's guilt. For one thing, Cobb was convinced that the white teddy that had been brought into court could not possibly be the one Karen had bought for herself before the murder. This conclusion was shared by almost everyone in the room, including many who had voted guilty. Totally unaware of how many hours the lawyers had devoted to fighting about the teddy, the majority of the jurors had already dismissed it. They had dismissed it for one simple reason: the teddy was a size small.

The jurors had never seen a picture of Karen alive. The prosecutors had not even tried to show such a photo, because they knew it would have been ruled irrelevant. But photos taken of Karen after the murder were admissible, and so the prosecutors had shown some of those. Having seen those pictures, most of them decided that Karen would have been too big for this teddy. Furthermore, they had seen Tonja Dishong and been struck by how thin and small she was. Karen, the jurors decided, never would have bought a piece of clothing that would have fit Tonja.

This logic was not so much a victory for the defense as a failure for the state. Because in two weeks of trial, the prosecutors had neglected one point. When Tonja was on the stand, they had not asked her, as she had been asked in her deposition, how the teddy fit. If she'd been asked that, Tonja would have explained again that the teddy was too big for her, even though it was a small.

The teddy was not the only thing the jurors had dismissed. Even before the first vote, almost all of them had discounted the defense's suggestion that Karen might have willingly had sex with someone before the murder. To them, the facts—and common sense—showed that Karen clearly had been raped. Aside from the semen that had been discovered during the autopsy, the jurors also considered that Karen's body had been found half-naked on the floor, not far away from a bed on which blood had been found. Obviously some of the struggle had taken place in the bedroom. There was also the strong possibility that she had been forced to wear the black teddy. In addition, Dr. Wood had testified that two "pricking wounds," shallow cuts on the skin, had been found on Karen's chest and neck. Wood explained that these possibly had been made as the killer lightly pressed the weapon against Karen's skin with just enough force to break it. Greg Blessing believed that these marks, one of which had been made in the area of Karen's breasts, were "torture wounds"—more proof of a sexually oriented attack.

Even if Karen had wanted to be unfaithful to David Mackey, taking advantage of the fact that he was out of town—and no evidence had been presented to prove such a possibility—the jurors knew she would have had little time for it in the hours before the murder. She'd been at work all day at her job as a graphic artist—a new job, one of them noted, where she would have been unlikely to fool around. After work, she'd gone home, made the moving run, gone to dinner at Neverne's, then left, telling Neverne how tired she was and how much she wanted to go home and go to sleep.

The jurors also had rejected another major component of the defense's case—the insinuations against Peter Kumble and Kenneth Kuhar. From the start of deliberations, few of the jurors seemed to put much stock in the notion that Kumble might be the real murderer and Kuhar the accomplice waiting out on the lawn. Blessing, for one, said he thought it was nothing more than a defense smoke screen.

A couple of the jurors did wonder how Kumble could have walked onto the front porch and not seen the blood on the door. They also wondered whether Karen really had invited him over for dinner. Still, there was nothing to prove that either Kumble or Kuhar were anywhere near Karen's house that night. There was no evidence to place Kumble inside the house, and Kuhar clearly did not match the original description Lewis himself had given of the man on the lawn. As for the composite drawing of the alleged intruder, some of the jurors thought it looked like Kuhar and some didn't.

Bit by bit the jurors were whittling away at the question before them.

Across the hall, within hearing distance of the buzzer, Karen Gregory's family and friends drifted in and out of a small office.

Kim, Karen's sister, was still angry that Ciarciaglino and Paver had pushed her out of the courtroom. Just as she'd suspected, they had never called her to the stand. She'd been forced to sit outside the whole time. Sophia, Karen's mother, had not been kicked out. She'd sat in court through virtually the entire trial, listening to the witnesses, trying to learn the facts of what had happened to her oldest child. She had only been asked to leave the one time, during Dr. Wood's testimony.

Roy and Mark, Karen's brothers, had sat beside Sophia. The two of them had arrived midway through the trial after driving from their homes in New York state. Out in the halls, they tried to keep some distance between themselves and Lewis and his family. One day Roy had found himself inside a cramped bathroom, only a foot or two away from Lewis. Roy did not want that to happen again. He was afraid of what he might do if he came that close to Lewis a second time. So he and Mark developed a system. They'd watch the bathroom, wait for Lewis to emerge, then go in.

Like the others, Mark had studied Lewis carefully during the trial. Now, after hearing so much of the evidence, he was convinced the police had arrested the right man. As far as he was concerned, it was clear that Lewis had treated Karen like garbage— raped her, killed her, then thrown her away. But Mark was not afforded the luxury of seeing Lewis as some monster. It was all too plain that he was a human being.

Mark had a young daughter of his own. Her name was Korey, and she was about the same age as Tiffany Lewis. And like Glenda Lewis, Mark's wife was pregnant with their second child. Mark found himself watching Tiffany in the hall. She reminded him of Korey. She looked vaguely like her, played like her, and ran to her father just like Korey ran to him. Mark stared at Lewis holding his little girl. He couldn't believe how tenderly Lewis touched her. He couldn't believe that this man could love a child so much.

A thought crossed Mark's mind: just how different are we?

At 5:15 P.M. the buzzer sounded. The jurors had a question. They sent a note to Judge Farnell, asking if they could listen to some of the testimony a second time. Specifically, they wanted to hear what Dr. Wood and Lewis had said on the stand, plus the tape of Lewis's final statement to the police. Farnell had the jurors brought back into the courtroom, and the court reporter pulled out her notes and began rereading the testimony. She started with Dr. Wood.

> Q. Doctor, you've gone through a lot of injuries. Could you please summarize the stab and cutting wounds for the jury? How many total stabbings or cutting wounds did you find on the body of Karen Gregory?
> A. There were nine stab wounds to the left—to the right neck, and three cutting wounds, for twelve wounds. There were four stab wounds to the left neck, so that's sixteen. At least two separate actions of cutting wound, seventeen, eighteen. A pricking injury to the skin of the left neck, which was not previously described, it was among those; it's nineteen. The injury on the front of her chest, twenty. And the injury to her hand, twenty-one.
> Q. The injury to the hand being the defensive wound that you had described earlier?
> A. Yes.

Sophia sat in the audience, listening with Roy and Mark beside her. This time no one asked her to leave. This time she heard for herself exactly what Karen had gone through. She had wondered for so long. For years she had not been able to understand why Karen did not escape her attacker that night. Karen was so strong, so fierce. Why didn't she fight harder?

Now Sophia understood just how hard Karen had fought.

> Q. Based on the number of wounds that you observed and your experience in this field, can you render an

opinion as to the minimum amount of time it would have taken to inflict all of these wounds upon Karen Gregory, or to the maximum amount of time?

A. I believe it could have taken five, ten, fifteen minutes. The minimum would probably be two or three minutes.

Sophia thought back to the first time she'd seen Karen and held her. Sophia was lying there in the hospital, and the nurses showed her this tiny child, and suddenly she was terrified. She realized she had no idea what to do with a baby. Maybe I can get up and run away, she'd thought. Maybe I can send her back.

Q. Dr. Wood, within a reasonable degree of medical certainty, can you give this jury and the court your opinion as to the cause of death of Karen Gregory?

A. Yes.

Q. And what is that opinion?

A. The cause of death of Karen Gregory was cutting and stabbing wounds to the neck, causing injury to the voice box and to the left outer jugular vein, draining blood from the head. Contributing to her death were multiple blows to the head with lacerations of the scalp and bleeding upon the left surface of the brain.

So much blood, Sophia thought. So much blood on that beautiful child's body. Sophia remembered how smooth Karen's skin had been when she was a little girl. She remembered brushing Karen's long brown hair. Karen had always been a bit vain about that, her mother recalled. She'd always been proud of how silky her hair was.

The court reporter had been reading for more than an hour when the defense attorneys asked to approach the bench. There was a problem. One of the jurors appeared to have fallen asleep.

It was Tim Green. Farnell had been glaring at him, trying to get his attention. If the lawyers saw him or anyone else sleeping again, the judge said, they were to let him know. For the moment, though, they were to continue.

"He'll perk up," said Farnell.

Several hours went by while the jurors reheard everything they'd asked for. When the late afternoon stretched into evening, they broke for dinner, came back, and kept going. Through it all, they were listening for specific details. They'd wanted to hear Dr. Wood's testimony again for several reasons. Dorene Cobb was still thinking about the rape charge. Though she thought Karen probably had been raped, she wanted to hear again what Wood had said about the semen and the "pricking wounds." At the same time, she and the others wanted to rehear Lewis's final statement to the police and his testimony in court so they could compare the two stories, side by side. Now, that was exactly what happened. First they listened to Lewis, on the tape, answering the detectives' questions. Then they listened to the court reporter, reading back what Lewis had said as he answered questions on the witness stand. One contradiction tumbled after the other.

First, on the tape:
"I wasn't even barefoot that night."
Then, in court:
"So you were barefoot then. Is that correct?"
"Yes, sir."
First:
"There wasn't any lights on in the house."
Then:
"When I got there, I noticed a little bit of light inside the house . . . A faint light."
First:
"I saw her laying there with her throat cut open."
Then:
"I couldn't tell what type of injuries she had."
First:
"I looked, and I saw her laying on the floor . . . I didn't do anything else."
Then:
"What did you do then after looking at her and seeing this blood?"
"I started to get sick, and I ran into what was the bathroom then, and I threw up."
Finally, at 9:50 P.M., after they'd stopped for dinner and then come back and continued, they'd heard everything. Back into the jury room they went. To many of them it seemed even clearer

now that the latest story from Lewis was another lie. But others weren't convinced.

It's unclear what doubts or questions were lingering inside Leif Bouffard. Of the four jurors voting not guilty, he was the only one who would later decline to talk about the deliberations. As for Ruth Wunder, she was still going through it all in her mind. If Lewis was telling the truth now—if he really had gone into that house to help, only to realize that he would be suspected—then she could understand why he initially would have denied being there. It also had occurred to her that once Lewis lied, he did not lie very well. The way he'd kept changing his stories reminded her of someone who didn't know how to lie because he normally told the truth. Could that kind of person, she asked herself, be capable of murder?

One of the other women on the jury had been struck by something as they'd listened again to Lewis on the tape, telling the police about the alleged man on the lawn. He'd said that the man was about five eight, maybe taller, with wavy hair that appeared auburn in color.

"Did you notice his description?" said the juror. "It was almost like he was describing himself."

They talked on for a half-hour or so before Blessing suggested they take another vote to see if they were any closer to a consensus. He borrowed the pocketknife again, cut up another sheet of paper, and passed around the ballots. Again the tally was eight to four. The same people—Bouffard, Cobb, Schafer, and Wunder—were still voting not guilty.

Shortly before 11 P.M. they sent a message to the judge that they were ready to stop for the night. This did not mean, however, that they were going home. It had already been explained to the jurors that they would be sequestered as long as they were deliberating. Already, reservations had been made for them at the Davis Brothers Motor Lodge. Knowing that it might come to this, the jurors had brought overnight bags and a change of clothes.

Before they were driven to the motel, Farnell gave them a few more instructions. Until they returned the next morning, he said, they were not to discuss the case or form any fixed opinions about Lewis's guilt or innocence. And though their motel rooms were equipped with TVs, they were on their honor not to watch them. There was one thing more: to make sure they did not discuss the case with any outsiders, the phones in their rooms would be cut off by the motel switchboard.

"All right," Farnell said. "No questions? Everybody satisfied with what the situation is and what we're going to do?"

The jurors nodded.

Thirty

Tim Green could not sleep. Earlier in the day, in court, he'd had trouble staying awake. Now, sitting inside his motel room, he was having trouble dozing off. Looking for something to do, he turned on his room TV and found a movie. It was a comedy, *Going Berserk*.

Off in their own rooms, other jurors were also finding it hard to fall asleep. Dorene Cobb lay in bed thinking about the case, asking God to help her see clearly. She did not know if George Lewis was guilty or not. She kept wavering back and forth. But she knew she did not want to spend the rest of her life wondering if she'd made a mistake.

Like the other three jurors voting not guilty, Cobb was a parent. She knew she was not supposed to be swayed by emotion, but she could not help harboring maternal feelings toward Lewis. She found it hard to believe that someone so nice and clean-cut could be guilty. He was out on bond, wasn't he? Didn't that mean he could be trusted? When he was testifying, Cobb thought she had detected something in his face—something wistful in his eyes. He'd reminded her of a little boy who knows an important secret and wants to share it with the grown-ups. To her, it seemed as if

Lewis had wanted to help the police by telling them what he knew about the murder. But he couldn't tell them everything, at least not at first. The man on the lawn threatened him, he'd said. The man knew where he lived.

There were so many unanswered questions pulling Cobb in opposite directions. She thought about Lewis walking into Karen's house and seeing her lying on the floor. He'd said he'd been too scared to call the police. But if he was so afraid, Cobb thought, couldn't he have called anonymously? Then there was the murder weapon. If Lewis was guilty, what had happened to his weapon? Why had the police never found it?

Cobb lay in bed, thinking through the night. She prayed, and went over the points, one by one, and then prayed some more. It was close to 5:00 A.M. when she turned her mind to the footprints. She thought about the trail of bloody footprints on the hallway carpet, the ones that were invisible to the naked eye until the technician, Timothy Whitfield, had sprayed them with Luminol. Cobb and the others had watched the videotape of the Luminol test, but the quality of the tape was poor and it had been difficult for the jurors to see much. But they had been able to make out a few prints, glowing in the dark, and they'd heard Whitfield describing others. If what he said was correct, there were at least a dozen footprints on that carpet.

On the stand, Lewis had said that he went into the house, saw Karen's body, ran to the bathroom, and then ran out. But if those footprints on the carpet were his, how could he be telling the truth? There were too many prints. They were all through that hallway, where so much of the struggle had taken place. Whoever left the footprints, Cobb thought, had obviously done more than run into the bathroom and run out. Was it Lewis? Were those footprints his? It was hard to tell. Whitfield, after all, had not been allowed to talk about the measurements and how they corresponded to the size of Lewis's feet. The jurors had been left in the dark on that point.

But Cobb remembered something. All of the bloody prints had been made by someone who was barefoot. How many people could that be? How many people, she asked herself, could have been walking through that house without any shoes? True, Karen was barefoot that night. But she couldn't have left those prints. The jurors had checked. Earlier that day, during the deliberations, they'd looked at the photos of her body lying on that hallway carpet, and they'd seen for themselves that there was no blood on the bottoms of her feet. That left Lewis. His print in the bathroom proved he'd been barefoot that night. But at first he had denied it. That bothered Cobb. Even though she wanted to believe Lewis, it bothered her that the man had denied being barefoot until he was cornered and forced to admit otherwise.

Suddenly Cobb knew. Her doubts were gone.

Outside, it was almost dawn.

At 9:30 that morning they assembled back in the jury room to begin their second day of deliberations. They'd talked for only a few minutes when they decided to vote again to see if anybody had had a change of heart during the night. Dorene Cobb quietly wrote a G on her ballot, folded it, and handed it in with the others. She sat there, not saying a word, as Greg Blessing tallied the vote. A headache pounded dully behind her temples.

Blessing finished counting. The vote was nine to three.

Now only Bouffard, Schafer, and Wunder were holding out for acquittal. The other nine tried to stay calm. Up to this point the deliberations had been polite and orderly. But the strain was starting to show. Schafer, feeling some pressure now, announced that she was not going to budge. After all, Lewis's life was at stake. It was important, she told herself, to be absolutely positive before she voted guilty. Yes, George had lied and lied and lied. But to Schafer that did not prove he was a murderer.

"You can go over this as many times as you want," she said. "But I'm not going to change my mind."

With that, one of the men was ready to quit.

"You might as well call the judge," he said. "There's no sense in us sitting here all day."

They didn't quit, though. They kept trying to talk it through. The ones who were voting guilty pointed to all of the bare footprints on the carpet. To many of them it seemed clear that the prints had been made by Lewis. Didn't that prove, they said, that he had done it? Weren't there too many prints to match his latest story?

Both Schafer and Wunder weren't sure that there really were as many footprints as the others believed. They'd all watched the videotape of the Luminol being sprayed onto the carpet and heard Whitfield, noting each footprint as it glowed in the dark. But the tape had been so murky. Schafer had not been able to see many of the footprints Whitfield was talking about. Wunder had made out only two or three. To accept that there were so many footprints on that carpet required her to take Whitfield's word for it, and Wunder didn't feel comfortable with that. She was still thinking about "Quincy" and all of the doubts that that had raised for her about the expertise of the state's witnesses.

They pulled out the carpet and unrolled it, there on the floor of the jury room. They tried to recall where the footprints had been found and which way they were pointed and how close they were to the bathroom. Finally they decided they needed to view the Luminol tape again, along with the videotape that the medical examiner's office had made of the interior of the crime scene. That way, they'd see the entire layout of the house—the hallway, the bathroom, everything—just as it had been found on the day Karen's body was discovered.

At 11:15 A.M. the jurors were brought back into the courtroom to view the two tapes again. This time Maytha Schafer saw the footprints. Sitting there in the dark, she found the proof she had lacked before. There were more footprints than she remembered. Too many, she told herself, for Lewis to be telling the truth. It's all just another lie, she thought. He was inside that house a lot longer than he'd said.

When they finished watching the tapes, the jurors returned to the jury room and had lunch. By this point, Wunder was wavering. Despite her doubts, she had decided to accept Whitfield's word. Like Schafer, she was finally convinced that those bloody footprints were all over the carpet. But she had a few more questions. She wanted to think some more. Schafer watched Ruth carefully as they went on talking. After spending so much time together, Schafer knew that Ruth's face grew red when she was upset. It was bright red now. As red, Schafer would later say, as fire.

Blessing said he thought they should take another vote. Again the slips of paper were cut, handed out, marked, folded, handed back. Again Blessing read each vote aloud. Wunder sat beside him, silently adding the tally to herself. She kept hearing Blessing read out the same word, over and over.

" . . . Guilty."

That was eight.

"Guilty."

Nine.
"Guilty."
Ten.
"Guilty."
Eleven.
"Guilty."
Twelve.

There was a hush around the table. Blessing handed the ballots to a couple of the other jurors, asking them to double-check and make sure he hadn't missed any votes for acquittal. He looked around the table.

"Did anybody vote not guilty?"

No one answered. He picked up the stack of verdict forms and found the one for conviction of first-degree murder and the one for conviction of sexual battery, then signed the bottom of both sheets.

"That's it," someone said. "We did our job."

Blessing stood up and pushed the buzzer. It was 2:21 P.M.

The door to the jury room opened and the jurors walked out in single file. Lewis studied their faces as they shuffled into the jury box. George's friends and family sat a few feet away in the audience along with Karen's friends and family. All of them had been allowed into the courtroom now.

"Mr. Blessing," said Judge Farnell. "You have a verdict?"

"Yes, we do."

"Hand it to the bailiff."

The bailiff handed the verdict forms to the judge, who read them over silently, then passed them to the clerk, a kind-looking man with glasses and thick white hair. Karen's brother Roy looked at the clerk and thought how strange it was that such a nice old man would be the one, after all this time, to deliver the news.

"Publish the verdict," said Farnell.

Roy stopped breathing. Everything around seemed to be suspended.

"*The State of Florida vs. George Alan Lewis,*" said the clerk, reading aloud from the first sheet. "We, the jury, find the defendant, George Alan Lewis, guilty of murder in the first degree. So say we all, dated this 14th of June 1987, Gregory H. Blessing, Foreperson."

He turned to the second sheet and began reading. But his

words were drowned out. Glenda Lewis had already begun screaming.

It was not one scream but several, each running into the next. There were no words, just the sound coming from deep inside her and filling the courtroom. She stood up. Her body was shaking. Her hands were curled and raised to her face. People rushed toward her. They half-walked her, half-carried her from the room. At the defense table, George sat with a sick look on his face, watching her go.

Farnell stared straight ahead.

"Does counsel wish the jury polled?" he said.

"Yes, sir," said Ciarciaglino.

"Poll the jury."

The clerk turned to Tim Green in the far seat in the back row.

"Mr. Green, is this your verdict?"

"Yes, sir."

Then to Elizabeth Carter, sitting beside Green, "Mrs. Carter, is this your verdict?"

"Yes, sir."

Down the rows the clerk went, asking each juror the same question. As each gave the same answer, Lewis looked at them in disbelief. When all twelve had spoken, he closed his eyes, bowed his head, and leaned forward over the table with his shoulders hunched together. Glenda's screams could still be heard, even though she was in another room, across the hall, with the door shut. The sound just kept going.

Karen's mother turned to Roy and grabbed his arm. "Those are Karen's last screams," she said.

Glenda's friends were with her in the room across the hall. Someone was trying to calm her down, but she was still crying out.

"They don't know him . . . I know him . . . I know, but it doesn't matter what we think . . . He didn't do it . . . They were sleeping in there . . . I just want to see him . . . What are they going to do?"

Amid all the confusion and the crying and the lights and TV cameras, a pregnant woman fainted out near the rotunda. She was one of Lewis's friends, and as she fell, a man caught her, picked her up, and carried her toward the room where Glenda had been taken.

"Open the door!" he said, the woman still cradled in his arms. "Open the door!"

David Mackey, who was out in the hall by now, saw what was happening, ran to a pay phone, and called for an ambulance. If there was irony in this—if it was strange for him to rush to help a friend of Lewis's after no one had called to help Karen— David did not have time to think about it. Quickly, he made the call, then went to the room of Lewis's supporters to say the paramedics were on their way. As he stepped inside, people began yelling at him, asking what he thought he was doing. Quietly, he stepped back outside. A few seconds later, when they realized he had only been trying to help, someone came out to thank him.

"All right," Judge Farnell said. "We have reconvened in chambers now at 2:52 by the clock . . . "

The bailiffs brought Lewis into the judge's chambers, away from the courtroom spectators.

"Let the record reflect," Farnell said, "that the defendant is now present."

Now that Lewis had been found guilty of first-degree murder, they would proceed with what is known as the penalty phase. On Wednesday the jurors would return to court to hear evidence on which sentence they should recommend: death in the electric chair, or life in prison with no chance of parole for twenty-five years.

Sitting in chambers, a few feet away from Lewis, Richard Mensh announced that the state would be seeking the maximum penalty. He did not use the words "death sentence." Just "maximum penalty."

Across the table, Lewis looked over in horror.

His eyes were red and blurry. He turned them toward the window. It was a beautiful Sunday afternoon. The sun was shining; trees on the courthouse lawn were swaying in the breeze.

From the next room came the sound of one of the prosecutor's voices. It was Beverly Andrews. She was on the phone, spreading the news.

"You hear we got a verdict? Guilty as charged."

Ruth Wunder cried all the way home.

Dorene Cobb walked into her house and sat on the porch and tried to enjoy the evening air. It was nice, she thought, to be out in the open. It was nice to be able to get up and walk outside if she wanted.

Karen's mother, exhausted by now, told reporters how badly she felt for the Lewis family.

"I am a mother like his mother," said Sophia. "I don't think I could ever sign a death paper for him."

Glenda Lewis was still crying hysterically when she left the courthouse. She was led out, surrounded by friends, who shielded her from the photographers.

George Lewis was taken to the Polk County Jail, a couple of blocks away. The officers there booked him and told him to empty his pockets and take off his clothes. They took and made an inventory of his tie, shirt, pants, jacket, belt, watch, wallet, and wedding ring, plus one Montgomery Ward credit card and $9 he'd been carrying. In place of his other clothes they gave him a jail uniform.

Dinner at the jail that night was corned beef, boiled cabbage, boiled potatoes, carrots, bread, iced tea, and mincemeat pie. The records do not show whether Lewis ate any of it. Concerned that he might try to kill himself, jail officials ordered that he be kept on a suicide watch. When it came time to decide whether he should be ordered to die, they wanted to make sure he was still alive.

Part
Five

Her Bare Hands

Thirty-one

When the verdict was announced and Glenda's screams filled the courtroom, there was a businessman sitting in the audience. It was Al Estes, the bonding agent. He had come to see that one of his accounts was closed properly.

As far as Estes was concerned, once the trial was over, so was the contract with the Lewis family. That was why he went to the Polk County Courthouse that day. He liked George. Still, he wanted to make sure there would be no misunderstandings. Lewis's family and friends would get back the property they'd put up as collateral, but the $30,000 cash fee would belong to Estes's company. Whether Lewis was convicted or acquitted, there would be no refund. That was the price they'd paid to have him out until the verdict. Later, if they needed help in posting bond again, they would have to arrange a new contract.

As it turned out, there was no need for that. Once the jury came back with its verdict, Judge Farnell returned Lewis to custody without bond. By that time he had been out of jail for 165 days, give or take a few hours. Each week of his freedom had cost about $1,271, each day about $182. Every dollar had bought him just under eight minutes.

*   *   *

On Wednesday, June 17—three days after the verdict—the jurors returned to the courthouse to consider Lewis's sentence. Early that morning Lewis was brought from the jail. By then he had been allowed to change from his jail uniform into his street clothes, but still he looked like a different man from the one who had entered this same courtroom two weeks before. The startling confidence had vanished; now he was a picture of despondency. He sat silently in a jacket and tie at the defense table, looking downward, leaning forward, hunching his shoulders together. It was as if he were made of paper and had been crushed.

Ciarciaglino had undergone a similar transformation. A week before, in the middle of the trial, the senior defense attorney had been striding around the courthouse, plotting strategy, firing accusations and insinuations at the state's witnesses. One day he had worn a tie pin shaped like the scales of justice. When someone asked him about it, a big grin had spread across his face. "Truth, justice, and the American way," he'd said. But the fire was gone now. Never before had a jury found one of his clients guilty of first-degree murder. Ciarciaglino sat motionless in his chair next to Lewis, staring into space. He didn't seem to hear what was being said around him; he barely spoke at all. Instead he let Paver do most of the talking. It was going to be a busy day for his partner. The defense had gathered dozens of Lewis's friends and family members to tell the jury about George's background and character.

The friends and family of Karen Gregory, however, would not be testifying about Karen's background or character. They wouldn't be saying a word, because the state was not calling them to the stand. This came as no surprise. In Florida, when defendants are convicted of first-degree murder, their relatives are routinely allowed to appear before the jury during the penalty phase and explain why they deserve mercy. Yet the family of the victim is rarely given a chance to talk about the pain of that person's loss.

On Monday, June 15, just two days before the penalty phase began in the Lewis trial, the U.S. Supreme Court had given its stamp of approval to this practice. Voting five to four, the court had ruled that in potential death sentence cases, families of murder victims generally should not be allowed to inform juries about the impact of the crime on their lives. Justice Lewis F. Powell, Jr., wrote that the trauma of the victim's family is "irrelevant" to the sentencing decision. Though he recognized the family's anger and grief, Powell said the jury might be inflamed into favoring the death sentence if those feelings were expressed in court. Such a decision, he said, must be "based on reason rather than caprice or emotion."

For years that kind of logic has been a sore point among advocates of victims' rights. If the family of the accused is allowed to speak, they say, why shouldn't the family of the victim? And if the goal is to erase emotion from the sentencing, then shouldn't both sides be forbidden to speak?

Still, the law was the law. David Mackey and the others finally would be admitted into the courtroom. But they would have to sit there with their mouths shut as a parade of Lewis supporters took the stand to talk about George.

Those who knew him kept slipping into the past tense, as if he were already dead.

Pamela Hackett, a friend, said: "He seemed to be a sweet kid, you know. He was real friendly. He'd say hi to you whenever you went by."

Edwin Eggert, a high school buddy: "He enjoyed helping everybody. He always—he was always the nice guy with a smile."

And Jan Radjeski, a fellow firefighter: "In the short time that I knew him, I knew that I could call on that man any time of day or night and he'd be there."

One by one they sat down in the witness chair, turned toward the jury, and searched for the right words to explain who Lewis was and why his life should be spared. George, the witnesses said, was "a good worker," "an all-around good guy," and a "perfect husband," who "more or less worshipped" Glenda. In addition, he was "very loyal," "very loving," "very level-headed," "always dependable," "conscientious, polite, and respectable," "never violent," and "the nicest guy."

After awhile the words began to blend together into one numbing blur. The witnesses just kept repeating the same glowing generalities, portraying him in such uncompromisingly favorable terms that they left no room for flaws or shortcomings, no hint that George had ever made a mistake or done anything foolish or acted petty. The person they were describing could never have raised his voice, much less committed a murder.

"I don't know anybody that perfect," one of the jurors would later say.

It was obvious that the witnesses cared about Lewis. But anyone who'd sat through the trial knew that much of what these people said did not match the testimony. Perhaps his friends had sheltered themselves from the facts. Perhaps they had accepted what they wanted to accept and pushed the rest from their minds. Either way, they did not know George as well as they wanted to believe, or at least as well as they wanted the jurors to believe.

At the defense table Lewis stayed slumped in his chair, with his head lowered and tears occasionally sliding down his cheeks. When his friends came into the courtroom, he would not look at them squarely. Some of them tried to make eye contact as they walked to the witness stand, but he would not lift his face in their direction.

Dale Martin, who had been George's neighbor for years, talked about how George was always such a good friend to Martin's stepson, Kenny Hackett. The two boys had grown up together, attending the same school, waterskiing, playing with their radio-controlled cars. George had helped Kenny become a volunteer firefighter in Gulfport. At one point, when Kenny was dating a woman of whom his parents disapproved, they'd asked George to "talk some sense" into him.

"So Georgie asked him which is the most important, being a Gulfport fireman or this young lady," Martin told the jurors. "And he said there's a lot more to life than this young lady. So, as a result, Kenny got away from her."

After Tiffany Lewis was born, Martin said, George used to babysit her. Glenda would be at work and he'd be off duty, so he took care of her.

"He loved that—dearly loved—that little girl," said the witness.

Neverne Covington was listening in the audience with Karen's family and other friends, taking notes. When she heard Martin say those words, she wrote:

Karen's mother dearly loved her "little girl."

Roy Ozmore, a fisherman who was a longtime friend of George's, told the jurors a story. One day, he said, he and George were waterskiing. Suddenly they saw some workers at a nearby construction site throwing rocks at a sea gull. The rocks hit the bird, causing it to fall from the air. George went over to the bird, picked it up, and carried it to safety, ignoring the workers who now were throwing rocks at him.

"Was that type of behavior unusual as far as George is concerned?" asked Paver.

"Not as far as George was concerned, no."

Neverne wrote:

Save a bird but not a human?

In the two weeks of trial before the verdict, thirty-one witnesses had been called. Now, during the single day of the penalty phase, the defense called another thirty-one. They moved in and out of the court at a breakneck pace, each person speaking for only a few minutes. The last to testify were the members of the Lewis family, including all six of George's brothers and sisters.

His sister Linda explained to the jurors that George was the youngest of the family. "He was a wonderful little baby," she said. "I mean, he would come toddling around, and he'd have a smile on his face, and he would just be delighted just to see someone there to talk to."

Anita, another sister, said that George was "a fun person . . . a loving person." She told how they used to fight with water guns until everyone was soaked. "And he just enjoyed life," she said. "He had a great time." She talked about how George had built rockets for her sons and how the boys were now "very worried" about their uncle.

"Anything else you want to say to the jury?"

"No."

Anita was crying. She turned toward the jurors.

"But I love him. Just don't forget that."

Milton, one of the brothers, said that George's desire to help people was the reason he had become a firefighter. George, he said, cared about any living creature. If George had any flaw, Milton said, it was that "he didn't hesitate to put other people first . . . he's a real human being in the truest sense, in my opinion."

James, another brother, said that George was "a very kind, very loving father" and alluded to the fact that young Tiffany was playing out in the hall. "As you can well see," James said, "he has a beautiful little daughter." George, the brother added, had no temper.

"There is no way that man is ever a violent person," he said.

Some of the jurors were getting tired of hearing such platitudes. They already had decided that Lewis had murdered Karen. That wasn't the issue anymore. Yet here were these friends and family members, suggesting over and over that George could not have done such a thing. Some of the jurors, meanwhile, were disturbed by the testimony of another of George's brothers, Carl Lewis, Jr., who made a point of telling them he'd been in the armed services and had been trained how to kill.

"It's easy to take life," he said. "I know this for a fact. In the service it can be done quick."

But George, he said, was trained to save, not take, lives. "All of his life, through school, he's never once had the idea—ever—to take anyone's life. Never had the reason for it; never had the need for it."

Carl kept going.

"It takes a lot of stamina and guts to keep from killing once you've learned how to do it. If you've never learned how to do it and never tried it, okay, you can't do it . . . "

At the lectern, Paver listened with a sick look on his face. He quickly tried to change the subject.

"Do you find George to be a gentle person?" he asked.

"Yes."

"What about George with Glenda and Tiffany?"

"Very gentle. Very gentle . . . Because neither one of them have any scars on them. Not a one."

"Call your next witness, sir."

"Glenda Lewis."

When she came in the courtroom, her eyes were red. She walked hesitantly, as if she'd almost forgotten how.

"Would you tell us please about George Lewis?"

Glenda paused, then began to talk. She and George, she said, had met in 1981. They started dating and she moved in with him a few months later. Glenda said that George was her first love. He had taught her to ride a motorcycle, she said. He tried to teach her to water ski, but she never got the hang of it. "And then we got married," she said, "and we had—we have our baby, Tiffany."

Glenda kept stopping, swallowing, looking up at the ceiling.

She was fighting not to cry. George, she said, was a wonderful father and husband. She said she couldn't ask for anyone else.

"I'm sorry," she said, tears streaming down her cheeks. She was rising from the witness chair to leave. "I can't say anything else."

The final witness was Evelyn Lewis, George's mother. Her youngest child, she told the jurors, was "a beautiful boy" who had always wanted to be a firefighter. Many times, she said, he used to draw pictures of fire trucks and of houses burning. His own father had been a volunteer firefighter, she said.

"And he would say, 'Mom, I want to be like Dad. I want to help people like Daddy helps people,' he'd say." George never lost that interest, she said. One night, after he became a firefighter, he drove proudly by the family's house so they could see him in a fire truck. "This is his life," she explained.

She began to wander through her memories. She said she and her husband loved their children dearly and had tried to raise their seven boys and girls as decent human beings. They'd made sure the kids had hobbies. They'd taught them how to swim and to plant flowers. They'd taken them to farms and showed them the animals.

Mrs. Lewis looked at the jurors. "All I can say, I know he's a good boy. I know he tells the truth, because this is what my children were always taught. No matter how bad or how hard it hurts them, I want the truth out of them. Their father demanded the truth, whatever it was. And we used to have round-table discussions after supper, and . . . "

Neverne had written down something else:

What went wrong?

After all the years and all the sleepless nights, Neverne was still trying to understand how all of them had ended up in this courtroom. How had such a horrible thing—such evil—come about? Neverne was not a religious woman. She did not believe in the devil. She had a hard time accepting that evil was some dark, supernatural force swirling under the surface of the earth. She thought it was something much more ordinary. It had to do with selfishness, she told herself. Evil was selfishness, taken to its ultimate extreme.

*   *   *

By the time Evelyn Lewis finished testifying, it was late in the afternoon. The lawyers had retreated to the privacy of the judge's chambers to discuss a few final details with Farnell when a bailiff appeared at the door with a note from the jury. It said:

> Judge, we as a group have put in a long day, and if we will not complete today's proceeding shortly, we would appreciate a recess until tomorrow at 9 o'clock.
> Gregory H. Blessing, Foreman

Blessing was eager to leave at a timely hour because his girl-friend was leaving town. A couple of days before he even had asked the judge that they not go late this day. Now Paver and Ciarciaglino remembered that request. A man's life was on the line, and the jury foreman was worrying about seeing his girl-friend. Ciarciaglino looked disgusted. Farnell said he wanted to press on. They were nearly finished. The only thing left was for the lawyers to deliver closing arguments and for the jurors to decide on a recommendation.

"Good afternoon, ladies and gentlemen," said Beverly Andrews.

Seated at the end of the first row in the jury box, Greg Blessing looked at his watch.

Quickly, Andrews summed up why the state was seeking the death sentence, The prosecution, she said, did not deny that Lewis was an able firefighter and emergency medical technician. Nor did the prosecution deny that Lewis had many friends. But the people who had testified on his behalf, Andrews said, did not know the facts of the case. They had believed in Lewis and given him their trust, she argued, and he had violated that trust.

"He let his family and friends down," she said.

Andrews pointed at Lewis, seated at the defense table. That man, she said, was a total fraud. She asked the jurors to picture him inside the house that night, standing over Karen in the hallway, a knife in his hand. She reminded them of the agony Karen must have suffered in the last minutes of her life. As for the motive behind the attack, she said that was clear; Lewis had murdered Karen to keep her quiet.

"They knew each other. They were neighbors," said Andrews. "He raped her, and then he had to eliminate her. Remember what, again, the defendant's mother said on the stand: Being a firefighter was his life. It meant the world to him. He raped that woman and then had to kill her, because it was his life or her life."

These words echoed something the jurors had heard earlier that day.

"So Georgie asked him which is the most important, being a Gulfport fireman or this young lady. And he said there's a lot more to life than this young lady."

When it was Paver's turn to speak, he asked the jurors to think about the kind of life George had led for the twenty-two years before the murder and then ask themselves whether that was outweighed by, as Paver put it, "a few frenzied moments." It wasn't as if he had gone on a crime spree through three counties. It wasn't, Paver suggested, as if George had killed several people.

"It's a crime . . . which occurred in a small segment of time," he said, "and that has to be weighed against the rest of Mr. Lewis's life and his family and his friends."

It would be horrible enough, Paver said, for George to spend his life in prison. He and Tiffany might never get to hold each other again. And when Glenda gave birth to their second child, he would not be there with her in the delivery room.

At opposite ends of the courtroom, George and Glenda were both crying. When Paver spoke of how Glenda would deliver her second child without her husband, she stood up and left the room.

Paver went on, talking about how the past would tear at George day after day in prison for the rest of his life.

"And I know you will think of the witnesses that you heard here today," he said, "and you'll think of the twenty-two years of existence that's all been good, and I hope that you will return the correct decision and recommend to the court that George's life not end in the Florida electric chair."

There was another thing the defense had considered doing to save Lewis's life. In chambers earlier in the day, outside the jury's hearing, Paver had requested that the judge approve the following sentence as one of the possible arguments for mercy:

The victim was a participant in the defendant's conduct
or consented to the act.

Andrews was startled.

"They're going to argue consent?"

Farnell, looking a little surprised himself, asked the defense
attorneys if they really wanted to use that argument. "You guys
want it?" he said. "You're going to be able to do this with a
straight face now?"

Paver thought for a second. They were withdrawing their
request, he said.

"That's what I thought," said Farnell.

Karen's mother was not in chambers to hear what the defense
had briefly suggested. Still, it was hard enough for Sophia to hear
what was said in open court. The worst—even worse than hearing
the cold details of how Karen had died—had come when Paver
suggested that Lewis should be spared because only one person
had been killed and because the murder was only "a few frenzied
moments."

When Paver spoke those words, Sophia wanted to climb over
the courtroom railing and strangle him. She'd heard a lot of mean
things in her life, she said, but that was the meanest. It was as if
her daughter had never existed, she said. As if Karen had been
nothing.

At 6:13 P.M. the jurors retired to choose between life and
death. This time their decision did not have to be unanimous. A
majority vote either way would be sufficient, the judge told them.
If they tied, that would be regarded as a recommendation for life.
There was no need, then, for more than one vote.

The jurors sat around the same table where they'd deliberated
for hours over the past weekend. For many of them, worn out
emotionally by that decision, this second phase of the trial had
been a frustrating experience. Several jurors could not understand
why they had not heard a single word of testimony about Karen
Gregory. Among those who felt this way was Ruth Wunder. Even
though she had been among the last jurors to be convinced that
Lewis was guilty, Wunder thought it made no sense that they had
not been told anything about the woman whose death had started
this case. Wunder had all sorts of questions. What kind of person
had Karen been? Why had she never had children? What had she

looked like? The jurors, after all, had never seen a picture of her alive. They had been allowed to see her only as a corpse.

Yet there seemed to be little disagreement as to which sentence they should recommend. Despite the brutality of this crime, they noted that Lewis had never been arrested before and had led, as far as they knew, a good life until the murder. He had been a dedicated firefighter and EMT. Furthermore, life in prison hardly seemed a lenient punishment.

Maytha Schafer had another reason for preferring a life sentence. She remembered how her husband had warned her, earlier on, that whatever decision they made would be overturned on appeal. Schafer didn't want to think that the past two weeks had been in vain. But she thought that possibility was more likely if Lewis were sentenced to death. If they voted for life, she told herself, maybe they wouldn't have to worry about years of appeals.

The jurors talked for almost an hour. Then Greg Blessing suggested they take a vote. Write down an "L" for life, he said, or a "D" for death.

The buzzer sounded at 7:05 P.M. The judge and the lawyers and the families returned once more to the courtroom, and the jurors were summoned back to their seats. Blessing handed over the recommendation form. Again a clerk read it aloud.

By a vote of twelve to zero, the jury advised and recommended that the court impose the sentence of life imprisonment upon George A. Lewis, without possibility of parole for twenty-five years.

"All right!" someone cried.

Lewis lowered his head and nodded.

Judge Farnell turned to the jurors. He said he knew how hard this case had been, both mentally and physically. But he said he hoped that they could find some reward in knowing that they'd served their country. Without citizens such as they, he said, our court system could not exist.

"So we do thank you," he said, "and you are free to go at this time."

It was almost dusk by now. The jurors walked together out of the courthouse to the parking lot. They hugged, said good-bye, joked about how they hoped they never had to see one another again. Before separating they agreed that they had done their jobs. Lewis, they said, had received a fair trial. They were sure of it.

*   *   *

Farnell would not be passing sentence immediately. He needed to give probation officials some time to prepare a pre-sentence investigation, commonly known as a PSI. In Florida the PSI is standard procedure in first-degree murder cases; it's designed to help the judge arrive at the proper sentence. An investigator would read the file, interview people involved in the case, then make a report on his or her findings. All of this would require at least a couple of weeks. When the sentencing was finally scheduled, it would be done back in Pinellas County. In the meantime, Lewis would stay in jail.

That evening the bailiffs allowed George and Glenda to hug and say good-bye in a waiting room. A few moments later Glenda walked out of the courthouse and joined a group of her husband's supporters at the foot of the steps as they faced the reporters and photographers who'd been waiting for them. Evelyn Lewis stepped forward, put on a pair of black-rimmed glasses, and read a statement handwritten on a piece of paper.

"We continue to have great faith in Georgie," she said, "and we will continue to fight for Georgie, and we hope he will be vindicated."

Karen's friends and family were giving statements to the press too. Three days before, after hearing Glenda scream, Karen's mother had said she could not sign a death warrant for Lewis. Now, sickened by what she'd heard over the past few hours, Sophia's compassion was gone.

"I think a life was taken and a life should be given," she said. "There has to be some justice."

Thirty-two

T hat night a summer thunderstorm swept over Polk County. Waves of thick raindrops fell to the streets; bursts of lightning illuminated great black stretches of the sky.

Once more Dorene Cobb was having trouble sleeping. She was praying again, this time for the Lewis family. She was asking God to help them accept what had happened. She tried to imagine how she would feel at that moment if one of her sons were in Lewis's place. She asked herself if she would stand by him. She thought she would. What else could she do?

Ruth Wunder was also torn by conflicting emotions. She'd tried so hard to do the right thing. But she kept thinking about Lewis and how she and the other jurors had recommended that he be locked up for the rest of his life.

"I'm not sure," she told her husband when she got home.

He asked her what she meant. What wasn't she sure about? The verdict?

"Not necessarily," she said. "I'm not sure that the so-called experts are experts."

The doubts that had nagged at Wunder during deliberations had returned. It still bothered her that Dr. Wood had belittled the significance of fingernail scrapings, even though they'd helped catch a killer on "Quincy." Wunder didn't know what to believe. During the trial, she remembered, Ciarciaglino had told them that the fingernail scrapings had been lost in this case. This was incorrect. The fingernail scrapings had not been lost. The FDLE had tested them and determined that they contained traces of human blood. But as a crime lab analyst had explained in her deposition, months before, there wasn't enough of a sample to determine the blood type.

Wunder did not know this. All she knew was that the scrapings were supposed to have been lost. Now, she had doubts about the validity of what she had heard from several prosecution witnesses. For instance, she remembered something that one of the crime scene analysts had said about fingerprints. The analyst had testified that people do not always leave fingerprints when they touch objects. That didn't sound right to Wunder either. She asked herself if maybe these witnesses had been wrong about all sorts of things. She wondered if maybe Technician Whitfield had been wrong too. May he'd been wrong about all of those footprints on the carpet—the footprints that finally had persuaded her to vote guilty.

The next day, Wunder and her husband began their own investigation. First they went to the public library in Lakeland, searching for technical books that might answer their questions. They found nothing there, so they went to the public library in Tampa. Nothing. So they went searching for some experts of their own. Wunder called the Polk County medical examiner's office and asked someone—she's not sure who—whether fingernail scrapings ever show anything of value. Yes, said the person on the other end of the line, sometimes they show a great deal.

Wunder's husband called the Orlando Police Department. He spoke to a supervisor in the crime laboratory—again, he's not sure who—and asked if people always leave fingerprints when they touch things with their bare hands. Yes, the supervisor said. The prints may be difficult to detect, but they're always there.

Hearing this, Ruth Wunder was more worried than ever. It seemed to her that the state's witnesses could very well have been wrong. And if they were wrong, she told herself, then it was possible that Lewis wasn't guilty. Wunder thought about calling the judge or the lawyers. But she wasn't sure it would do any good. Even if she wanted to change her vote, was that possible?

Or would she simply have to learn to live with the verdict? She struggled with these questions for days. Then one night she had a dream. In the dream she was talking to a man. It wasn't George Lewis. But suddenly she realized that this person was the real murderer and that he had a knife and that he was after her.

Wunder woke covered with sweat.

"What's the matter?" asked her husband.

"Just hold me," she said. "I'm so scared."

The day after the trial ended, George Lewis was transported to Pinellas County's maximum security jail, where he was to stay until the sentencing. Already his lawyers were fighting to have the convictions overturned, putting together several written motions to be filed with the judge. First they wanted Judge Farnell to set aside the jury verdict and find Lewis not guilty; if the judge was not willing to do that, they asked that he grant a new trial.

These were standard motions, routinely filed with trial judges—and routinely denied. A higher court might grant them, but it was uncommon for the judge who had presided over the case to decide that he or she had allowed something to go wrong and that now the verdict should be thrown out. In fact, in all of his years as a lawyer, Farnell could not recall a single trial judge ever making such a decision in a first-degree murder case. Still, Ciarciaglino and Paver were determined to persuade Farnell that he should do just that. In a massive, twenty-six-page motion, they spelled out more than sixty grounds for why they believed that the verdict from the first trial should be overturned.

Among their arguments:

- The jury should not have been allowed to consider the white teddy, because the prosecution had notified the defense of the teddy's existence only several days before the trial, forcing them to split their time between defending their client and attempting, outside the courtroom, to investigate the new evidence. Furthermore, they pointed out again, it had never been proved that Lewis had stolen the teddy from Karen Gregory's belongings.
- The jury should not have been allowed to consider the hallway carpet on which the bloody footprints were found, because the police had left the carpet in the

house for weeks before taking it into evidence. It had not been proved, the lawyers said, that the carpet was in the same condition as it was when Karen's body had been found. In addition, they said, there was no proof that the footprints on the carpet had been made by Lewis.

- The defense had been handicapped when it learned partway through the trial that Karen had kept a diary.
- Karen's family and friends had potentially prejudiced the case because they had been "constantly present in a narrow hallway through which the jurors had to pass."
- The prosecutors had made improper comments in front of the jury, such as saying that Lewis had allowed Karen's body to "rot" for two days.

The prosecutors filed a massive motion of their own, responding to the defense's points. If they wanted, Ciarciaglino and Paver could try to make a fuss about Karen's friends and family standing in the courthouse hall. But all of those people, the prosecutors pointed out, had been either spectators or witnesses. They had had reason to be there. Besides, the prosecutors said, if anybody was harmed by such behavior, it was the state. Hadn't Lewis been outside the courtroom, hugging his daughter?

Still, there wasn't much the state could gain by harping on such arguments. This was one of the ironies of criminal law. Prosecutors, who carry the burden of proof on their shoulders, simply cannot afford to step out of line with the same impunity as the other side. If they don't present their case in the strictest accordance with the rules—if, say, they allow the victim's family to cry in front of the jury—they risk having a mistrial declared or a conviction thrown out. But defense attorneys can do the same and know that, strategically, they have much less to lose. They can let their witnesses weep in front of the jury. They can even hurl highly emotional but irrelevant bombshells into the testimony. They might get a tongue-lashing from the judge or even a contempt citation. But if the jury votes to acquit, none of the lawyers' breaches will count against their client.

"It's a one-way street in this business," Ciarciaglino had told Mensh one day. "You know that."

"Yeah," Mensh replied. "I know that."

There was a reason it was a one-way street: no one stood to lose more than the person on trial. It was true that Karen had been horribly murdered. George Lewis, however, was still alive. If he had been convicted unfairly, it would be one more injustice added to the first.

Even so, those close to Karen were angry. To them, it seemed that Ciarciaglino and Paver had been given free rein to attack Karen. They had pushed their way inside her diary and searched for dirt about her past and made insinuations about her "lifestyle" and fought repeatedly, throughout the case, to have her friends silenced. They had tried to make it hard for the jurors to see Karen's friends—and Karen—as human beings. In fact, they had made it hard to see or hear or think of Karen and her friends at all. They had gone, Neverne said, beyond the beyond.

Neverne said this on Friday, July 10, three days before the scheduled date of the sentencing. She was sitting in her house in Gulfport, talking about the case. She said she was tired and disillusioned. Yes, she was happy that the jury had come back with the verdict she thought was correct. But the verdict had not exactly restored her faith in the system. It had been luck, she said. It easily could have gone the other way. Besides, she said, how did they know that the conviction would stand? Lewis hadn't even been sentenced yet, and already his lawyers were demanding a new trial. Just to cover all of the bases, they had also filed a motion asking that none of Karen's friends or family be allowed to speak at the sentencing about the impact of the murder on their lives. They also were asking that the judge not read letters from the friends and family. Yet the defense intended to call Lewis's supporters to speak at the hearing. If necessary, Ciarciaglino said, they'd call thirty-one people again.

Neverne closed her eyes, rubbed her forehead. There was no end to it, she said. There was no parole . . .

That same Friday, Ruth Wunder was still searching for peace of mind. By now she was less certain than ever that the right man had been convicted. She knew that the sentencing was approaching. She knew, too, that Judge Farnell was considering the motion for a new trial. But what could she do?

"If it were me," her husband told her, "what I'd do would be to call the judge."

The next morning, the two of them tried. It was a Saturday, but they figured that Judge Farnell might be at the criminal courthouse in Pinellas County, researching his decision. They tried to get through there, but there was no answer. Then they tried to reach Farnell at home. But directory information said he had an unlisted number. They would have to wait until Monday.

The judge wasn't at home much that weekend anyway. He was too busy, working overtime inside his office at the civil courthouse in downtown Clearwater, where he usually presided. He was pondering the questions before him. Should he overturn the jury verdict? Or should he go ahead and sentence Lewis? If so, what should be the sentence? The jury had voted for life, but the presentence investigation had been completed and it recommended that Lewis be executed.

Judge Farnell had no problem getting tough with criminals. Several years before, in another murder case, he'd overridden a jury's recommendation for life and sentenced the defendant to death, calling him "a rabid rat." Yet Farnell had not forgotten his duty to uphold the rights of the accused. This was not always the most popular thing to do. People love to complain about how defendants get off on "technicalities." Yet if those same people would ever find themselves on trial, then suddenly those so-called technicalities, which can be as basic as the right to have a lawyer, would not seem so technical.

Now Farnell was faced with a difficult choice. He was sympathetic to what Karen's friends and family had endured over the past three years. But he thought Ciarciaglino and Paver had raised some questions worth serious consideration. They still maintained, despite the jury verdict, that it never really had been proved that Karen was raped. Not by Lewis, not by anyone. It wasn't enough, they said, to simply say that she probably had been raped. The judge thought they had a point. He also thought there was merit to their contention that it had been improper for the prosecution to tell the jury that Lewis had allowed Karen's body to "rot" inside the house.

There was more. Reading through the defense's motion, Farnell agreed there were real problems with the admissibility of the teddy and the carpet. He didn't think he should have allowed the jurors to see either of them. Nor did he believe he should have allowed them to view a Luminol tape of such shabby quality, much less allow them to view it twice, the second time during what had obviously been a crucial stage of the deliberations. On top of all these other problems, there was no denying that the late discovery of the diary, like the late discovery of the teddy, had forced Ciarciaglino and Paver to divide their time and attention between the trial and a side investigation into a potentially explosive new piece of evidence. Once they found the diary, the judge thought, he should have at least granted their motion for continuance. He should have done the same, he thought, when the teddy surfaced.

From the start of the trial, when he'd been brought in at the last minute, Farnell had been at a disadvantage. He had done his best in Bartow to sort through the complicated disputes that had been laid before him. But looking back, it was clear to him that he had made mistakes. The question was, were the mistakes serious enough to have deprived Lewis of a fair trial?

The judge worked through the weekend, puffing on his cigars, poring through his notes and stacks of law books, studying the cases the lawyers had cited. He was there until midnight Sunday.

At 8:00 Monday morning, the day of sentencing, Ruth Wunder's husband was back on the phone, trying to reach the judge at the courthouse. There was no answer. He called several more times. Still no answer. Finally, at about 9:00, he reached Farnell's secretary. He identified himself as the husband of one of the jurors in the Lewis trial. He said his wife wanted to speak to Farnell before he made his decision.

"He already has," said the secretary.

At 8:00 that morning there had been a short hearing. Farnell had walked into court, bid the lawyers good morning, then made an announcement.

"At this time," he told the defense, "I will grant your motion for judgment of acquittal as to the sexual battery. Accordingly, I will grant a new trial on the accumulative effect of matters that you have raised in your motion."

That was it. The judge was overturning the jury's verdict—throwing out the rape charge altogether and ordering a new trial on the murder charge.

Dick Mensh didn't seem to believe what he was hearing.

"You have granted a new trial as to the murder," he said.

"Yes, sir."

Mensh struggled for a few moments. He said he was trying to understand, for the record, what had happened. The judge was granting a new trial based on the totality of the defense's motion? Again, the judge said it was based on the "accumulative effect" of "matters" that had been raised in the defense motion.

That was about all he said.

"Anything further?" he asked the lawyers.

"No, sir," said Paver.

"This court will be adjourned."

Ciarciaglino was triumphant.

"It means," he said, "that the war continues."

The prosecutors were almost speechless.

"We have to start all over," said Beverly Andrews, "and we don't know why."

Maytha Schafer, the juror who had hoped that a life sentence would preclude appeals, was watching the news that night when suddenly she saw a picture of herself and the rest of the jury, sitting in court. When she heard what Farnell had decided, Schafer thought she was dreaming. She felt as if all the jurors' work had been for nothing. If so many things had gone wrong, she wondered, why hadn't the judge stopped the trial?

Ruth Wunder was relieved. "Now it's going to be up to somebody else," she told her husband.

Greg Blessing, the foreman, was angry. "I have no doubt in my mind," he said, "that he's guilty of both."

Lewis's sister Linda said: "The boy is innocent, that's all. I don't know why people don't believe him."

Lewis's brother Carl: "We're glad. . . . Personally, I'd like to give him a big spanking for not calling the cops that night."

Tammy Ozmore, one of Lewis's friends: "George is a very good person, and if there were more people like him, the world would be better off."

David Mackey: "I'm not going to give up. I'll go to my grave before I give up."

Karen's sister: "Here we go again. Back at square one. I just feel a sense of complete despair."

Karen's mother: "Are we going to be victims forever and ever? . . . It's all another waste of time. It's just a great big joke. Was it a show?"

Finally, there was this thought from Karen's brother Mark:

"If he's acquitted on the rape . . . how are they going to prove a motive?"

Thirty-three

T he case against George Lewis was teetering at the edge. Once Farnell had ruled, it was unclear how much of a case the state had left. Karen's brother had asked a good question. Although prosecutors are not required to prove motive to win a conviction, they know that jurors often hunger for the answers and context that a motive provides. Now that the rape charge against Lewis was gone, it was possible that the next jury would find it all the harder to believe that he had indeed wandered across the street that night and approached Karen. Then there was the problem of the white teddy and the carpet. Did the judge's decision mean that those items of evidence were to be permanently excluded? Without the carpet, which had been so instrumental in the first jury's verdict, was there any chance at all of proving the case?

All of these questions turned out to be moot.

On February 17, 1989, after the state filed a lengthy challenge to Farnell's decision, the Second District Court of Appeal overturned the ruling and reinstated both the rape and the murder convictions. In a backhanded compliment to the judge, the appeal court ruled that Farnell had done a worthy job presiding over a difficult trial—so worthy that there had been no reason for him to throw out the convictions. The court said he had properly given the defense a chance to investigate both the teddy and the diary and had properly allowed the teddy and the carpet into evidence. In fact, the court said that the only real error Farnell had made was in deciding, once the trial was over, that he had erred.

On the final page of its twenty-three-page opinion, the court delivered an especially stinging blow to the defense. In their arguments, Ciarciaglino and Paver had insisted that case law dictates that in a purely circumstantial case the accused must be acquitted unless the evidence excludes any reasonable hypothesis of innocence. In this case, they said, George's account of why he'd gone into the house was entirely reasonable.

The appeal court did not agree. As the acting chief judge wrote:

> In this instance, we find that there was substantial, competent evidence that was consistent with Lewis's guilt and inconsistent with any reasonable hypothesis of his innocence.

In plain English:

We think he did it, too.

Thirty-four

The sentencing took place on June 2, 1989, a radiant summer day that fell exactly two years after the start of the trial in Bartow. By now the proceedings had returned to Pinellas County. They were back in the Slum of Justice, back in the same fourth-floor courtroom where the defense had reigned over the first attempt at jury selection and Ciarciaglino had stolen the prosecution's chair.

That afternoon the courtroom was jammed. Squeezed together in the front row, shoulder to shoulder—in a physical metaphor for how all of their lives had been drawn together—were Evelyn Lewis, Glenda Lewis, Karen's sister and her mother, David Mackey, Anita Kilpatrick, and Neverne Covington. Larry Tosi sat off to the side, almost invisible in the crowd. Several of Lewis's friends were there too, wearing their uniforms and showing their support, but their numbers had dwindled to a conspicuous few. Gone now were the dozens of firefighters and paramedics who had congregated at the bond hearing months before, staring at the prosecutors.

The prosecutors again arrived early, and while they waited for the hearing to begin, Dick Mensh carried his chair, a plain straight-backed chair, across the courtroom and exchanged it for a black cushioned swivel-back chair from behind the table where Ciarciaglino and Paver would be sitting. If he was making a symbolic gesture—if he was paying back the old insult—Mensh did not say so. He was merely looking, he explained, for a comfortable seat.

"First come, first serve," he said.

Ciarciaglino and Paver walked in a few minutes later, and then the bailiffs brought in Lewis from a holding cell behind the courtroom. He was in street clothes, wearing a chocolate brown jacket and light brown pants he'd often worn during the trial, and as he took his seat between his lawyers, he searched the gallery for Glenda and his mother and then greeted them with a nod. The months of waiting in jail had left their mark. He was pale, his eyes had lost a degree of luster, and his mouth seemed smaller and tighter, with the peculiar fixed quality of someone wearing dentures. Only twenty-seven, he looked incalculably older.

If his appearance gave the impression that he was beaten, though, he soon proved that wrong. When the sentencing began and his turn came to speak, Lewis stepped forward, pulled a written statement from the pocket of his jacket and read a lengthy indictment of the police, the prosecutors, and the *St. Petersburg Times*, all of whom, he said, had worked together to convict the wrong man. He thanked Judge Farnell for his efforts to grant him a new trial. He thanked his friends and family for their continued support and vowed to them that he would never stop fighting the charges against him. And he apologized to Karen's family, saying that he was deeply sorry that he had fled that night after discovering the body. If he hadn't run—if he had stayed in the house and called the police—he was sure, he said, he would have ended up as a key witness for the state and not the defendant. Even so, he said, the prosecutors had been unable to produce any solid evidence against him. In fact, he said, their case was so weak that at one point they had tried to cut a deal with him. In exchange for a change of plea, he said, they had offered to drop the murder charge to manslaughter and drop the rape charge altogether.

"I don't think it's right to try to plea bargain away the rights of this victim, Karen Gregory," he said. "It just proves that they themselves were not sure."

A few minutes later, when the speech was concluded, Mensh stood up and argued that Lewis was still pointing the finger at others, still trying to blame his guilt on everyone but himself. It was all just more lies, said Mensh, denying that the state had ever made Lewis any such plea offer.

"The truth still seems to escape him," said the senior prosecutor. "As a matter of fact, the truth is still a long way from his vocabulary."

A few others stepped forward as well. Evelyn Lewis proclaimed her son's innocence and said that George was a victim of the system. David Mackey asked that Lewis be sentenced to two consecutive life terms in prison, one for the murder and another for the rape, so that he would never again have the opportunity to walk among civilized human beings.

Finally, after listening to everyone, Judge Farnell spoke. He recognized that this was a brutal case—as brutal, he said, as any he had ever seen—but he was not about to give a second life sentence, he said, on the rape charge, the validity of which he already had questioned. Accordingly, he said, he was sentencing Lewis to life in prison on the murder charge and to a concurrent twelve-year term on the rape.

"Good luck to you," the judge told him.

Throughout the hearing, a bevy of silent bailiffs had stood at the doors and other strategic points around the room, carefully watching Lewis from a polite distance. Now that the sentence had been passed, they moved forward, led him to a table, and began to fingerprint him right there in the courtroom. It was a standard procedure, but one that defendants often find humiliating, and as they took his hands and pressed them to the ink and the paper, Lewis stood with his back to his wife and family, refusing to turn around.

Watching him, Neverne Covington again was struck with feelings of profound empathy. There was something in his face, some human quality that made it hard for her, despite everything she knew, to believe that this was the man who had murdered Karen. For a second she asked herself if maybe he hadn't done it. Was it possible?

A moment later, she was embarrassed by her own gullibility.

Epilogue

October 1990

At the time of this writing, George Lewis is serving his life sentence at the Tomoka Correctional Institution in Daytona Beach. He is no longer a St. Petersburg firefighter, because the city fired him at 8:00 A.M. on Monday, June 15, 1987, the first business hour of the first business day after the verdict. Back at his old house in Gulfport, the neighborhood crime watch sign still stands in the yard.

Glenda Lewis has been forced to raise a family without her husband. On February 8, 1988, at 6:48 A.M., she gave birth to their second child, an eight-pound eight-ounce girl named Brittany, at Bayfront Medical Center in St. Petersburg. Afterward, she went on living with her daughters in Pinellas County for a while and continued working at the bank; however, she was assigned to a different branch from Debbie Tosi, with whom she no longer spoke. In the years since the trial, Glenda has repeatedly shown her support for George in his legal battle, appearing at his hearings with his mother and the other members of his family. Just this past June, however, she filed for divorce. A few months later, in a brief hearing in St. Petersburg at which George was not present, a judge granted her petition and awarded her sole parental responsibility. At the hearing, Glenda said she and the girls have moved out of Florida and are trying to start a new life for themselves.

The criminal case, meanwhile, goes on. George Lewis's lawyers are still pursuing a new trial or a judgment of acquittal; this past spring, in a courtroom at Stetson University College of Law in Gulfport, only a few minutes from the site of the murder, they offered another round of oral arguments before the Second District Court of Appeal. However, in a decision released a few days before Glenda filed for divorce, the court denied the appeal and again affirmed the convictions. His lawyers say they'll fight on.

More than four years after they came onto the case, Ciarciaglino and Paver continue to represent Lewis. Though they have spent hundreds of hours on the case and have turned to a Miami lawyer to assist them in the appeal, they will not answer a question raised by Karen's friends. Namely: Who is paying for the defense? That, the lawyers say, is nobody's business but theirs.

Beverly Andrews and William Loughery still serve at the state attorney's office. Richard Mensh, however, recently resigned as the office's chief assistant and now devotes himself entirely to private practice. The Lewis case, he says, was his "swan song." When he left the office, the local chapter of the Police Benevolent Association awarded him a plaque commemorating his years of service; the plaque was handed to him by the PBA's attorney, Joe Ciarciaglino.

Sgt. Larry Tosi is now completing his second decade of service with the one police department that did not care how tall he was; today he heads Gulfport's detective division. He still drives the yellow Barracuda, still tries daily to forge some sense of order out of the chaos on top of his desk. To this date, he says, he has not completed the paperwork on the Lewis case. Persistent as always, he carried on with the investigation even after the verdict. In 1988, as genetic fingerprinting became a popular new forensic tool across the country, he tried to determine if the recent advances might be used to test the semen found during the autopsy. He was informed, however, that it was not possible in this case.

Some of those close to Karen Gregory have gone on working with the homicide survivors organization founded by Lula Redmond. Now called the Center for Crime Victims and Survivors, it continues to spread support for those whose loved ones have been murdered, as well as for other crime victims. This case, after all, is only one of many. Every year approximately twenty thousand people are murdered in the United States; in each of those cases, the center estimates that between seven and ten people are left to struggle with severe emotional turmoil.

At the center's office, the members of the organization have covered a wall with photos of the loved ones who are gone. After the murder they placed one there of Karen, sitting in a chair, looking over her shoulder with a hint of a smile. Her Mona Lisa look.

David Mackey has continued counseling Vietnam veterans; at the moment, he has just returned to school to work on a doctoral degree in clinical social work. At the same time he has taken his struggle for survivors' rights to the national level, appearing on the Phil Donahue show and speaking at a convention of NOVA, the National Organization for Victims Assistance.

Anita Kilpatrick still lives and works in Pinellas County. To this day, she carries in her wallet the note Karen wrote her on the night she died.

Neverne Covington has moved from the house in Gulfport where she and Karen had dinner on their last evening together. Since then, Neverne says, she has learned that those you love are gifts. She has learned, she says, that it takes an act of faith to get through every single day.

Even now, she wonders about Lewis. She says it makes her angry, and profoundly sad, to realize how much time she has spent thinking about this stranger who, as she puts it, only grows more strange. She finds herself looking for a thread that will tie everything together, searching for some glimpse or clue that will help her finally understand. She wonders if the answer might lie in Lewis's "obsession" with being a firefighter. As she put it to me in a letter after the trial:

> Surely one could call it an obsession. I think his friends described it as that. To be a firefighter for one's job, to volunteer for it in his spare time and to even marry in a firefighter's "cage" seems to me to be beyond an avocation. How does this fit? If evil is selfishness taken to its ultimate and logical extreme—if this is evil in humankind—then, what is fire in nature? I ask myself. Fire

is, among other things, a force of violence and evil in nature—a force of death and destruction. Is it far-fetched to think if George Lewis's obsession with fighting this sometimes wild, random and uncontrollable force in nature pertains to his inability to control his own fires, his own destructive forces? Is this a way of controlling these external forces in nature—does this pertain to his internal forces? I wonder, I just don't know. Maybe this is too far-fetched but I keep trying to see reason (not to be confused with the reason).

There is something else Neverne cannot help thinking about. Lewis, she points out, has had years to fight for his life and freedom. He also has had the help of his lawyers, dozens of friends, and a long list of constitutional rights, courtroom rules, and legal procedures. This is the way of the law. Neverne knows that. But she cannot get it out of her mind that when Karen was struggling for her life, there was no law. That night, when she cried out, there were no rules, no procedures, no sense of fair play. There was only Karen, fighting alone in the dark with her bare hands.

—　—Thomas French

Acknowledgments

S o many people have helped with this book that I could not begin to list them all. Yet there are a number who deserve special thanks—all of those close to Karen Gregory who shared such painful memories; Lu Redmond, who shared her invaluable insights; the officers of the Gulfport Police Department who shared their time and expertise; my agent, Jane Dystel, who had faith from the start; and my editor at St. Martin's, Charles Spicer, and Associate Editor Bill Thomas, who gave me confidence and guidance.

What appears on these pages is based closely on articles I originally wrote for the *St. Petersburg Times*; in fact, the book would not have been possible without the generous support of numerous people at the *Times*, including Sandra Thompson, Michael Foley, Andrew Barnes, Eugene Patterson, Don McBride, Rick Holter, Steve Small, George Sweers, Barbara Hijek, and everyone in the *Times* library. I also am indebted to George Rahdert and Pat Anderson for their counsel and heartening words; to Suzanne Klinkenberg for identifying the flora and fauna; to Kati Kairies of the *Times* Tallahassee bureau for cheerfully tracking down a dozen different addresses; to Frances Purdy of the Gulfport

Historical Society, as well as to the society's book on Gulfport, for providing historical details; and to Terri McKaig for spending countless hours trying to explain to me the inner workings of the courts.

I have had the good fortune of knowing some of the best writers and writing coaches in the country, many of whom have given me their encouragement, suggestions, and friendship through several years of reporting and writing. Among them are Roy Peter Clark and Donald Fry of the Poynter Institute for Media Studies; Donald Murray, writing coach for the *Boston Globe* and other newspapers; Pat Meisol of the *Baltimore Sun*; Tim Nickens of the *Miami Herald*; Christopher Scanlan of the Knight-Ridder Washington bureau; and David Finkel, Anne Hull, Sheryl James, Jeff Klinkenberg, and Wilma Norton of the *St. Petersburg Times*. I am especially indebted to Karl Vick of the *Times* Washington bureau for all of his patience and advice. Deepest thanks to Neville Green, deputy managing editor at the *Times*, who always believed and was always there with the ablest hand. It is impossible to convey how much of Neville's judgment and commitment run through these pages.

Finally, much love to my son, Nat, for lifting my spirits during hard times, and to my wife, Linda, for all of her proof-reading, listening, and understanding.